Corporate Turnaround and Restructuring

AF528772

Bharat Gupta

Copyright © 2025 Bharat Gupta

This book is a work of nonfiction, drawing on real events, incidents, and experiences of the author. While the core facts, strategies, and outcomes described are accurate and based on actual occurrences, certain details have been altered to protect confidentiality and proprietary information. This includes changing names of individuals, companies, and organizations; modifying identification characteristics; condensing timelines and events for narrative clarity; and reconstructing dialogues based on recollections and records. These adjustments ensure the protection of sensitive business matters while preserving the essential lessons and insights for readers.

All Rights Reserved.

First Edition: December 2025
Printed in India

Printed at: Gapmeta Ventures Pvt.Ltd, Mumbai
Typeset in Adobe Garamond Pro

ISBN: 978-93-6070-130-7

Cover Design: Prajakta Sawant

STORYMIRROR
Stories that reflect you

Publisher: StoryMirror Infotech Pvt. Ltd.
Unit No-F/705, 7th Floor, Kailas Corporate Lounge,
Veer Savarkar Road, Vikhroli Park Site,
Vikhroli West, Mumbai-400079,
Maharashtra, India.

Web: storymirror.com
Facebook: @storymirror
Twitter: @story_mirror
Instagram: @storymirror
Email: marketing@storymirror.com

No part of this publication may be reproduced, distributed, stored in a retrieval system, or transmitted in any form or by any means, electronic, mechanical, photocopying, recording, or otherwise, without the prior written permission of the publisher. Furthermore, no portion of this work may be used to train artificial intelligence technologies, large language models, or similar systems without express written consent from the author. All rights reserved.

To all turnaround experts,
whose heart aches and who clinch their fists,
when they see a business in distress.

Acknowledgments

I would not have been able to take a bold decision to take a break from a prestigious full-time role to finish writing this book and pursue my other passions, without the strength and confidence I have gained from my family and friends. It is the culmination of many years of work and many starts and stops.

I owe my deepest gratitude to my parents, who (despite their limited means and struggles) encouraged me to dream and allowed me to fly far away from home. During all my travels far from home, my elder brother and sister-in-law have been the family elders and kept us all together. My younger sister has grown beyond her age into a spiritual guide to our family. As I changed careers and countries, my constant companion and source of strength has been my wife, without whose encouragement this book would not have been possible. To my niece, nephew, son and daughter, I owe you all lots of love for the joy and excitement that you bring to the family and wish for your bright future.

I am sincerely indebted to Mr. J M Seth - Senior Partner at A F Ferguson & Co. for the faith he placed in me (and the scoldings), Mr. Paul D'Silva - CFO at SABMiller India for being my mentor over the years, Ms. Helen Mastrantonis - Director HR at SABMiller Africa & Asia for giving me the wings to see the world outside India, Mr. Sankar Krishnan - Senior MD at Alvarez & Marsal whose turnaround stories inspired me to pursue corporate turnarounds with all my heart, Mr. Abizer Diwanji - Senior Partner at EY LLP for giving me India's best platform to pursue my passion and my friend Vishal Bansal - Senior Partner at EY LLP, who made EY feel like home.

I am indebted to my friends from London Business School - Mohit Midha, João Pedro Ladeira, Philipp Schaefer, Nishant Mehta, and Kartik Prabhakara, with whom I had the privilege of forming the Turnaround Club and organising some amazing events.

I am grateful to Alvarez & Marsal and EY India for giving me the opportunity to practice, refine, and test my craft in real-world situations. To my colleagues and teams at both firms, thank you for your dedication, insights, and for tolerating me. To my clients and business partners, many of whom have now become lifelong friends, thank you for trusting me and sometimes going out of your way to help me.

Finally, my thanks to StoryMirror for partnering with me in bringing this book to life and supporting me through the publishing journey.

Foreword

By Michael G. Jacobides

Sir Donald Gordon Professor of Entrepreneurship & Innovation and Professor of Strategy, London Business School

Over the last two decades, I have had the privilege of teaching turnarounds and corporate restructuring to generations of executives at London Business School. In that time, I've watched many students leave the classroom to grapple with distressed firms in the real world, but only a handful have gone on to build a career that spans the full arc of the profession: from global restructuring firms, to Big Four partnerships, to independent practice. Bharat is one of those few.

His journey – from India to London to Dubai and ultimately back to India – mirrors the globalisation of the turnaround profession itself. In London and the Gulf, he absorbed the hard-earned lessons of mature restructuring markets, where early intervention, creditor discipline, and specialist leadership are now accepted parts of the corporate toolkit, rather than signs of failure. And then he made, in my view, the more important move: bringing that experience home, and asking what a truly Indian turnaround practice should look like.

That is what makes this book distinctive. It does not simply import Anglo-American recipes and reheat them for an Indian audience. Bharat has seen enough failed "cut-and-paste" efforts to know that doesn't work. Instead, he takes the best of what he has learned abroad – early warning indicators, structured independent business reviews, professional Chief Restructuring Officers, disciplined stakeholder orchestration – and subjects it to a very practical test: does this make sense with Indian promoters, Indian lenders, Indian courts, and Indian regulators? Where it does, he adopts it. Where it doesn't, he adapts or discards it. The result is a framework that is global in its intellectual roots but unmistakably Indian in its application, without a whiff of useless imports.

This is especially timely because the world of turnarounds has itself been changing. Over the past few decades in the US, UK, and Europe, restructuring has evolved from a late-stage "work-out" activity into a recognised profession with its own tools, standards, and career paths. Dedicated restructuring funds, private credit investors, and specialist advisory teams have proliferated, and boards are far more willing to bring in CROs, interim CEOs, or transformation executives when trouble looms. Surveys of restructuring professionals show a sustained high level of activity globally, but also a shift in mindset: interventions are happening earlier, and are framed less as admissions of defeat and more as disciplined capital recycling and value preservation.

Alongside this professionalisation, the stigma once attached to corporate distress is gradually being eroded. Scholars of insolvency and corporate law have documented how, in many jurisdictions, policy has moved away from "shame and punishment" towards rescue, rehabilitation, and going-concern preservation. Liquidation is increasingly seen as the last resort, not the default. While this cultural shift is uneven and incomplete, it matters: when failure is treated as an irredeemable stain, managers and promoters delay action; when it is treated as a problem to be addressed early and professionally, firms, creditors, and employees all stand to gain.

India's own evolution on this front has been dramatic. For years, its financial system struggled with mounting non-performing assets and a fragmented, debtor-friendly insolvency regime that made it difficult to resolve distress quickly. The Insolvency and Bankruptcy Code (IBC) of 2016 fundamentally altered that landscape: it created a time-bound, creditor-in-control framework, empowered professional insolvency practitioners, and signalled that failure would be dealt with transparently and promptly rather than hidden or endlessly rolled over.

The results are beginning to show. Resolution outcomes under the IBC have been markedly better than under earlier mechanisms, both in terms of recovery rates and in the growing share of cases resolved as going concerns rather than liquidated. Recent data suggest that, for every company going into liquidation, roughly two now achieve resolution; and tens of thousands of stressed exposures are reportedly being settled even before formal admission, as the mere presence of an effective regime sharpens incentives for early negotiation. India is building not only a stronger banking system, but also the institutional scaffolding for a genuine turnaround ecosystem.

Why does this matter beyond the obvious? Here, the work of Nicholas Bloom, John Van Reenen, Raffaella Sadun and co-authors offers a powerful lens. Their research, based on large-scale surveys of management practices across countries, shows that national productivity is not just about a few excellent firms at the frontier. It is the distribution of firm-level productivity – and management quality – that determines aggregate performance. Many economies, including India, have a long "tail" of poorly managed, underperforming firms that drag down overall productivity.

From that perspective, effective turnaround and restructuring are not merely niche technical activities. They are key mechanisms through which resources move from less productive to more productive uses – or through which underperforming firms are pushed to improve their management practices or exit. When we fix ailing firms quickly, or when we acknowledge failure early and redeploy capital and talent, we compress that long tail. That, in turn, can have an outsized impact on the prosperity of a country like India.

Adopting and adapting global best practices in turnarounds will help India recycle capital efficiently, preventing long lock-ups in non-performing assets; preserve jobs and productive capacity, ensuring continuity of economic activity; enhance competitiveness by repositioning viable companies for future growth; Improve governance and transparency, especially in promoter-led enterprises; and increase productivity, a critical enabler for sustaining long-term economic expansion. Turnarounds, when executed early and professionally, do more than rescue distressed firms—they strengthen the entire economic architecture by ensuring that resources flow to their most productive uses.

Bharat's book sits squarely at this intersection of firm-level practice and macroeconomic consequence. It takes the abstract ideas of productivity dispersion and capital reallocation and embeds them in the practical realities of promoter psychology, bank credit committees, court timelines, and cash-starved operations. It explains, with examples and tools, how to move from denial to diagnosis, from crisis to structured action; how to get promoters, lenders, employees, and sometimes the state onto the same page; and how to decide when a business can and should be saved, and when the honest answer is that value lies elsewhere.

On a personal note, it is a pleasure – and a source of pride – to see one of my former students chart this path: from the classroom to Alvarez & Marsal, to EY's restructuring practice, to independent advisor; from global hubs like London and Dubai back to India; and now from practitioner to author. Along the way, he has returned to the classroom as a guest speaker in many iterations of our turnaround course in Dubai, sharing candid war stories and practical lessons. That willingness to give back and to educate his peers on the realities of turnaround work is very much in evidence in this book as well.

This book is not a consultant's brochure dressed up as scholarship, nor an academic treatise remote from reality. It is the product of someone who has sat with promoters in denial, lenders under pressure, and employees fearing for their livelihoods – and who has had to make the hard trade-offs that case studies often gloss over.

As India advances toward its ambition of becoming a developed, high-income economy, it will need not only new firms and new technologies, but also better ways of dealing with the old, the stuck, and the struggling. Turnarounds, done early and well, are one of the quiet enablers of that journey: they free capital, preserve viable jobs, and raise the average quality of management in the corporate sector. Books like this help build the mindset and skill base required to make that happen.

I hope that Bharat's timely book will be read not only by turnaround specialists, but by promoters, bankers, investors, regulators, and students

– anyone who has a stake in how India handles distress, and in how quickly it can turn today's stressed assets into tomorrow's productive enterprises.

London, November 2025

Preface

If a book can change someone's life, for me, that book was Corporate Turnarounds by Stuart Slatter and David Lovett. I still remember that sunny October 2006 morning in London, I stepped into the bookstore, outside the London Business School campus. Forever curious about new topics to learn (as long as it doesn't come in a thick book), I noticed this thin book with a title named Corporate Turnarounds. With time on my hands, as my family was still in India and I was leading a bachelor student life, I felt this book would be a good companion for the next few days (after all, books are an introvert's best friend). Little did I know that the book itself would change the course of my life and turnarounds would become the central theme of my professional life. It sparked in me a fascination with how businesses, often left for dead, could be revived with the right mix of strategy, leadership, and execution. Over the years, as I worked with Middle Eastern and Indian companies, both large and mid-sized, this fascination grew into a lived reality. I found myself not merely advising on numbers, but stepping into situations where survival, jobs, reputations, and sometimes entire communities were at stake.

In my seventeen years with professional services firms, particularly in restructuring and turnaround advisory, I have had the privilege of witnessing this world up close. I saw promoters who had built empires with grit, now staring at bankruptcy. I sat across the table from bankers carrying the burden of mounting NPAs, searching for hope in balance sheets drowning in red ink. I watched management teams struggle with cash starvation, talent flight, and declining morale. And occasionally, I saw the magic when everything came together: the business stabilized, trust was rebuilt, and growth returned.

This book is my attempt to bring those experiences together into a coherent framework. It is written for promoters, entrepreneurs, lenders, private equity investors, and aspiring turnaround professionals. It is also for students of business, who will shape the next generation of corporate leadership in India. While global literature on turnarounds is rich, very little has been written with a clear focus on the Indian context.

Why This Book and Why Now?

The past two decades have transformed the corporate credit landscape in India. In the early 2000s, lenders often had little recourse when borrowers defaulted. The Sick Industrial Companies Act (SICA) dragged cases for years in BIFR courts, locking capital and eroding value. The SARFAESI Act of 2002 was a step forward, giving banks the ability to seize assets, but it was often resisted by promoters and limited in scope. RBI's schemes like CDR (Corporate Debt Restructuring), SDR (Strategic Debt Restructuring), and S4A (Scheme for Sustainable Structuring of Stressed Assets) provided temporary relief, but rarely led to sustainable recovery.

It was only with the introduction of the Insolvency and Bankruptcy Code (IBC) in 2016 that creditor rights were decisively strengthened. For the first time, lenders had a credible legal framework to resolve stressed assets within strict timelines. This shifted the balance of power from promoters to creditors and fundamentally changed the culture of credit in India. From a peak of over 10% gross NPAs just a decade ago, Indian bank NPAs today are at multi-year lows. Promoters have become far more cautious in how they structure and service debt.

And yet, law and regulation are only one part of the story. For every successful resolution under IBC, there are cases where value was lost due to delay, indecision or the absence of professional turnaround leadership. In India, unlike in Western economies, promoters and lenders have been reluctant to appoint Chief Restructuring Officers (CROs) or turnaround specialists with operational control. Advisory firms are often brought in to prepare financial models or negotiate with lenders, but rarely to lead operations. As a result, opportunities to save viable businesses are sometimes missed.

This book argues that turnarounds in India need to be seen as more than financial restructuring. They are about people, trust, execution discipline and cultural sensitivity. A crisis cannot be solved by numbers alone. It requires leadership that can win the confidence of stakeholders, make hard decisions, and create a roadmap for recovery.

What This Book Offers

The chapters that follow are structured around a six-step framework for corporate turnaround. This is not an abstract model; it is built from practical experience in different countries, diverse industries, and many different contexts. The framework moves from diagnostic reviews, to crisis management, to stakeholder alignment, to operational restructuring, to financial restructuring, and finally to implementation and handover.

Each chapter is written with a deep focus on the Indian context. Where relevant, I have drawn on examples, both successful and unsuccessful, from Indian corporate history. I have also referred to regulatory developments like RBI circulars, Companies Act provisions and IBC jurisprudence that shapes the playing field for turnarounds.

But this book is not just about frameworks and case studies. It is also about the softer side of turnarounds. How does one rebuild trust when lenders and promoters no longer believe each other? How do you keep employees motivated when salaries are delayed, and rumours of closure abound? How do you make investment decisions in a cash-starved business? How does a leader make an entrance in a company under siege, and how does he or she exit gracefully once stability has been restored?

I have tried to answer these questions not from a distance, but from the vantage point of someone who has rolled up their sleeves and worked alongside management teams.

A Word on Style and Approach

You will find in these pages a blend of analysis and storytelling. I have used analogies from cricket, cinema, and medicine to make the concepts more relatable. I have leaned on financial analysis where necessary, but avoided excessive jargon. My aim is to make this book accessible not only to restructuring professionals, but also to business owners, investors, and students.

The approach is hands-on. Just as in my advisory practice, I believe theory must meet execution. Ideas are of little value if they cannot be implemented on the ground.

Closing Thought

Turnarounds are not just about rescuing companies. They are about resilience, about second chances, about the belief that decline is not destiny. They remind us that failure is not final, and that with the right leadership, even the most distressed situations can be transformed into stories of renewal.

It is in that spirit that I offer you this book. Just as a book changed the course of my destiny, I hope this book may impact the readers in a positive way and may it serve as a bridge, a Dharma Setu, to righteous outcomes for businesses, stakeholders, and society at large.

Contents

Section II

Section I

Chapter 01

Why Corporate Turnarounds?

"Turnarounds are capitalism's reset button!"

Over the last two decades, some very large corporations have succumbed to a variety of factors - ranging from intense competition, regulatory changes, poor capital allocation, poorly designed capital structure, mismanagement, and white collar fraud. News headlines below will refresh the readers' memory about the situations being referred to:

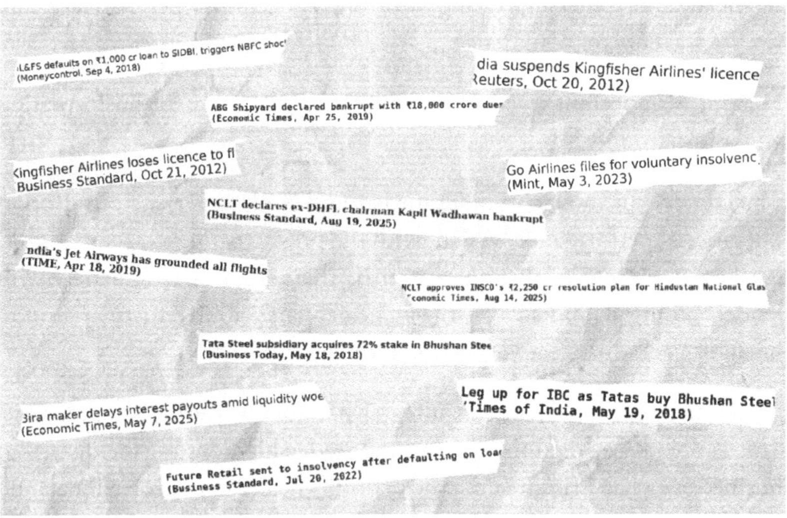

News clippings above show these businesses are in financial distress, where they have either defaulted on the debt obligations or not paid core business expenses like salaries, taxes and suppliers.

Definition of Corporate Turnaround

There are several meanings of the word "turnaround" but Merriam-Webster's definition, "to change for the better", is a good starting point. It denotes value creation, an improvement in the existing situation and alleviation of stress or challenges. In the context of business, it could have a narrow or a wider meaning. Narrow definition would include everything from arresting a falling market share to gaining market share, from net attrition in manpower to net additions, etc. However, we are concerned about the wider and holistic corporate performance, which has an impact across the organization and its supply chain.

We are not just referring to improvement in the rate of change but to a complete change in direction from a loss-making to a profit-making business or from a business losing operating cash to generating positive free cash for its stakeholders. In other words, a corporate turnaround is the process of reinventing a struggling or failing company into a profitable and sustainable business again. It usually involves strategic, operational, financial, and leadership changes to reverse declining performance and restore stakeholder confidence.

Here, it is important to explain the difference between a transformation and a turnaround:

The context for most corporate turnaround situations is a steep drop in operational performance, which, with the presence of leverage, manifests itself as an overwhelming liquidity crisis. There is a deep trust deficit, with lenders losing confidence in the management's ability to turn around business performance and meet their obligations.

Crisis management forms an integral part of the turnaround process. This is the phase when the turnaround leadership does for the distressed businesses what paramedics and critical healthcare professionals do for individual medical emergencies. Quick diagnosis, cash generation (external infusion), stabilization initiatives, and asking lenders to step back (by signing a standstill agreement) are some of the steps taken during this phase.

Given the steep decline in enterprise value of the business and presence of debt, turnarounds involve significant equity reductions and a restructuring of the debt. Resetting expectations regarding enterprise value and negotiations between equity and lenders is a critical component of the process. For a financial restructuring to be successful and sustainable, a robust, well-tested business plan that is executed with precision is an absolute necessity.

Leadership skills to drive a turnaround are very different from typical growth CEO or transformation CEO roles. Firm, decisive, passionate about winning, objective, detail-oriented, excellent stakeholder management, etc. are some of the key attributes of good Turnaround leaders. Once the business is stabilized and has a sound capital structure in place, turnaround leaders hand over the reins of the business to growth CEO / Leader and move on to the next challenge.

On the other hand, contextual setting for a Transformation is usually a mature business that has been struggling to increase revenue and/or profitability but is still many quarters away from a cash crisis. Often, the revenue and market share are declining for several years and the business may be incurring losses. It helps if the business is not heavily leveraged, as the level of urgency is alleviated and there are fewer stakeholder issues to deal with.

Given the absence of an immediate or ongoing cash crisis, there is a longer time horizon available to address the business challenges and a longer perspective can be taken when developing solutions. E.g., developing new products/markets and/or new marketing campaigns with longer lead times are solutions that work well in Transformations but will not be pursued in Turnaround situations due to cash/resource constraints. Similarly, disposal of non-core business can be done at a measured pace and time taken to find a buyer at the right price, whereas in a Turnaround situation, often, sales happen at distressed valuations due to paucity of time.

Key stakeholders pushing for a Transformation of a business are usually the Board of Directors and large shareholders. The new CEO driving the Transformation will have to actively engage with these stakeholders and manage the expectations. However, unlike a Turnaround, the Transformation leader most likely would not have to deal with a large group of lenders with conflicting agendas and vendors/employees who have not been paid for months.

Having successfully led a Transformation, the Board of Directors would like the leader to continue to lead the organization to maintain continuity of vision.

We will deal with more details about the difference between Turnarounds and Transformation later in the book. For now, I hope the reader has a flavor of what a Corporate Turnaround is and how it is different from a Corporate Transformation.

The Business Life Cycle

The S-curve is a powerful concept used to understand the life cycle of a company, product, or industry. It shows how growth typically follows an S-shaped path: slow at first, then rapid, and finally tapering off. A business starts small as a "start-up", grows rapidly with greater product acceptance and market share expansion. Over the years, business growth slows down as its products attain market saturation and competition absorbs surplus ROCE. Businesses without any differentiation and competitive advantage will start to stagnate and often experience a decline in revenue, profitability and cash generation. A stagnant business will always exhibit symptoms of stress, similar to mild illnesses shown by human beings (like fever, cough, etc.) prior to the onset of a more severe illness. If these symptoms are not dealt with appropriately through the right business strategies or visionary transformation programs, a crisis will develop, forcing tougher Corporate Turnaround strategies to be implemented that, at times, can be traumatic for employees, vendors, lenders, shareholders and other stakeholders of the business.

The S-curve on the next page provides an indication wherein a business lifecycle transformation and turnaround sit.

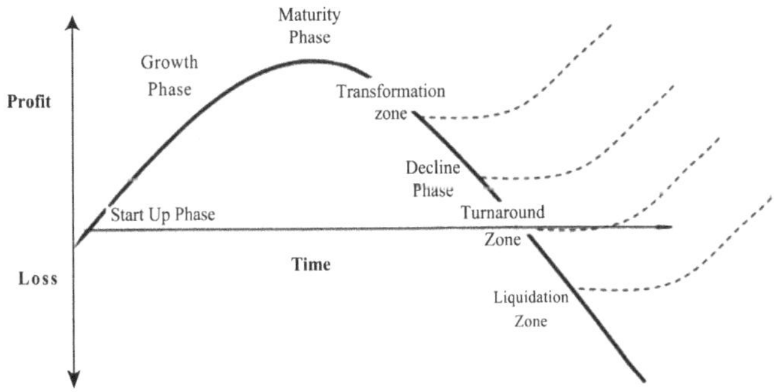

It is pertinent to note that the mere existence of profits is not an indication of a healthy business. A profitable business that is not generating adequate operating cash to invest in its future growth and provide adequate return to its stakeholders, will soon enough find itself in a turnaround situation. Similarly, one year of loss does not necessarily mean that the business is in a crisis and requires a turnaround. It is possible that the business suffered a one-time loss due to an asset write-off, a large provision, etc., but it could still have a healthy, profitable business and large cash reserves. Successive years of lower profits with poor cash generation and/or continued losses will most likely lead to a difficult situation requiring urgent recovery steps.

Here is another way to look at potential turnaround situations:

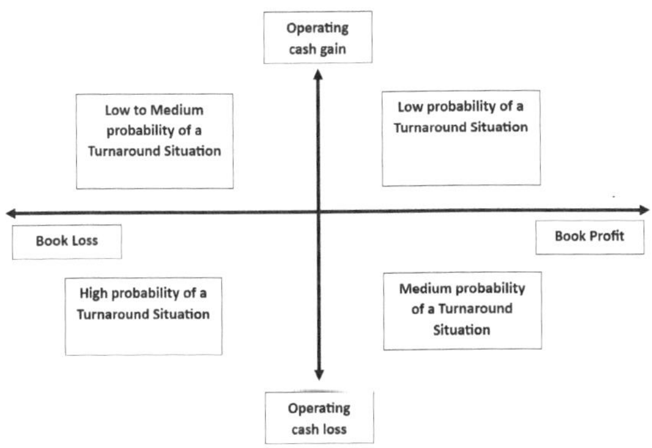

Above is a simple illustration to show the importance of cash generation in a business. However, the analysis of whether a business requires transformation or turnaround would require a deeper analysis of financial performance over a period of time, in addition to the reliability of books and the existence of leverage.

If managements are unable to take corrective action or their steps aren't able to reverse the business performance, they may resort to inflating profitability. Hence, at times, stakeholders commission a forensic analysis of books or an independent business review.

The existence of leverage compounds a crisis, just like an alcoholic may suffer greater complications vis-à-vis a non-alcoholic. Businesses borrow money as interest is tax-deductible, making debt a cheaper source of finance compared to equity. Judicious use of debt helps improve return on equity. However, bank debt comes with more stringent conditions than trade credit. Banks provide debt against security of assets and put stringent conditions (also called covenants) around business performance. Breach of repayment obligations (either interest, principal or both) or covenants may lead to banks calling for repayment of their debt, compounding an existing business crisis. Higher the leverage, the earlier the business will go into a crisis. Readers will recall the massive surge in bank non-performing assets (NPAs) during 2012 – 2016 period, requiring the government to come up with the Insolvency and Bankruptcy Code, 2016, to save these distressed businesses and find a suitable closure for all stakeholders.

Due to the existence of leverage, as shared in the previous graph, the medium and even low to medium probability situations can become a cash crisis, if the business is not generating sufficient cash to pay its debt obligations. Either the business will have to borrow more (increasing leverage in the business) or shareholders will have to provide new equity funds. If new funds are not available to meet capital expenditure and/or debt repayment requirements, then most likely both stakeholders (lenders and shareholders) doubt the business's ability to generate incremental cash returns that compensate for the risks involved. In such a situation, a financial restructuring is required immediately, a concept which we will discuss in a separate chapter.

Hopefully, the reader has understood what a turnaround situation is, the context in which such situations arise and the dynamics involved. Here are some non-business examples that involve a turnaround, which may help the reader to better understand turnarounds in a business context.

Example 1: Medical Emergency

Corporate Turnaround as a Medical Emergency

When a company plunges into crisis, cash flows drying up, creditors knocking, morale collapsing, it's not unlike a person involved in a serious road accident. The body goes into shock. Systems begin to fail. Immediate intervention is the only way to survive.

In such cases, time becomes the most precious resource. Just as a critically injured patient needs rapid response from paramedics and trauma doctors, a distressed company needs turnaround professionals, interim leaders, crisis managers, and financial advisors to stabilize it before irreversible damage occurs.

This isn't about strategic planning or long-term vision just yet. It's about survival. Bleeding must be stopped. Vital signs must be monitored. Quick decisions, often painful, must be made.

Over time, if handled right, the company transitions from the equivalent of the emergency room to the ICU, where deeper diagnosis and restructuring happen. Once stable, it can begin the process of recovery, rehabilitation, and eventually, transformation.

The Business as a Patient: Corporate Turnaround Through a Medical Lens

Medical Stage	Corporate Equivalent	Explanation
Accident / Trauma occurs	Major business crisis: cash burn, fraud, market crash	An external/internal shock destabilizes the company.
Loss of blood	Operating cash losses	Just like blood carries life to organs, cash sustains operations.
Paramedics rush to stabilize Emergency Room (ER)	Turnaround consultants / interim management	Experts provide immediate support to stabilize the bleeding.
Emergency Room (ER)	Crisis management phase	Rapid assessments, triage decisions, and firefighting (short-term survival)
ICU admission	Deep restructuring and turnaround planning	Intensive monitoring, debt restructuring, asset sales, cost-cutting.
Specialist intervention (surgeons)	Strategic advisors, lenders, board changes	High-level intervention to address core structural issues.
Monitoring & gradual healing	Cash flow stabilization, morale recovery	Business stabilizes but needs careful watch and minimal shocks.
Recovery room	Transition to steady-state operations	Business regains rhythm, team morale returns, trust rebuilds.
Physiotherapy & rehab	Capability building, process strengthening	Investing in new systems, skills, culture — prevent relapse.
Discharge from hospital	Back to growth track / Transformation	Company exits turnaround mode, repositions itself for future success.

Key Takeaways:

- Time is critical: In both ER and business crises, delay can be fatal.
- Stabilize first, then diagnose: Focus on survival, then work toward recovery and growth.
- Multidisciplinary team effort: Doctors, nurses, therapists ≈ Board, consultants, bankers, employees.
- Recovery is not instant: Long-term healing needs discipline, monitoring, and leadership commitment.
- Relapses happen: Without reforming underlying issues, companies can fall sick again, just like patients.

Example 2: Indian cricket

A powerful corporate turnaround analogy from Indian cricket history is India's comeback under Sourav Ganguly's captaincy after the 2000 match-fixing scandal.

India's Revival (2000–2003) = Classic Corporate Turnaround

In 2000, Indian cricket was at its lowest point. The match-fixing scandal had tarnished the sport's image, top players were banned or under suspicion, and public trust was shattered.

Enter Sourav Ganguly as captain. What followed was one of the most iconic turnarounds in Indian cricket history, akin to a company pulling itself back from the brink.

Turnaround Elements:

Loss of trust	Fans felt betrayed; brand India was tainted.
Leadership overhaul	Ganguly became captain - aggressive, fearless, and unafraid of reputations.
New talent pipeline	Backed young players like Sehwag, Yuvraj, Harbhajan, Zaheer — long-term bets.
Culture reset	Introduced team-first mentality, resilience, and pride in the jersey.
Bold decisions	Took on opposition fearlessly — even challenged Australia's dominance.
Stakeholder revival	Regained fan support, media respect, and international competitiveness.
Result	Finalists in the 2003 World Cup; laid the foundation for future dominance.

Why This is a Textbook Turnaround:

- The scandal was like a corporate fraud—it destroyed brand value and stakeholder faith.
- Ganguly acted like a turnaround CEO—decisive, fearless, and people-focused.
- His leadership attracted and retained fresh talent, critical for long-term transformation.
- The Indian team regained credibility, competitiveness, and fan loyalty.

Corporate Parallel:

Just like a company after a reputational crisis, Indian cricket restructured its core, brought in new leadership, and built a new culture of performance.

Example 3: Bollywood Movie "Guru"

A great and relatable Bollywood movie example of a corporate turnaround is "Guru" (2007) — inspired by the life of Dhirubhai Ambani and the rise of Reliance Industries.

Plot Summary with Turnaround Lens:

In Guru, the protagonist Gurukant Desai starts small but dreams big. He faces resistance from established players, bureaucracy, and scandals. At one point, his business empire faces major public backlash and regulatory pressure due to alleged unethical practices. Instead of giving up, Guru:

- Restructures his approach to business.
- Faces regulators and the media head-on, defending his vision.
- Redefines the narrative: Instead of being painted as a villain, he positions himself as a visionary for India's middle class and small investors.
- Streamlines operations, cuts waste, and focuses on scaling production and exports.

Turnaround Elements in "Guru":

In Guru, the protagonist Gurukant Desai starts small but dreams big. He faces resistance from established players, bureaucracy, and scandals. At one point, his business empire faces major public backlash and regulatory pressure due to alleged unethical practices. Instead of giving up, Guru:

Visionary leadership	Guru's relentless drive to grow and break norms.
Crisis moment	Public and media opposition, SEBI investigation
Reputation risk	Accusations of manipulation and corner-cutting.
Strategic pivot	Transparent engagement with regulators & public.
Outcome	Public support returns; business expands further.

Lesson:

"Guru" shows that a turnaround is not just about fixing numbers: it's about restoring confidence, realigning strategy, and resilient leadership.

Example 4: 2001 India – Australia Test Series

The Eden Gardens Miracle: A Corporate Turnaround in Whites

In March 2001, India found itself up against a near-invincible Australian team, riding a 16-Test winning streak. After losing the first Test of the series in Mumbai, India was staring at defeat again in the second Test at Eden Gardens, Kolkata. Forced to follow-on after a poor first innings, the match seemed all but lost.

What followed was nothing short of a miracle.

VVS Laxman (281) and Rahul Dravid (180) crafted a legendary 376-run partnership, turning the match on its head. India not only avoided defeat but went on to win the match, and ultimately, the series 2-1.

This isn't just cricket history. It's a masterclass in turnaround strategy.

Mapping the Match to a Corporate Turnaround

Cricket Event	Corporate Parallel	Turnaround Insight
Australia's dominance, India follows on	Market leadership of competitors; company suffers major losses	A crisis caused by competition, missteps, or market shift puts the company in retreat.
First innings collapse	Operational breakdown, liquidity crisis	The company is overwhelmed and forced into emergency response mode.
Forced to follow-on	External pressure (banks, regulators, stakeholders) intensifies	Pressure mounts; management may lose hope, stakeholders prepare for exit.
Laxman–Dravid partnership begins	Leadership and team resilience emerge	A new leadership mindset and team resolve become visible under pressure.
Laxman's 281 – patient, composed, daring	Bold turnaround plan with a long view	Requires stamina, clarity, and the ability to shut out noise and focus on fundamentals.
Dravid's support role – anchoring the side	Collaborative execution with aligned teams	Turnarounds are not solo efforts—supportive teams matter as much as bold leadership.
The tide turns – Australia on the back foot	Cash flows improve, operations stabilize	Momentum shifts with disciplined execution and belief in the plan.
India wins the Test and series	Full recovery and transformation	A company not only survives but emerges stronger, repositioned for long-term success.

Lessons for Corporate Turnaround Professionals

1. Don't panic when the follow-on hits: Setbacks are part of the game. The second half is still yours to play.
2. Anchor your turnaround with resilient leadership: Laxman and Dravid didn't look at the scoreboard, they focused on one ball, one run at a time.
3. Believe when others don't: Turnarounds require unshakable belief, even when everyone expects you to fold.
4. Partnerships are key: Just as no batter can win alone, no CXO or turnaround expert can either. Build the right team.
5. Turn the tide, then press the advantage: Once momentum shifts, move from survival to offense—innovate, grow, transform.

Closing Thought

If you were watching the Eden Gardens Test in 2001, you weren't just seeing a cricket match—you were witnessing a masterclass in turnaround leadership. For business leaders, CFOs, and crisis managers, this story reminds us that even when all seems lost, disciplined execution, belief, and team synergy can reverse the tide and rewrite history.

Hopefully, the reader by now has a good understanding of what turnaround situations are all about and why we need corporate turnarounds. On the latter point, in later chapters, we discuss at length the impact on businesses due to macro-economic cycles, industry-specific cycles, disruptions due to changes in technologies and supply chain shifts, etc. Some changes can be drastic and hit at the heart of a business, leading to immediate survival challenges. Others can be slow, gradual change, where if businesses fail to innovate and adapt to a changing environment, they will reach a turnaround situation.

Sample Indian Case Study: The Kingfisher Saga - A Flight into Liquidation

(based on publicly available data)

The story of Kingfisher Airlines is a cautionary tale of corporate ambition, financial mismanagement, and the harsh realities of the aviation industry. It is a journey that began with a flourish of luxury and ended in a cascade of debt, legal battles, and the painful lesson on how quickly a company can unravel. The narrative is not just about a business failure; it's about the very public journey of a high-profile company as it transitioned from a symbol of extravagance to a textbook case of liquidation.

The First Signs of Turbulence

The initial whispers of financial distress at Kingfisher Airlines began to surface well before the dramatic collapse. While the airline launched in 2005 with a reputation for premium service, it never posted a profit. The acquisition of the low-cost carrier Air Deccan in 2007, and its subsequent rebranding as Kingfisher Red, was a pivotal moment. The move, intended to expand the airline's market share, instead saddled it with enormous debt and a business model that was at odds with its premium image.

By late 2010 and early 2011, the financial pressure became palpable. News reports began to highlight stress on Kingfisher's balance sheet. The company's auditors, in their annual report for 2010-11, pointed out that accumulated losses had exceeded 50% of its net worth. This was a clear red flag, a warning that the airline was operating on a razor's edge.

The Cascade of Defaults

The stress on the balance sheet soon translated into concrete, and increasingly public, defaults. The first defaults were on smaller, but critical, payments. In late 2011, the airline's bank accounts were frozen by the Service Tax Department for non-payment of dues. This was a turning point. A company that cannot pay its taxes is a company in deep trouble. While the accounts were temporarily unfrozen after a partial payment, the incident was a clear signal of the airline's precarious cash position.

The defaults became more frequent and severe in 2012. The airline failed to pay its dues to airports, oil companies, and aircraft lessors. A consortium of 17 banks, led by the State Bank of India (SBI), which had lent a total of around ₹7,500 crore (approximately $1.2 billion at the time) to the airline, became increasingly concerned. Kingfisher was on the verge of being declared a "non-performing asset" (NPA), a technical term for loans on which principal or interest payments are overdue. To stave off this classification, the company would make a last-minute, one-month interest payment. It was a strategy of survival, but one that was unsustainable.

The Human Cost: Unpaid Salaries and Vendor Woes

While the financial news was a matter of balance sheets and corporate announcements, the human dimension of the crisis was far more immediate and painful. Kingfisher's employees, the very people who had made the airline a symbol of luxury, began to feel the pinch. Salary delays, which had first surfaced as early as 2009, became a regular occurrence and then a prolonged agony. Pilots, engineers, and cabin crew went months without pay.

The frustration escalated into public protests and strikes. Employees would report sick en masse, leading to widespread flight cancellations. The airline's operations were thrown into chaos. At one point, engineers went on strike, refusing to certify the planes for flight, effectively grounding the entire fleet. The airline was forced to declare a partial lockout. These strikes were a direct result of the company's inability to pay its staff, and they had a devastating impact on Kingfisher's ability to operate and generate revenue.

Vendors, too, were left in the lurch. Kingfisher had failed to pay for everything from jet fuel to ground services. The International Air Transport Association (IATA) even suspended the airline from its clearing house, which meant travel agents could no longer book tickets on Kingfisher. This cut off a vital revenue stream and hammered the final nails into the coffin of its operational viability.

Vijay Mallya's Statements and the Final Curtain

As the crisis deepened, all eyes were on the airline's charismatic chairman, Vijay Mallya. Known as the "King of Good Times," Mallya's public persona of a high-flying tycoon seemed at odds with the crumbling empire he presided over. Initially, he maintained a defiant optimism, often blaming external factors like high fuel prices and government policies. In statements to the media and employees, he would promise a turnaround, assuring them that a debt recast package was in place and that the government would soon allow foreign direct investment in airlines, which he believed would be a silver bullet.

However, as the situation worsened, Mallya's statements took on a more defensive tone. He later claimed he had a revival plan and even approached the then-Finance Minister, Pranab Mukherjee, to downsize the airline and lay off employees, but was allegedly told to continue operations and that banks would provide support. He also stated that money to pay employee salaries was tied up in legal proceedings and that banks had objected to its use for that purpose.

The endgame was swift and brutal. On October 20, 2012, the Directorate General of Civil Aviation (DGCA) suspended Kingfisher's flying license after it failed to present a credible revival plan. This was the final, fatal blow. The airline was grounded for good. The final demise of the company was sealed in the legal and financial labyrinth that followed. The banks moved the Debt Recovery Tribunal to recover their dues, and Mallya, who had by then fled to the UK, became the subject of a high-profile extradition case. The company's assets, including its Mumbai headquarters, were seized and put up for auction, a long and complex process that continues to this day.

The Kingfisher saga is a stark illustration of how a company's financial health is a delicate ecosystem. It shows that initial balance sheet stress, if unaddressed, can lead to a domino effect of debt defaults, loss of trust from vendors and employees, and, ultimately, the complete cessation of operations and the painful process of liquidation. The high-flying airline's descent serves as a powerful and enduring lesson for businesses and regulators alike.

Sample Indian Case Study: Essar Steel - A Corporate Debacle and a Landmark Resolution

(based on publicly available data)

The saga of Essar Steel is not a story of a company going into liquidation in the traditional sense. Instead, it is a landmark case in India's corporate history, a litmus test for the country's new Insolvency and Bankruptcy Code (IBC). It's a tale of a company's massive debt, a protracted legal battle, and a new paradigm of resolving corporate distress. Essar Steel's journey from a leading steel producer to a stressed asset is a powerful illustration of how a company's downfall can be a complex mix of business decisions, market forces, and the evolution of legal frameworks.

The Weight of Ambition and Debt

Essar Steel's financial woes were not an overnight phenomenon. The company, a major player in the Indian steel industry, had a history of high debt, even going through a corporate debt restructuring in the early 2000s. However, the seeds of its final crisis were sown in a massive expansion plan at its Hazira plant in Gujarat. This expansion, aimed at significantly increasing its steel-making capacity, was fuelled by large-scale borrowing from a consortium of banks.

By 2015, the expansion plan had faltered. A combination of factors, including delays in environmental clearances and the non-availability of natural gas, a crucial input for its plant, left the company saddled with an enormous debt load. To make matters worse, a global slump in commodity prices, particularly steel, eroded the company's profitability and ability to service its loans. As a result, Essar Steel's financial condition deteriorated rapidly, with its debt soaring to over ₹49,000 crore (approximately $7.5 billion at the time) by 2017.

The Dawn of a New Legal Era

The introduction of the Insolvency and Bankruptcy Code (IBC) in 2016 provided a new, time-bound framework for addressing corporate defaults.

Unlike the old system, which was often slow and inefficient, the IBC gave creditors the power to initiate a "Corporate Insolvency Resolution Process" (CIRP) against a defaulting company.

In June 2017, Essar Steel was among the first on the "dirty dozen" list of large defaulters referred to the National Company Law Tribunal (NCLT) by the Reserve Bank of India (RBI) for immediate insolvency action. This was the beginning of a high-stakes legal and financial drama. The case was admitted to the NCLT in August 2017, and a resolution professional was appointed to take control of the company's management and assets.

The Battle for Essar Steel

The insolvency proceedings for Essar Steel became one of the most high-profile and complex cases under the new IBC. Several global giants, including ArcelorMittal and Vedanta, submitted bids to acquire the company. The bids were not just about financial offers; they also had to navigate the intricate legal landscape of the new insolvency law. The Essar promoters, the Ruia family, made a last-ditch attempt to retain control of the company by offering to pay back all the creditors, but their offer was ultimately rejected by the courts.

The battle for Essar Steel was marked by fierce legal challenges, particularly between the bidders, ArcelorMittal and Numetal, and the Committee of Creditors (CoC). The Supreme Court of India was called upon to clarify critical sections of the IBC, including the eligibility criteria for bidders. The court's judgments played a crucial role in shaping the future of India's insolvency law, as they set important precedents regarding the rights of different classes of creditors and the primacy of the CoC's commercial decisions.

A Resolution, Not a Liquidation

While Kingfisher Airlines' story ended in liquidation, Essar Steel's journey took a different turn. The goal of the IBC is not to liquidate a company but to revive it as a "going concern", if a viable resolution plan can be found. In this case, the efforts of the creditors and the legal process bore fruit.

After a two-year-long legal marathon that saw multiple appeals and a series of landmark judgments from the NCLT, NCLAT (National Company Law Appellate Tribunal), and the Supreme Court, the resolution plan submitted by ArcelorMittal, in partnership with Nippon Steel, was finally approved in November 2019. The plan involved an upfront payment of ₹42,000 crore to the financial creditors, giving them a significant recovery on their loans. ArcelorMittal and Nippon Steel took control of the company, which was renamed ArcelorMittal Nippon Steel India (AM/NS India).

The resolution of the Essar Steel case was a monumental victory for the IBC and a clear signal to both domestic and international investors that India's new bankruptcy law was effective and credible. It demonstrated that even in cases of massive debt and complex ownership structures, a time-bound and transparent resolution process could work. The Essar Steel saga, therefore, is not a tale of a company's final demise but rather a story of a high-stakes corporate rescue and the birth of a new era of business resolution in India.

Sample Indian Case Study: Videocon Industries - From Television Screens to the Insolvency Court

(based on publicly available data)

The downfall of Videocon Industries is a complex narrative that reflects the shifting tides of the Indian economy, the perils of aggressive diversification, and the critical role of corporate governance. Once a household name and a pioneer in India's consumer electronics market, the company's journey from a market leader to a distressed asset is a stark reminder of how a company can lose its way.

Losing the Plot: The Technology Gap

In its heyday, Videocon dominated the Indian consumer electronics market, especially in televisions and washing machines. However, as the new millennium dawned, the company failed to adapt to the rapid technological advancements sweeping the industry. The market shifted from cathode ray tube (CRT) TVs to sleek, high-definition flat-screen liquid-crystal display (LCD) and light-emitting diode (LED) TVs.

Videocon's foreign rivals, like Samsung and LG, were aggressively investing in research and development (R&D) to bring these new technologies to market. They built strong brands, cultivated consumer loyalty, and established a reputation for cutting-edge products. While Videocon did make some investments in R&D, its efforts were not on par with its global competitors. This lack of strategic foresight and insufficient investment in new technologies led to a gradual but irreversible loss of market share. Consumers, drawn to the superior technology and features of foreign brands, began to abandon Videocon products. The once-dominant brand became a symbol of outdated technology, and its core business, the very foundation of its success, started to erode.

A Web of Debt and Diversification

The decline of the core business was exacerbated by a strategy of aggressive and often misguided diversification. Videocon Industries ventured into a wide range of capital-intensive and unrelated sectors, including oil and gas, telecommunications, power generation, and DTH services. To fund these ambitious projects, the company took on massive amounts of debt from a consortium of banks.

By 2017, Videocon's debt had ballooned to over ₹49,000 crore. Its ventures outside consumer electronics, particularly its telecom business which suffered significant losses after the Supreme Court revoked its 2G licenses, failed to generate sufficient revenue to service this debt. A key issue was the intermingling of finances across the group's many subsidiaries. The company operated as a single economic unit, with loans taken jointly by multiple group entities. When the financial crunch hit, this complex corporate structure made it nearly impossible to resolve the debt on a company-by-company basis, creating a legal and financial quagmire for creditors.

The Corporate Structure maze

The company's complex corporate structure played a significant role in its ultimate downfall. Instead of focusing on its core strengths and investing in innovation, the management pursued a high-risk, debt-fuelled expansion. This led to a situation where even the profitable consumer electronics division could not compensate for the losses in other ventures.

The tangled web of subsidiaries and their interdependent operations became a major point of contention during the insolvency proceedings. When a consortium of banks led by the State Bank of India (SBI) filed for insolvency under the new Insolvency and Bankruptcy Code (IBC) in 2018, the National Company Law Tribunal (NCLT) was forced to invoke the "doctrine of substantive consolidation" to deal with the debt. The court recognized that the assets and liabilities of 13 of the 15 Videocon group companies were so intertwined that they could only be resolved as a single entity. This landmark decision highlighted how the company's opaque and convoluted structure had a direct and negative impact on its management and made a resolution nearly impossible without a drastic legal measure.

Statements from the promoter to the NCLT itself underscored this complexity, with the promoter arguing for consolidation of the corporate insolvency resolution process (CIRP) of the group companies. The promoter and others were also later embroiled in a high-profile case related to alleged irregularities in loans sanctioned by ICICI Bank, which further damaged the company's reputation and trust among creditors and the public.

The Final Chapter

The story of Videocon Industries culminated in a protracted legal battle under the IBC. The first

resolution plan, submitted by Twin Star Technologies (a Vedanta Group company), was approved by the Committee of Creditors (CoC) but later set aside by the National Company Law Appellate Tribunal (NCLAT). The case has since been through multiple appeals, highlighting the challenges of resolving complex corporate defaults in India. Videocon's journey is not a simple case of liquidation; it's a profound lesson in how a lack of focus on core business, failure to embrace technological change, and an overly complicated, debt-ridden corporate structure can bring down even a once-thriving business empire.

Chapter 02

Identifying a Turnaround Situation

"Turnaround truth: Foresight buys time; hindsight just buys regrets"

In this chapter, we will try to understand the following:

1. Difference between stress and distress
2. What ratios, data sources, and news must be used - to evaluate if a business is facing stress?
3. Common causes of businesses ending up in a turnaround situation

Stress and Distress

We have gained a broad understanding of what a turnaround situation looks like. However, as with everything in life, generalisations rarely capture the full picture. There are always nuances, and it is important to recognise and respect them. Much like a doctor diagnosing a patient, it is critical to understand whether a business's illness requires medication or surgery.

In the previous chapter, we touched upon the business life cycle, where mature companies may enter a decline phase if management fails to innovate or lead a bold, forward-looking transformation. Often, management teams do attempt to counter competition and revive performance. However, their efforts may fall short due to flawed strategies, poor capital allocation, or weak execution. At times, the actions taken are simply not ambitious or courageous enough, given the scale of disruption facing the business or industry.

The early stages of a decline (let's call it the Stress phase) often exhibit one or more of the following symptoms:

- **Loss or stagnation of market share**

  A once-dominant player may begin losing ground to nimbler or more innovative competitors. This could be due to shifts in customer preferences, technological disruption, or a failure to respond effectively to market trends. In some cases, market share may stagnate despite efforts, indicating a loss of relevance or value proposition.

- **Declining product margins**

  As competition intensifies or as the product portfolio becomes outdated, businesses may face pricing pressures. Discounts and promotional spending to push sales eat into gross margins. This often reflects a loss of pricing power and declining customer perception of value.

- **Shrinking profit margins and overall profitability**

  Operational inefficiencies, increased overheads, and strategic missteps contribute to reduced profitability. Even if top-line revenue holds steady, the bottom line erodes. This is often the clearest financial indicator that the business is under stress.

- **Increased working capital requirements**

  In an attempt to sustain revenues, companies may offer more generous credit terms or build up inventories, leading to higher working capital needs. This can strain cash flows, leaving less room for investments in innovation or growth. Often, this is a sign of a company buying time rather than building strength.

- **Constrained budgets for future growth initiatives**

  As financial pressures mount, investments in R&D, marketing, or strategic initiatives are often scaled back. This creates a vicious cycle where the lack of forward-looking investment further accelerates decline. The business starts focusing on survival rather than growth, weakening its competitive edge.

In such conditions, morale within the organization typically deteriorates. Leadership finds itself navigating a constrained environment, often dealing with setbacks in the marketplace. The mood is marked by uncertainty, and decision-making becomes reactive rather than strategic.

The slow & gradual decline, combined with a constrained budgetary environment and low morale, can numb a business into falsely believing it has the luxury of time to execute a transformation.

Until one day, it runs out of time.

An apt analogy is that of a frog in a pan of water, being slowly heated. The frog does not perceive the rising temperature until it is too late, eventually succumbing to the heat. For cricket aficionados, a familiar scenario is the slow run rate during a tight chase in a 50-over match. The chasing side, reassured by wickets in hand, allows the required run rate to rise steadily. While some teams manage a final-overs flourish, more often than not, wickets fall at key moments, creating a crisis, and they lose the match.

Similarly, if the right turnaround strategies are not employed during the **Stress** phase, the business can slip into deeper operational and financial challenges. We refer to this as the **Distress** phase, marked by a combination of one or more of the following symptoms:

- **Sharp decline in revenue**

  A significant drop in top-line performance indicates either customer attrition, market irrelevance, or severe competitive pressure. This is often a red flag for stakeholders.

- **Consecutive quarters of book losses**

  Sustained net losses begin to erode shareholder value and highlight systemic inefficiencies or flawed business models.

- **Consecutive quarters of operating cash loss**

  When core operations consistently consume rather than generate cash, it signals a severe breakdown in the business's ability to sustain itself without external support.

- **Significant extension of trade credit, far exceeding industry norms**

  Suppliers begin to worry as payables are stretched. This may be a desperate attempt to conserve cash, but it compromises credibility and long-term supplier relationships.

- **Departure of key senior management personnel**

  Loss of leadership at such times can further destabilise the organisation, damage morale, and indicate a lack of internal alignment or confidence in recovery.

- **Delays in employee bonuses, or worse, salary payments**

  A clear sign of cash crunch. When compensation is delayed, employee trust collapses, often leading to attrition and a breakdown in productivity.

- **Headcount reduction**

  Often positioned as a cost-control measure, layoffs can harm morale and signal to the market that the business is struggling to stay afloat.

- **Halt in existing or new capital expenditure plans**

  Freezing investments in growth or maintenance initiatives suggests financial stress and limits future competitiveness.

- **High-cost borrowings**

  As risk perception rises, lenders demand higher returns. Resorting to expensive debt only worsens the financial position and reduces room for manoeuvre.

- **Company debt put on credit watch or facing a rating downgrade**

  Rating agencies and financial institutions begin to flag concerns about solvency and repayment ability, triggering further scrutiny and potential investor exit.

- **Delay in payment of interest or principal and/or breach of debt covenants**

  This is often the tipping point—an explicit sign that the business is veering toward insolvency unless immediate and drastic corrective action is taken.

As the business slips deeper into distress, perhaps the most damaging development is the breakdown of trust among stakeholders viz., employees, lenders, suppliers, customers, and even internal leadership. Trust begins to erode when promises are missed, communication becomes reactive or opaque, and key decisions appear inconsistent or self-preserving. Employees grow anxious about job security and compensation. Creditors and suppliers tighten terms or disengage altogether. Customers may begin to question the company's reliability and long-term viability. Even within the leadership team, differing opinions on survival strategies can cause misalignment and friction. This erosion of trust doesn't just reflect the crisis, it accelerates it. Once stakeholder confidence begins to collapse, the window for a smooth or internally-driven turnaround narrows sharply. At this point, any revival effort demands not just operational and financial fixes, but a concerted effort to rebuild credibility, often under intense scrutiny and time pressure.

Another critical yet less visible dimension of the Stress and Distress phases is the growing temptation within management to manipulate or "adjust" financial reporting in an attempt to present a healthier picture of the business. In the early stages of stress, this may begin subtly e.g., accelerating revenue recognition, under-reporting provisions, deferring expenses, or overly optimistic assumptions in forecasting models. The belief is often that these adjustments are temporary: a bridge to get through a rough patch, with the intention of "cleaning up" the books once performance improves.

However, if the hoped-for turnaround does not materialize or, worse, if the situation deteriorates further, these accounting manoeuvres become increasingly difficult to unwind. What starts as tactical short-term smoothing can evolve into systemic misrepresentation, eroding the reliability of the financial statements and severely damaging the credibility of the management team. In distress, the pressure intensifies. With limited options left and external scrutiny mounting, some teams may resort to aggressive or even unethical accounting practices in a last-ditch effort to maintain stakeholder confidence, meet debt covenants, or avoid triggering defaults.

This behavior creates a vicious cycle. Stakeholders, including lenders, investors, and auditors begin to question not just the numbers, but the integrity behind them. Once doubt creeps in about the trustworthiness of reported financials, access to capital dries up, partnerships weaken, and turnaround opportunities shrink. Even if the company survives, the damage to its reputation can linger for years.

Thus, a key leadership challenge during a turnaround is to resist the urge to obscure reality, however uncomfortable it may be. Transparent, timely, and honest financial reporting is not just a compliance requirement; it is a strategic imperative for rebuilding stakeholder trust and enabling a viable path to recovery.

Identifying a Turnaround Situation

Investors, lenders, suppliers, and other stakeholders must remain vigilant when engaging with a business showing signs of stress, as discussed earlier. Early identification of a potential turnaround scenario is critical not just for risk mitigation, but also to assess whether there may be an opportunity for value creation if the company successfully navigates the crisis.

A proactive approach begins with direct engagement with the company's management team. Stakeholders should seek to understand what corrective measures are being taken, and critically evaluate whether these are adequate, timely, and well-aligned with industry realities. Conversations should be anchored in data and context, i.e., how the company is performing relative to its peers, both domestic and international, and how management interprets its own underperformance. Equally important is to study how industry leaders or agile competitors are navigating similar challenges. Benchmarking responses across companies often reveals whether the business is acting boldly or merely reacting defensively.

An in-person interaction with management can also reveal intangible, yet important signals such as confidence, energy, coherence, and ownership. A follow-up, a few quarters later, to assess whether the announced initiatives are delivering the promised results, offers valuable insight into execution quality and adaptability.

That said, not all stakeholders have the luxury of regular access to management. In such cases and even otherwise, a structured analysis of financial and non-financial indicators can help assess whether a business is in need of a turnaround and whether it is on the right path.

Non-Financial Red Flags

Management & Governance Signals

- Resignations of key executives such as the CEO, CFO, or Independent Directors
- Sudden change of auditors, or delays in audit sign-offs
- Absence of formal guidance, or unrealistic forward-looking statements in contrast to recent performance
- Repeated failures to meet targets set in previous investor calls or earnings guidance
- Delay or stalling of strategic capital projects (expansion, tech upgrades, cost efficiency)

External Market Signals

- Credit rating downgrades or placement on a negative watch (CRISIL, ICRA, CARE in India; S&P, Moody's, Fitch globally)
- High or rising promoter share pledging (especially >50% of promoter holding)
- Increase in short interest in the company's stock (for listed companies)
- Shift in shareholding patterns—reduction in DII/FII stake and a rise in retail public holding
- Rising cost or tightening of trade credit insurance
- Regulatory or tax changes threatening the core business model (e.g., 2023 GST changes affecting real-money gaming companies)

Financial Red Flags

Deteriorating Financial Trends (vs. industry & peers)

- Consecutive quarters of stagnant or declining revenue
- Persistent decline in operating or EBITDA margins
- Increase in working capital as a percentage of revenue
- Worsening working capital cycle (days receivable, inventory, payable)

Extraordinary or One-Time Adjustments

- Large write-offs, impairments, or reclassifications that significantly alter reported earnings or balance sheet strength

Cash Flow Stress

- Steep decline in operating cash flow as a percentage of EBITDA, suggesting poor earnings quality

Leverage & Solvency Pressure

- Declining interest coverage ratio (EBIT / Interest)
- Rising debt-to-EBITDA ratio—especially if breaching covenant thresholds

These red flags are early indicators that merit deeper analysis. Once a business shows multiple signs across the categories above, stakeholders must go beyond surface-level metrics and undertake a deeper review of:

- Market share dynamics and trends
- Product-market fit and competitive positioning
- Input cost structure and margin vulnerability
- Order book trends (where applicable)
- Segment-wise performance and customer concentration risk
- Capital allocation history and strategy

Identifying a business in need of a turnaround is as much about recognizing distress as it is about assessing recovery potential. The ability to distinguish between temporary setbacks and structural weaknesses can make all the difference in strategic decision-making: be it for lenders extending credit, investors seeking value, or vendors managing risk.

Here's a Diagnostic Checklist that can be used as a quick reference to assess whether a business is showing signs of stress and may require a turnaround. It's structured into four categories, with yes/no checks and brief indicators.

Turnaround Diagnostic Checklist

Financial Performance & Liquidity

Question	Yes/No Notes
Has revenue declined in 2 or more consecutive quarters?	☐ / ☐ Compare with industry peers
Are operating or EBITDA margins deteriorating consistently?	☐ / ☐ Check against historical levels
Is the company generating negative operating cash flow?	☐ / ☐ Even if profitable on paper
Is working capital rising as a % of revenue?	☐ / ☐ Suggests pressure in receivables or inventory
Has there been a large write-off, impairment, or provisioning recently?	☐ / ☐ Indicates stress or cleanup

Solvency & Capital Structure

Question	Yes/No Notes
Is the interest coverage ratio below 1.5x?	☐ / ☐ EBIT / Interest Expense
Is debt-to-EBITDA rising significantly or > 3.5x?	☐ / ☐ May breach covenants
Has the company raised high-cost debt or bridge funding recently?	☐ / ☐ Emergency funding = stress
Are there signs of cash crunch (e.g. delays in bonuses, vendor payments)?	☐ / ☐ May also reflect in audit notes

Governance & Management Signals

Question	Yes/No Notes
Have key executives (CEO, CFO, etc.) recently resigned?	☐ / ☐ Especially if abrupt or unexplained
Has the auditor changed suddenly or delayed sign-off?	☐ / ☐ Governance concern
Is the company missing guidance or investor commitments repeatedly?	☐ / ☐ Signals poor execution
Are there signs of accounting adjustments or earnings management?	☐ / ☐ e.g., aggressive revenue recognition

Market, Competition & External Indicators

Question	Yes/No Notes
Has the company lost market share to competitors?	☐ / ☐ Look for customer churn or product weakness
Are there significant regulatory or tax headwinds impacting the model?	☐ / ☐ e.g., policy changes in digital or ESG
Has there been a credit rating downgrade or increase in pledged promoter shares?	☐ / ☐ Financial market signals
Are DIIs/FIIs exiting, and public shareholding rising?	☐ / ☐ Red flag in listed companies

How to Use This Checklist

- 5 or more "Yes": Immediate attention needed; turnaround likely required.
- 10+ "Yes": Business is likely in Distress or at high risk of entering that phase.
- <5 "Yes": Monitor closely; evaluate trend lines and external risks.

Common Causes of Businesses Ending Up in a Turnaround Situation

Earlier in this chapter, we discussed the symptoms of stress and distress in a business's lifecycle and how to identify them. Now, before we embark on understanding how to turn around a distressed business, it is essential to ask a more fundamental question: How do businesses end up in distress in the first place?

This question is not academic—it is foundational. Just as a skilled doctor must differentiate between a fever and the infection that causes it, a turnaround professional must distinguish between symptoms (falling revenue, rising debt, poor cash flows) and root causes (mismanagement, flawed strategy, market disruption, etc.). Only by identifying the real underlying issues can effective and sustainable solutions be devised.

Importantly, distress rarely stems from a single cause. It is almost always a combination of internal and external factors. While management must often take a lion's share of the responsibility, some crises are genuinely driven by forces beyond their control such as macroeconomic shifts, regulatory shocks, geopolitical upheavals, or technological disruptions.

It is this nuanced understanding that ensures a turnaround strategy doesn't "throw the baby out with the bathwater." The goal is not just survival. It is a revival with purpose.

Let us now look at some of the most common causes of corporate distress, especially as seen in the Indian business context:

1. Mismanaged Growth

Businesses often falter when they grow too fast without building the foundational capabilities to sustain that growth. During periods of strong industry tailwinds, the businesses that are buoyed by easy capital and customer demand, may chase aggressive expansion strategies. However, businesses are not just about acquiring customers and funding working capital.

Growth puts stress on every part of the organization:

- People and talent pipelines
- Operational systems and controls
- Governance and compliance
- Training, culture, and internal processes

When these elements are neglected in favor of just "top-line" growth, the business begins to fray at the edges. Shortcuts in execution, inadequate internal controls, and a lack of preparedness can unravel even a fundamentally good business.

Case Example

Mismanaged Growth Despite Strong Fundamentals

Consider the case of a 100% promoter-owned company, led by a high-integrity and capable entrepreneur, that chose to partner with a private equity (PE) fund to finance its next phase of growth. At the time of the investment, the business was fundamentally sound with healthy margins, profitable operations, and a stable revenue base of around ₹100 crore. The company specialized in installing surveillance camera networks and fire alarm systems in residential and commercial buildings, a niche but growing segment.

The timing seemed perfect. Post-2003, India was witnessing a real estate boom, fuelled by easy credit, low interest rates, and massive demand for residential and commercial infrastructure. This wave created significant opportunities for ancillary service providers like this one.

With fresh capital from the PE fund, the business scaled rapidly, securing large orders that required upfront inventory investment. Monthly revenue run-rate surged. On the surface, it looked like a textbook case of growth capital at work.

But internally, cracks began to emerge. The business had underestimated the complexity of scaling execution capabilities.

- Project execution teams were overwhelmed, and large numbers of untrained recruits were hastily pushed into field operations.
- Financial controls were weak, and there was no institutionalized system for real-time project monitoring.
- Standard operating procedures were either undefined or inconsistently followed.

As operational chaos grew, project delivery timelines slipped. This triggered penalties, delayed receivables, and customer dissatisfaction. New orders dried up. Meanwhile, the company had already drawn down its working capital lines to the limit, expecting incoming cash flows to replenish liquidity. When those inflows stalled, the business found itself in a full-blown liquidity crisis.

This is a classic example of how a fundamentally good business, in the right market at the right time, can slide into distress not because of flawed strategy, but because of mismanaged execution and inadequate readiness for growth.

2. Overestimating Demand

One of the most critical responsibilities of any management team is to anticipate future demand and plan investments accordingly. Whether it is capacity expansion, product development, or geographic diversification - these decisions require a long-term horizon and are often capital-intensive. Misjudging future demand trends can therefore be costly, particularly when such expansion is debt-funded, leaving the business vulnerable to external shocks.

The situation becomes especially precarious when the anticipated demand fails to materialize, but input costs rise or competitive intensity increases. This results in a double whammy: weaker revenue coupled with higher costs and fixed obligations.

Case Example

The Perils of Demand Overestimation

Around 2010, a leading Indian manufacturer of packaging material for the FMCG sector found itself at the top of its game. With over 50% market share and a pan-India footprint, the company had built strong relationships with large domestic FMCG brands.

A wave of consolidation in the FMCG sector began in the mid-2000s. One after another, these Indian brands were acquired by global industry giants, bringing with them expectations of larger product portfolios, aggressive marketing, and increased consumption. The packaging supplier saw this as a massive opportunity and embarked on an ambitious growth plan.

To protect its market share and capture the expected surge in demand, the company:

- Undertook a major capacity expansion;
- Acquired a competitor with a large manufacturing facility (despite known challenges with a unionized workforce);
- Took on significant debt to finance both the acquisition and capex.

Unfortunately, the demand expansion never materialized at the projected pace. Consumer uptake was slower than anticipated, and the international FMCG players focused more on supply chain efficiencies and price competitiveness than simply ramping up volumes.

To make matters worse, the following issues arose:

- The newly acquired plant struggled with labour unrest, affecting productivity;
- Rising input costs squeezed margins;
- The business faced high interest obligations, owing to the leveraged expansion;

- Customers resisted price hikes and encouraged rival suppliers to reduce dependency on a single player.

The company's financial position deteriorated quickly. As profitability dropped and loan covenants were breached, lenders lost confidence. Working capital limits were frozen, triggering a liquidity crisis.

In less than five years, a business that once held a dominant position in a growing market found itself in distress, with an over-leveraged balance sheet, rising costs, and eroding customer loyalty: all because of a strategic misjudgement in demand forecasting.

3. Overdependence on a Single Client

In the pursuit of growth and stability, businesses often take comfort in large, anchor clients, especially when those clients offer consistent volumes, timely payments, and long-term contracts. However, overreliance on a single client or a very small group of clients can be deceptively risky. When a disproportionate share of revenue, production capacity, or strategic focus is tied to one customer, the business becomes exposed to external shocks it cannot control.

Even minor disruptions such as changes in the client's procurement strategy, a pricing dispute, or a management reshuffle can have a cascading effect on the supplier. In more serious cases, the loss of that client can be existential.

Case Example

A Cautionary Tale in B2B Manufacturing

Consider the case of a mid-sized engineering components manufacturer based in western India, specializing in precision parts for the automotive sector. Over a period of years, the company built a deep and profitable relationship with a leading Indian auto OEM (original equipment manufacturer), which eventually grew to constitute nearly 70% of its annual revenues.

The business expanded capacity specifically to serve this client, customized its production lines, and even opened a satellite facility near the OEM's main plant. On paper, the relationship appeared to be a stable annuity—high volumes, long-term visibility, and a prestigious customer name.

But the risks were lurking beneath the surface:

- Pricing power lay entirely with the OEM, which routinely negotiated tighter margins with suppliers.
- Product design decisions were made solely by the client, making it hard for the supplier to innovate or diversify.
- The manufacturer neglected building a wider client base, choosing to deepen the single relationship instead of de-risking it.

Trouble began when the OEM underwent a global strategic realignment, deciding to shift a large portion of its sourcing to a different region in Asia to optimize costs. Almost overnight, the Indian supplier lost a significant chunk of its business.

With no alternative customers of similar scale and fixed costs tied to capacity that was now idle, the business quickly slipped into financial distress. Working capital cycles stretched, bank facilities were maxed out, and cash reserves were depleted. The company scrambled to diversify its customer base but by then, the distress was too deep, and turnaround required a complete reimagining of the business model.

This case is a reminder that customer concentration risk is not just a sales issue, it's a strategic vulnerability. A healthy business must continuously diversify revenue streams, build redundancy into its client portfolio, and ensure no single customer holds undue influence over its financial or operational health.

4. External Shocks

No matter how well-run or fundamentally strong a business is, it is not insulated from the external environment. Economic cycles, regulatory changes, geopolitical disruptions, commodity price swings, pandemics, and currency volatility are just some examples of external shocks that can rapidly destabilize even a healthy enterprise.

What makes external shocks particularly dangerous is that they are:

- Unpredictable in timing,
- Broad in impact, and
- Difficult to mitigate, especially for businesses that are not structurally resilient.

While no management can fully prevent the impact of such shocks, many businesses slide into distress because they failed to build buffers such as financial prudence, diversified markets, or agile operations that can help absorb the blow.

Case Example

Regulatory Shock in Infrastructure Services

Consider the case of an infrastructure services company that specialized in logistics and handling operations for coal-based thermal power plants. The company operated in several Indian states and had long-term contracts with power producers for coal yard management and intra-plant logistics.

In the early 2010s, with India's power generation capacity expanding and coal usage remaining high, the company scaled operations rapidly and invested in mechanized handling systems at several locations. The business had stable cash flows, long-term visibility, and comfortable debt servicing ability.

Then came the coal block deallocation ruling in 2014 by the Supreme Court of India, which cancelled over 200 coal block allocations on grounds of procedural irregularities. Several coal-fired power plants under development or early commissioning were suddenly thrown into disarray. Some clients lost their captive coal supply; others went into arbitration or litigation. Payments slowed. New contracts were frozen. Some plants mothballed their expansion plans altogether.

The infrastructure services provider, despite doing nothing wrong operationally, saw a sudden collapse in business volumes and stuck receivables. Fixed costs remained high, and bank loans taken to invest in capital equipment became difficult to service. With no immediate alternative markets or clients, and contractual disputes delaying cash flows, the company went into distress.

This example highlights how regulatory actions or policy shifts, even if well-intentioned at the national level, can disrupt the operating model of dependent businesses. Other examples of external shocks include:

- The COVID-19 pandemic, which upended supply chains and consumer behaviour;
- Currency depreciation, affecting import-heavy industries;
- Geopolitical conflicts, impacting energy prices or export markets;
- Ban on specific inputs or environmental restrictions, which can render capacities idle overnight.

In each case, the companies that fared better were those that had:

- Diversified customer and product portfolios,
- Lean cost structures,
- Low leverage, and
- Scenario planning mechanisms in place.

While external shocks may not be preventable, business fragility is often self-created through poor risk management.

5. Financial Mismanagement

At the heart of many business failures lie not a bad product, weak demand, or even external shocks but poor financial management. A company can have a strong market position, innovative offerings, and operational capabilities, yet still slide into distress if it mismanages cash flow, leverage, working capital, or capital allocation.

Financial mismanagement takes many forms:

- Over-leveraging the balance sheet without corresponding return on capital.
- Mismatch between asset-liability tenures, such as using short-term loans to fund long-term assets.
- Lax controls over working capital, leading to receivables build-up or inventory bloat.
- Undisciplined capital expenditure, without realistic ROI expectations.
- Failure to track early financial red flags, such as covenant breaches, rising finance costs, or poor cash conversion.

Such practices not only create fragility but also reduce management's ability to respond when stress does arrive.

Case Example

Growth Without Guardrails in a B2B Services Firm

Take the case of a rapidly growing B2B facilities management company, which provided services such as housekeeping, security, and catering to large corporate campuses and industrial facilities. The business model was inherently working capital intensive: employees had to be paid monthly, while clients typically paid after 45–60 days.

To win large contracts, the company aggressively underpriced its services, hoping to later increase pricing or cross-sell. While revenue grew quickly, margins were razor-thin, and the gap between billing and collections widened. The company failed to put in place:

- Periodic account reconciliation with clients;
- Receivables management systems;
- Cash flow-based budgeting;
- And contingency planning for delays in client payments.

Instead of addressing the cash flow crunch, the management chose to fund the gap by rolling over short-term loans, opening up new overdraft limits, and stretching vendor payments. Over time, finance costs ballooned, and vendors started withholding services. Payrolls were delayed. Several key clients, sensing instability, exited at the time of renewal.

By the time the company acknowledged its financial fragility, it had already accumulated unsustainable debt, had no available banking lines, and was facing operational disruption. Despite having a strong brand and client base, the business fell into distress not due to a lack of demand, but due to poor financial discipline.

This case underlines an essential truth: Revenue is vanity, profit is sanity, but cash flow is reality. Businesses that do not ground their growth in solid financial controls are essentially building castles on sand. The problem is not always the absence of finance professionals. It's often the lack of integration between finance and strategy at the leadership level.

Understanding the causes that push a business into distress is the critical first step in any turnaround journey. As we've seen, there is rarely a single trigger; more often, it is a combination of internal missteps and external pressures, compounded over time. Whether it's unchecked ambition, flawed financial decisions, overreliance on key customers, or a leadership blind to change, these root causes must be surfaced and acknowledged with honesty. Just as a doctor cannot cure an illness without diagnosing the disease, a turnaround professional cannot prescribe solutions without first identifying what went wrong and why. Moreover, the same cause can manifest differently across businesses depending on industry structure, life-cycle stage, and management quality. Hence, a nuanced diagnosis is essential not only to develop effective strategies but also to avoid repeating past mistakes. In the chapters ahead, we will move from diagnosis to action, laying out frameworks and approaches that have helped struggling businesses recover, transform, and rebuild value.

Chapter 03

Successful Corporate Turnaround Process

"Process beats panic; cadence turns chaos into momentum."

Before we learn more about the process of leading Corporate Turnarounds, it's important that we internalize certain principles that must be followed by any practitioner. Hopefully, the reader has understood that Turnarounds are a niche area of management and not for everyone. It requires a very different kind of leadership and approach to save a business. We will go into details of leadership style later in the book, but here we will deal with certain principles that must be followed for the Corporate Turnaround Process to have any chance of success.

Principles are necessary because they serve as foundational guideposts, helping us navigate complex situations, make consistent decisions, and live with integrity. Here's a deeper breakdown of why principles matter:

1. Clarity in Decision-Making

Principles offer a mental compass. When faced with dilemmas, you don't need to start from scratch every time you refer to your core values.

2. Consistency and Integrity

Acting on principles makes your behavior predictable and trustworthy, both to yourself and to others.

- It aligns your actions with your values, reducing inner conflict.
- It builds credibility with people personally and professionally.

3. Resilience During Adversity

In tough times, principles provide the anchor for the leader and the team. They offer stability when emotions, pressure, or chaos threaten to derail progress.

4. Better Relationships and Leadership

Working with principles builds a common ground for the team to operate. It brings a team together around core values and makes it stronger.

Principles That Matter

Build Trust and Credibility

- **Key Focus:** Establishing credibility quickly is critical in turnaround situations, where trust may have been compromised. Rebuild the stakeholders' confidence by demonstrating competence and integrity.
- **Practical Steps:**
    - Engage Stakeholders Early: Actively involve key stakeholders in the process from the start. Provide them with a clear roadmap of the turnaround plan, and ensure timely communication about progress and setbacks.
    - Be Transparent and Accountable: Regularly update the board, creditors, employees, and other stakeholders with clear, honest assessments of the situation. Avoid over-promising and under-delivering; instead, focus on delivering small, visible results quickly.
    - Visible Leadership: Leaders' presence must be felt at all levels of the organization. Hold town halls, meet employees on the ground, and demonstrate that you're committed to the company's turnaround, not just as a figurehead but as an active participant.

Operate with Complete and Unquestionable Integrity

- **Key Focus:** In distressed situations, where corruption or misconduct may have taken place, operating with integrity becomes not just important but essential for regaining stakeholder confidence.
- **Practical Steps:**
  - Implement Strict Compliance Measures: Establish clear internal controls and processes to prevent further misconduct. For example, tighten procurement processes with the introduction of oversight committees and implement a robust whistleblower policy.
  - Lead by Example: The tone set by leadership will filter down the ranks. Be transparent with actions and decisions.
  - Consequences for Misconduct: Take decisive action against any individuals caught engaging in unethical practices. While the focus should be on reform, the organization needs to see that misconduct won't be tolerated.
  - Employee Engagement Programs: Incorporate integrity into performance evaluations, ensuring that employees understand the company values and their role in upholding them.

Hands-On Leadership

- **Key Focus:** A turnaround leader needs to be actively involved, not just in high-level strategy but also in day-to-day operations, especially in the early phases.
- **Practical Steps:**
  - Direct Engagement: Involve yourself in the key operational aspects of the turnaround, be it renegotiating contracts, addressing customer concerns, or solving supply chain bottlenecks. Your involvement will signal your commitment to action.

- ¤ Quick Decision-Making: Time is critical during a turnaround. The leader must be capable of making informed, yet swift, decisions even with incomplete data. This requires a combination of gut instinct, experience, and the ability to learn from real-time data.
- ¤ Lead from the Front: Don't just sit in the boardroom. Spend time on the ground, talking to employees, customers, and suppliers. Identify issues directly from the source.

Detail-Oriented, but Focus on Important Issues

- **Key Focus:** In the chaos of a turnaround, it's easy to become overwhelmed by the sheer number of issues, but effective leaders know how to cut through the noise.
- **Practical Steps:**
  - ¤ Identify Key Priorities: Constantly assess what issues need attention immediately and what can be deferred. Some aspects may need immediate decision-making, such as liquidity crises, while others can be dealt with later.
  - ¤ Data-Driven Decision-Making: While speed is critical, ensure decisions are informed by data wherever possible. Even in the absence of perfect information, use available data to make reasonable estimates.
  - ¤ Establish Crisis Management Protocols: Create a crisis management team that focuses on the immediate issues at hand while another team can begin working on longer-term strategic issues. Separate the urgent from the important.

Balance Urgent with Big Picture

- **Key Focus:** While immediate actions are required, it's critical not to lose sight of the company's long-term viability. Balancing short-term gains with long-term strategy is key.

- **Practical Steps:**
  - Create a Dual-Track Strategy: Address immediate financial and operational issues while working on strategic restructuring (product offerings, business model, and market entry). Ensure both tracks are aligned.
  - Stakeholder Communication: Ensure the big picture is clear in stakeholder communications. While you're managing immediate concerns, convey the company's long-term vision for stability and growth.
  - Resilience Planning: Prepare the company for periodic setbacks by ensuring that the turnaround plan is adaptable. The big picture plan should include recovery from failures and a plan for potential market or operational disruptions.

Focus on Cash

- **Key Focus:** Cash flow is often the most critical issue in a distressed business. Managing liquidity effectively is a top priority.
- **Practical Steps:**
  - Cash Flow Monitoring: Create a real-time cash flow monitoring system. Daily or weekly cash flow reports will give you immediate insight into whether the business can survive in the short term and help identify where cash is being spent inefficiently.
  - Cost Reduction Initiatives: Immediately reduce non-essential expenditures. Prioritize payments that are critical for the operation and long-term survival of the business (e.g., supplier payments, employee wages).
  - Raise Short-Term Capital: Consider raising capital via asset sales, interim finance, or injecting fresh equity if necessary. Having a

strong relationship with investors and creditors will enable faster access to funds when required.

Communication with Stakeholders

- **Key Focus:** Consistent and transparent communication can prevent panic and keep all stakeholders aligned with the turnaround plan.
- **Practical Steps:**
  - ¤ Be Transparent and Honest: Clearly communicate the challenges the company faces but also outline the roadmap for turnaround and how you plan to overcome obstacles.
  - ¤ Regular Updates: Set up a communication rhythm. Whether it's weekly board meetings, monthly stakeholder reports, or frequent updates to employees, regular communication ensures everyone is on the same page.
  - ¤ Manage Expectations: Communicate realistic timelines for progress. Stakeholders may expect quick results, but setting realistic milestones will help avoid disappointment.

Resilience to Periodic Setbacks

- **Key Focus:** In a turnaround, setbacks are inevitable. A strong leader remains calm, focused, and adaptable during these periods.
- **Practical Steps:**
  - ¤ Build Contingency Plans: Prepare for potential disruptions—whether financial, operational, or market-based. Having contingency plans can help minimize the impact of setbacks.
  - ¤ Lead with Confidence: Demonstrate resilience in the face of setbacks. Show your team that challenges are part of the process, and the focus should remain on moving forward.

- Adapt the Strategy: Be open to adjusting the strategy when things don't go according to plan. Recognize the need for flexibility and adapt to changing circumstances.

The principles above represent the core values and actions necessary for leading a successful corporate turnaround in India. They emphasize the importance of leadership credibility, integrity, hands-on management, and focus on cash. The key to a successful turnaround lies in staying focused on both the immediate crisis and the long-term recovery, balancing both urgency and strategic vision. The leader's role is not only to steer the company through the crisis but also to restore confidence, revitalize operations, and ensure that the company emerges stronger and more resilient.

Corporate Turnaround Process

A complete Corporate Turnaround process is a multi-step process, starting from diagnosis to crisis management to leading a turnaround, and in between developing a robust plan, managing stakeholders, and negotiating a new capital structure for the business.

Below is a six-step process, each step explained in a summary manner and in detail in later chapters.

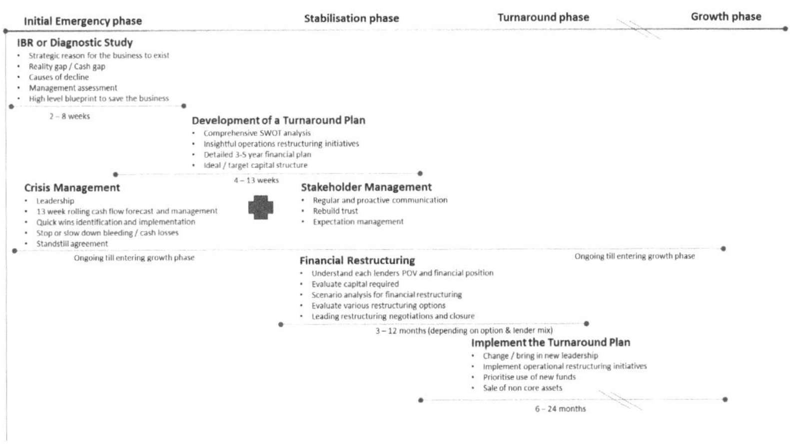

Independent Business Review (IBR) or Diagnostic Study

IBR or Diagnostic Study perfectly encapsulates the critical first step in any successful corporate turnaround process. Before any effective restructuring or strategic redirection can occur, a deep and honest assessment of the current situation is paramount. This initial diagnostic phase is not merely about identifying problems but about gaining a comprehensive and unvarnished understanding of the business's predicament and its potential for recovery.

The first point, "Strategic reason for the business to exist," serves as the fundamental starting block. In a turnaround scenario, this goes beyond a simple mission statement; it's a vital re-evaluation of the company's core purpose and its continued relevance. Is the original value proposition still valid in the current market landscape? Has the competitive environment fundamentally shifted, rendering the business's offerings obsolete or less appealing? This diagnostic step forces an introspective look at whether the company has a reason to continue operating in its current form. If the strategic rationale is weak or non-existent, then even the most robust operational fixes will only delay the inevitable. Understanding this provides the foundational context for all subsequent turnaround efforts.

Secondly, and crucially, "Reality gap / Cash gap" highlights a common and often dangerous delusion within struggling organizations. As noted by Stuart Slatter and David Lovett in their "Corporate Turnaround" book, the "reality gap" specifically refers to the chasm between what management believes about the depth and nature of the problems and the actual, often far worse, reality. Management teams, particularly in declining businesses, can be prone to optimism bias, denial, or simply lacking the objective data to fully grasp the severity of their situation. A diagnostic study aims to brutally expose this gap by providing an objective, data-driven assessment of financial performance, operational inefficiencies, and market position. The "cash gap" then quantifies the immediate financial shortfall, revealing the stark reality of liquidity constraints and the urgency of the situation. This unflinching analysis is vital because true turnaround can only begin when the entire organization, especially leadership, acknowledges the true scale of the challenges.

Thirdly, "Causes of decline" involves a forensic investigation into the root factors precipitating the business's woes. This isn't just about identifying symptoms like falling sales or shrinking margins, but rather unearthing the underlying disease. These can be multifaceted, including internal dysfunctions such as poor strategic choices, outdated processes, lack of innovation, excessive costs, or internal political conflicts. External factors like disruptive technologies, changing consumer preferences, intensified competition, or economic downturns also play a significant role. A thorough diagnostic study employs various analytical frameworks to systematically identify all contributing factors, ensuring that the turnaround strategy addresses the fundamental issues rather than merely patching over symptoms.

Fourthly, a "Management assessment" is an indispensable part of this initial phase. The effectiveness and capability of the leadership team are often a direct reflection of the company's performance. In a turnaround, this assessment scrutinizes the skills, experience, decision-making capabilities, and leadership styles of key personnel. It evaluates whether the existing management possesses the necessary acumen and drive to steer the company through crisis, or if changes in leadership, skill sets, or organizational structure are required. This assessment can be uncomfortable, but it's essential for building a team capable of executing a demanding turnaround plan.

Finally, the "High-level blueprint to save the business" is the immediate outcome of this initial diagnostic phase. It is not yet a detailed implementation plan, but rather a strategic outline based on the raw, objective findings. This blueprint identifies the critical strategic shifts, operational improvements, financial restructuring needs, and potential talent changes required to stabilize the company. It provides a preliminary roadmap for stakeholders, setting the direction for more granular planning. This high-level blueprint serves as the foundation upon which the entire corporate turnaround process will be built, transforming the bleak reality into an actionable path toward recovery.

Crisis Management

Crisis Management is a crucial and often brutal phase in a corporate turnaround process. Unlike the diagnostic phase, which focuses on understanding the problems, crisis management is about immediate stabilization and stopping the haemorrhaging. This stage is akin to a paramedic or ICU doctor in the medical industry; his or her primary goal is to stabilize the patient, stop the bleeding, and ensure vital functions are maintained, often before a full diagnosis or long-term treatment plan is even finalized. Most regular professionals, accustomed to growth or stable environments, have little to no experience in this high-stakes, time-sensitive environment.

"Leadership" in crisis management is distinctly different from leadership in prosperous times. Crisis leaders are the "paramedics" of the corporate world. They need to be decisive, resilient, and possess an unwavering ability to make tough calls under immense pressure. Communication must be clear, frequent, and honest, both internally to rally employees and externally to calm nervous stakeholders. They must quickly build trust, demonstrating credibility and a firm grip on the deteriorating situation. This isn't about consensus-building but about taking charge and executing with precision.

The "13-week rolling cash flow forecast and management" is the lifeblood of crisis management. In a turnaround, cash is the central element of all decision-making. Profitability becomes secondary to liquidity. A business can be profitable on paper but still fail if it runs out of cash. This short-term cash flow forecast, updated weekly or even daily, provides the "vital signs" of the corporate patient. Every decision, from operational changes to vendor payments, is filtered through its impact on cash. It helps identify immediate cash shortfalls and surpluses, enabling leaders to prioritize payments, negotiate terms, and forecast when the business might run out of oxygen. Without this granular control over cash, a company in crisis is flying blind, accelerating towards collapse.

"Quick wins identification and implementation" are the immediate interventions. These are actions that can generate a positive impact on cash flow or morale within days or weeks. This could involve aggressively collecting receivables, negotiating immediate discounts with suppliers, reducing non-essential spending, or even launching a quick promotional sale. These wins provide much-needed breathing room, demonstrate progress to internal and external stakeholders, and build momentum, signalling that the company is actively fighting for survival.

"Stop or slow down bleeding / cash losses" is the direct objective of all these efforts. This involves ruthlessly cutting non-essential expenditures, renegotiating contracts, streamlining operations, and eliminating unprofitable activities. It's about conserving every last drop of cash. This phase often involves difficult decisions, such as workforce reductions, asset sales, or temporary halts on investments, all aimed at stemming the outflow of cash that threatens the company's existence.

Finally, a "Standstill agreement" is a critical, though often challenging, tool in crisis management. In developed countries, particularly in jurisdictions like the UK or the US, a standstill agreement is a formal pact between the struggling company and its lenders and creditors. It typically involves lenders agreeing to temporarily suspend or "stand still" on their rights to demand repayment, accelerate loans, or initiate bankruptcy proceedings, usually in exchange for information, partial payments, or a commitment to a restructuring plan. This provides the company with breathing room to implement crisis measures and develop a comprehensive turnaround strategy without the immediate threat of legal action. However, it's important to note that while this is a common practice in developed countries, in India, lenders may just hold off any formal workout or bankruptcy action, but will not sign any such agreements formally. Indian banks and financial institutions, while often engaging in informal forbearance or a wait-and-see approach, are generally reluctant to put formal standstill agreements in writing due to various regulatory, legal, and operational complexities. This informal nature can add another layer of uncertainty to an already volatile crisis management phase in India.

Stakeholder Management

Stakeholder management isn't merely about informing various parties; it's a sophisticated and continuous effort to navigate the complex web of relationships that define a struggling business. Effective stakeholder management can be the difference between a successful rescue and a catastrophic collapse, often preventing a formal bankruptcy or a piecemeal sale of the business.

A significant challenge in a distressed company is the trust deficit that inevitably develops over time. This deficit isn't accidental; it's often a direct consequence of a cycle where management, facing mounting pressure, makes promises it cannot keep, or worse, deliberately misrepresents the true state of affairs. Initially, these broken promises might be due to genuine unforeseen circumstances, but as failures accumulate, stakeholders, viz., employees, customers, suppliers, and critically, lenders, begin to lose faith. They become wary of every new pronouncement, viewing it with skepticism. This erosion of trust is insidious; it paralyzes operations as suppliers demand cash upfront, customers seek alternatives, and employees become disengaged. Lenders, feeling misled or ignored, become increasingly rigid, unwilling to grant concessions or provide new funding.

Rebuilding trust is therefore absolutely critical for a turnaround to succeed. Without it, negotiation becomes impossible, critical support dries up, and the company finds itself isolated. It starts with transparent and honest communication, even when the news is bad. Acknowledging past failures and taking responsibility for them is the first step towards re-establishing credibility.

The qualities of a corporate turnaround leader who excels at stakeholder communication are distinct and vital. They must possess unwavering integrity and courage, willing to deliver unvarnished truths, even if unpopular. They need empathy to understand the varied concerns and anxieties of different stakeholder groups, from employees fearing job losses to lenders worried about their capital. Crucially, they must have exceptional communication skills, capable of articulating a clear, consistent message across diverse audiences, whether it's a reassuring message to the shop floor or a pragmatic proposal to a syndicate of banks. Finally, they require strategic foresight and negotiation prowess, knowing when to push, when to compromise, and how to frame solutions that offer mutual benefit.

Such leaders can often create the foundation for successful negotiations among lenders and with equity holders. In a distressed scenario, lenders often have conflicting interests; some might be secured, others unsecured; some might have short-term exposures, others long-term. Without a unified understanding and a sense of shared purpose, infighting among lenders can derail any rescue effort. A skilled turnaround leader acts as a central, credible information conduit, providing consistent data and realistic recovery scenarios. By fostering open dialogue and ensuring all parties feel heard and adequately informed, they can gradually align divergent interests towards a common goal i.e., maximizing recovery. This often involves presenting a credible turnaround plan that demonstrates how concessions made today could lead to a better return tomorrow.

Similarly, with equity holders, who often face significant dilution or even complete loss, the leader must manage expectations carefully while still seeking their cooperation for necessary restructuring (e.g., approving share issuances or debt-to-equity conversions). By demonstrating competence, transparency, and a viable path forward, these leaders can convince stakeholders to give the company the breathing room it needs. This proactive and skilled management of relationships, built on rebuilt trust and clear expectations, can often avert the finality of a formal bankruptcy filing or the value-destroying process of a piecemeal asset sale, allowing the company a fighting chance at survival and revival.

Development of a Turnaround Plan

Development of a Turnaround Plan marks a pivotal shift from the urgent stabilization of crisis management to formulating a sustainable path to recovery. If crisis management is akin to the paramedic or ICU doctor stabilizing a critically ill patient, the development of a turnaround plan is when the hospital's specialists, like surgeons, oncologists, and physical therapists, collaborate to devise a comprehensive treatment strategy for the patient still in the ICU or under observation. This is emphatically not a time for abstract strategy consulting advisors or "30,000-foot thinking." Instead, it demands practical, actionable changes on the ground, executed under severe resource constraints.

A "Comprehensive SWOT analysis" forms the analytical backbone of this plan. While SWOT (Strengths, Weaknesses, Opportunities, Threats) is a common strategic tool, in a turnaround context, its application is far more rigorous and brutally honest. It probes the true internal capabilities and deficiencies, and critically probes the external environment that offers both potential pathways and significant risks. Beyond SWOT, other analytical tools become highly relevant during distress. Porter's Five Forces can provide a deep understanding of industry attractiveness and competitive intensity, revealing if the fundamental market structure is conducive to long-term recovery. A Value Chain Analysis can pinpoint exactly where inefficiencies lie within the company's operations, from procurement to delivery, identifying specific areas for cost reduction or value enhancement. A Customer Segmentation Analysis can reveal which customer groups are still profitable and loyal, guiding efforts to conserve resources and focus on core markets.

"Insightful operations restructuring initiatives" are the bedrock of a sustainable financial turnaround. A robust operations turnaround plan provides a solid foundation for a sustainable financial restructuring because without fixing the underlying operational issues that caused the decline, any financial band-aid will be temporary. You can renegotiate debt, secure new funding, or sell assets, but if the business continues to leak cash due to inefficient processes, poor product quality, or excessive costs, it will inevitably return to distress. Operational fixes are about making the business fundamentally healthier and more efficient.

In distress situations, operational turnaround initiatives can be stark and immediate. These include:

- Aggressive cost reduction: Beyond immediate cuts, this involves fundamental re-evaluation of all expenditure, perhaps by consolidating suppliers, renegotiating terms, or outsourcing non-core activities.
- Working capital optimization: Rapidly converting inventory to cash, tightening credit terms for customers, and extending payment terms with suppliers (where feasible and ethically sound).
- Process re-engineering: Streamlining workflows, eliminating redundant steps, and automating tasks to improve efficiency and reduce errors.
- Product/service rationalization: Ruthlessly cutting unprofitable product lines or services to focus resources on those that generate positive cash flow or hold strategic importance.
- Supply chain rationalization: Identifying and mitigating risks within the supply chain, diversifying suppliers, or renegotiating contracts for better terms.
- Quality improvement initiatives: Addressing product defects or service failures that lead to customer churn and reputational damage.

A "Detailed 3-5 year financial plan" translates the operational strategies into concrete financial projections. This isn't just about showing profitability; it's about projecting cash flow, balance sheet movements, and key financial ratios under various scenarios. It provides a roadmap for lenders and investors, demonstrating the viability of the turnaround and the projected returns. This plan must be realistic, conservative, and stress-tested against various assumptions (e.g., lower sales, higher costs).

Finally, defining the "Ideal / target capital structure" is crucial. This involves determining the optimal mix of debt and equity that the restructured business can realistically support, considering its projected cash flows and risk profile. This often necessitates tough conversations with lenders and equity holders about debt write-downs, debt-to-equity conversions, or fresh equity injections. The goal is to arrive at a capital structure that is sustainable, that allows for future investment, and that is attractive to potential new funders or investors, ensuring the company isn't burdened by an unsustainable debt load as it attempts to recover.

Financial Restructuring

"Financial Restructuring," is often the most complex and contentious phase of a corporate turnaround. This stage involves realigning the company's financial obligations with its capacity to generate cash, and it's where the rubber meets the road in terms of debt reduction, new funding, and ownership changes.

Time is of the essence in financial restructuring. A distressed business is like a patient bleeding cash; every day that passes without a definitive agreement on financial terms means further deterioration of its operational health, erosion of its market position, and depletion of its remaining value. The longer it takes to secure the required additional funding for healing and growth, the higher the risk of asset stripping, loss of key employees, and irreversible damage to customer and supplier relationships. Delays transform a solvable problem into an intractable one, often leading to liquidation or a piecemeal sale, which typically yields far less value for all stakeholders.

A significant challenge, particularly in the Indian context, is that Indian promoters can often be their own worst enemy by holding on to the business in the hopes of a larger "haircut" (debt write-off) from lenders. This stems from a combination of emotional attachment, a desire to retain control, and sometimes a miscalculation of the time and value erosion occurring. They might deliberately frustrate the negotiation process, hoping that as the business's condition worsens, lenders will become more desperate and offer more favourable terms. However, this strategy is profoundly self-defeating. By prolonging the agony, they not only erode the business's operational viability but also destroy the very asset they are trying to save. The longer the delay, the less there is to salvage, ultimately leading to a worse outcome for everyone, including themselves.

This often explains why it sometimes takes more than a year to close these financial restructuring negotiations in India. The multi-lender environment (some under RBI supervision and others outside of it), coupled with the reluctance of promoters to accept early, albeit painful, compromises, creates a protracted negotiation cycle. By the time the negotiations finally close, the business is in a much worse position. The operational turnaround plan, meticulously crafted months earlier, may have become outdated, rendered irrelevant by the continued deterioration of market conditions, technological shifts, or the loss of critical talent. What was once a viable path to recovery becomes a desperate scramble, often with insufficient resources.

The components of financial restructuring are designed to navigate this complex landscape:

- **Understand each lender's POV and financial position:** Lenders are not a monolithic entity. They have different exposures (secured vs. unsecured), different internal policies, and different risk appetites. Understanding their individual perspectives, their internal pressures, and their financial capacity to absorb losses or provide new funds is crucial for crafting a viable solution. For each lender, understanding what their best alternative is if a deal isn't reached (e.g., liquidation, legal action, selling their debt) helps in framing proposals that are more attractive than their alternatives. This requires a deep understanding of legal frameworks and recovery rates in distress scenarios.
- **Evaluate capital required:** A distressed business is starved of capital and resources. It has multiple demands for cash in various areas of the business. Operational restructuring initiatives will identify several areas to invest in, which would be crucial for the turnaround of the business. There would be a long list of supplier and employee dues that would not have been paid, sometimes for many months. On the other hand, not many lenders and investors are oriented to invest in turnaround situations and where they do agree, they want to invest in a phased manner based on outcomes of agreed initiatives or assurances made by the turnaround leader. So, evaluating required capital, prioritising it in a phased manner to give the distressed

business and its new investors the highest probability of success is a fine skill.

- **Scenario analysis for financial restructuring:** Finding the right capital structure is a fine art even for companies operating in normal circumstances. In a distress situation, where the survival itself is in question, finding the right capital structure becomes very complicated. Forecast free cash flows are tenuous and committing interest payments or a repayment schedule is challenging. Scenario analysis allows management, lenders, and equity holders to test capital structures against multiple future states of the world, instead of relying on a single-point forecast. It forces alignment around resilience and downside protection rather than just upside potential. Scenarios could be management scenario, prolonged stress scenario, liquidation scenario, and an upside scenario. Each scenario has to be tested for debt service coverage ratio, interest coverage, liquidity headroom, and refinancing requirements. The goal is flexibility and resilience, not minimal cost of capital.

- **Evaluate various restructuring options:** As of 2025, Indian regulators – the RBI, SEBI, and the Government of India – have built a wide spectrum of mechanisms to deal with financial distress. This has given turnaround leaders and company boards several pathways to navigate stress, ranging from out-of-court bank-led restructurings to market-driven alternatives and, ultimately, the formal insolvency process. For a turnaround leader, the decision is not simply about "which framework exists" but rather which framework best suits the company's context. The choice depends on the composition of lenders, the alignment (or conflict) among them, the relative negotiating power of each class of creditor, the willingness of promoters to inject or forgo capital, and the realistic trajectory of the business under different turnaround scenarios.

  The toolkit today includes:

  - **Restructuring under the RBI Prudential Framework (June 7, 2019):** The mainstay for lender-led resolution outside IBC, but reliant on consensus and strict timelines.

- **One-Time Settlements (OTS) under RBI's June 8, 2023 norms:** A quicker route for closure where promoters can raise funds for settlement, but often involving significant haircuts for banks.

- **Transfers to ARCs (Asset Reconstruction Companies):** Allowing lenders to clean up their books and bringing in a specialized resolution entity, though ARC capital and execution bandwidth can vary.

- **Capital solutions via AIFs / Special Situation Funds: SEBI-**regulated investment vehicles that bring in new money and sophisticated structuring, albeit at higher cost and with promoter dilution.

- **The Insolvency and Bankruptcy Code (IBC):** A creditor-in-control, court-supervised process that provides legal finality and market discovery of value, but also strips promoters of control and can be highly disruptive.

Each pathway carries trade-offs: speed versus value maximization, confidentiality versus transparency, promoter continuity versus new ownership, consensual negotiation versus judicial imposition. The turnaround leader's role is to map these trade-offs against the company's immediate liquidity runway, the lenders' provisioning incentives, and the long-term viability of the business.

Ultimately, the art of choosing the right restructuring route lies in aligning the resolution framework with the business realities and stakeholder psychology. A company with a dominant consortium lender and cooperative promoters may benefit from a June 7 restructuring. A promoter with access to cash might prefer OTS to preserve control. When banks are unwilling to take bold steps, selling to an ARC or attracting an AIF/SSF may be the pragmatic choice. And when conflicts among lenders are deep or the viability gap is large, IBC often becomes the unavoidable endgame.

- **Leading restructuring negotiations and closure:** This requires exceptional negotiation skills, patience, and the ability to find common ground amidst conflicting interests. It involves structuring complex financial instruments (e.g., new debt, equity infusions, debt-to-equity swaps), drafting intricate legal agreements, and coordinating multiple parties to reach a consensual resolution. The goal is not just to reach an agreement, but to close it swiftly and effectively, providing the distressed business with the financial stability it desperately needs to recover and eventually thrive.

Implement the Turnaround Plan

This is the decisive phase of the corporate turnaround process. This is where all the previous analysis, crisis management, stakeholder negotiations, and plan development converge into concrete execution. It's the period where the "patient," having been stabilized and diagnosed, now undergoes the rigorous treatment plan designed for long-term recovery, aiming for a sustainable future before it can even dream of a growth phase.

A critical aspect often overlooked but foundational to successful implementation is the "Change / bring in new leadership." The Turnaround leader, brought in to manage the crisis, should continue to lead the turnaround. This leader, often a Chief Restructuring Officer (CRO) or a newly appointed CEO, needs to be a highly skilled executor and motivator. They must possess unwavering resolve to push through difficult changes, exceptional organizational skills to coordinate complex initiatives, and strong communication capabilities to continuously align stakeholders. They must be able to inspire and rebuild morale among a workforce that has likely endured significant stress and uncertainty. Crucially, the Turnaround leader should be adept at hiring and attracting good talent, not just any talent, but individuals who thrive in challenging environments, are results-oriented, and can contribute directly to the turnaround objectives. Existing talent may be fatigued or resistant to change, necessitating strategic additions to the team. The Turnaround leader's excellent execution skills are vital to implement the turnaround plan at a brisk pace, as time is of the essence.

"Implement operational restructuring initiatives" is the engine of the turnaround, and it's here that the Turnaround leader's qualities truly shine. Success in this phase hinges on the leader's ability to drive execution with relentless focus and urgency. They must be a master of prioritization, capable of distinguishing between critical tasks and distractions under immense pressure. This requires hands-on involvement, often getting into the weeds of operations to ensure changes are happening on the ground, not just on paper. The leader must foster a "mission mode" environment across the entire team, where every employee understands the gravity of the situation and their role in saving the business. This means creating a culture of accountability, swift decision-making, and continuous problem-solving. Aligning incentives of the team becomes a powerful tool in this phase; tying performance bonuses, recognition, or even future career opportunities directly to the achievement of turnaround milestones can galvanize employees and ensure everyone is pulling in the same direction towards the shared goal of survival and revival.

"Prioritize use of new funds" is paramount. Having secured fresh capital through financial restructuring, the turnaround leader must be incredibly disciplined in its allocation. These funds are not for business-as-usual spending or speculative ventures. They are specifically earmarked for critical initiatives that directly support the turnaround plan, such as funding operational restructuring, investing in essential technology upgrades, or providing necessary working capital. Every dollar spent must be justified by its contribution to stabilizing the business and enabling its recovery. Misallocation of these precious new funds can quickly send the business back into a downward spiral.

This entire phase is often referred to as the "stabilization" or "rebuilding" phase before the business can even consider entering a growth phase again. It's about getting the company back to a state of health and viability, eventually laying the groundwork for future growth. Without successful implementation, even the most brilliant turnaround plan remains just a document, and the distressed business risks succumbing to its challenges.

Tilaknagar Industries: A Turnaround Case Study

(based on publicly available data)

Tilaknagar Industries Ltd. (TIL), best known for its flagship brand Mansion House Brandy, is a compelling example of a highly leveraged Indian consumer business that fell into deep distress by 2019–20 and then engineered a remarkable turnaround. From losses, negative net worth, and over ₹1,100 crore of debt, the company managed to restructure its liabilities, stabilize operations, and ultimately return to profitability with a net cash balance sheet by FY25. This case study examines how the decline unfolded, what restructuring measures were undertaken, and how operating discipline and brand strength combined to restore financial health.

The Downfall: A Cocktail of Debt and Losses (2014-2019)

The period between 2014 and 2019 was tumultuous for Tilaknagar Industries. The company's financial statements from this era paint a grim picture of mounting losses, a burgeoning debt pile, and an eroding net worth.

Financial Performance at a Glance:

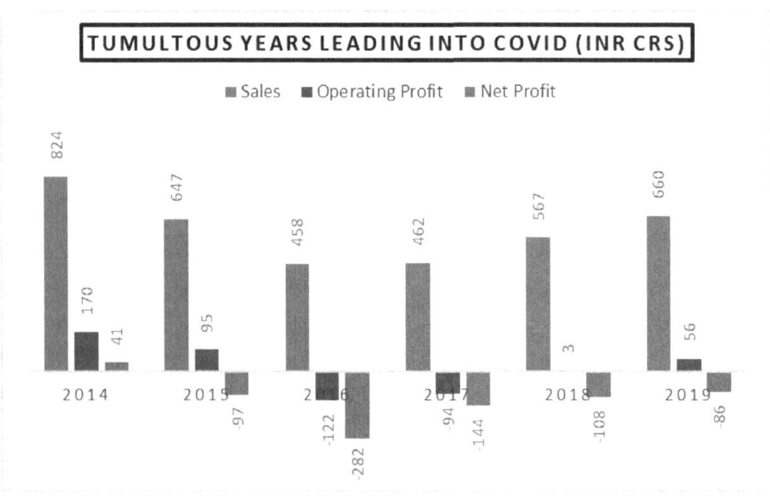

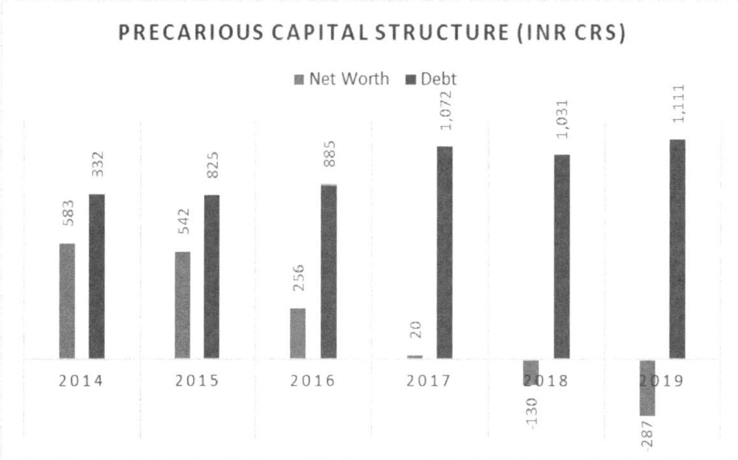

Leverage Ratios	2014	2015	2016	2017	2018	2019
D/E(X)	1.43	1.52	3.46	52.45	-7.93	-3.87
Interest Cov(X)	2.66	0.98	-0.98	-0.60	0.02	0.30

WC Days	2014	2015	2016	2017	2018	2019
Debtors	99	72	91	106	109	133
Inventory	124	237	134	194	206	252
Accounts Payable	68	289	218	365	418	502

Source: Screener.in

As is evident from the above charts and tables, the company's sales witnessed a significant decline after 2014, and it consistently posted net losses for five consecutive years. This led to a substantial decline in its net worth and an increase in its borrowings, which peaked at over ₹1,000 crores. The company's capital structure became precarious and it wasn't able to pay its suppliers, as is evident from the increase in its Accounts Payable days.

Key Reasons for the Decline:

- **Aggressive Expansion and Acquisitions:** Prior to 2014, TIL had embarked on an aggressive expansion drive, including the acquisition of brands from IFB Agro and a push into new markets. As per Crisil, "Over fiscals 2010-2014, the company undertook several asset-heavy backward integration capital expenditure (capex) programmes aggregating ₹720 crore through a mix of debt, equity and internal accruals to improve efficiency and take advantage of benefits under government subsidy schemes for which some of the projects were eligible."

- **Regulatory Headwinds:** The alcoholic beverage industry in India is subject to complex and varied state-level regulations. Changes in government policies and taxation structures in key markets adversely impacted the company's operations. As per Crisil, "The operational disturbances created due to bifurcation of Andhra Pradesh and Telangana, delay in receipt of subsidy and licensing complications led to significant impact on volumes sold."

- **Operational Challenges:** In 2015, TIL's main bottler in Tamil Nadu (a key market for TIL with 30% of its sales) ceased operations resulting in sudden collapse of a key market, which contributed 30% of its sales (source: Brickworks Rating, December 2015).

- **Debt default and liquidity challenges:** As a result of a combination of operational setbacks and high leverage, TIL defaulted on its loans, leading to complete drying up of liquidity.

- **Subsidiary default and insolvency:** Prag Distilleries, a subsidiary of TIL, was admitted into formal bankruptcy in June, 2017 and in March 2018, the Committee of Creditors (CoC) decided to liquidate the company, as it could not find any buyers for the business.

The Restructuring: A Lifeline from Edelweiss ARC

By 2019, TIL was in a precarious position. A crucial turning point in its journey was the extensive OTS efforts with public sector banks and the agreement with Edelweiss ARC to restructure its debt in 2020.

- **One-Time Settlement (OTS):** TIL entered into an OTS with its lenders – SBI, IDBI, and BoI. Based on publicly available data, the OTS was executed at 35-40% of the total debt.

- **Master debt restructuring agreement with Edelweiss ARC:** Remaining debt of approximately ₹523 Crores held (acquired) by Edelweiss ARC was restructured into a sustainable portion of ₹344 Crores at 9% and balance of ₹178 Crores was to be paid as a long-dated instrument at 0.001% interest, significantly reducing TIL interest obligations. Part of the long-dated instrument (unsustainable debt) was converted to 10% equity at ₹24.36 per share.

- **Asset Monetization:** To fund the OTS and improve its financial health, the company undertook a strategic sale of non-core assets.

- **Infusion of Fresh Capital:** The promoters infused fresh capital into the company, demonstrating their commitment and confidence in the turnaround plan.

This comprehensive debt restructuring was instrumental in cleaning up the company's balance sheet and providing it with the much-needed financial stability to implement its turnaround plan.

The Turnaround: A Story of Operational Excellence (2020 Onwards)

With its debt burden significantly reduced, TIL embarked on a multi-pronged strategy to improve its operating performance and regain its lost ground.

Strategic Initiatives:

- **Focus on Core Brands:** The company sharpened its focus on its flagship brands, particularly Mansion House and Courier Napoleon brandies, which have a strong market presence in Southern India.

- **Premiumization and Product Innovation:** Recognizing the changing consumer preferences, TIL launched new premium products like Flandy and Chambers to cater to the evolving market demands.

- **Geographic Expansion:** While consolidating its position in its core markets, the company also selectively expanded its presence in other regions.
- **Strengthening Distribution Network:** TIL revamped its distribution network to ensure wider availability of its products and improve its market reach.
- **Manufacturing Agreement with Pernod Ricard:** A 10-year manufacturing agreement with Pernod Ricard in Maharashtra provided a steady revenue stream and improved capacity utilization.
- **Prudent Financial Management:** The company adopted a disciplined approach to financial management, with a focus on cost control, working capital optimization, and maintaining a healthy balance sheet.

Improved Financial Performance:

The positive impact of these measures is reflected in the company's recent financial performance.

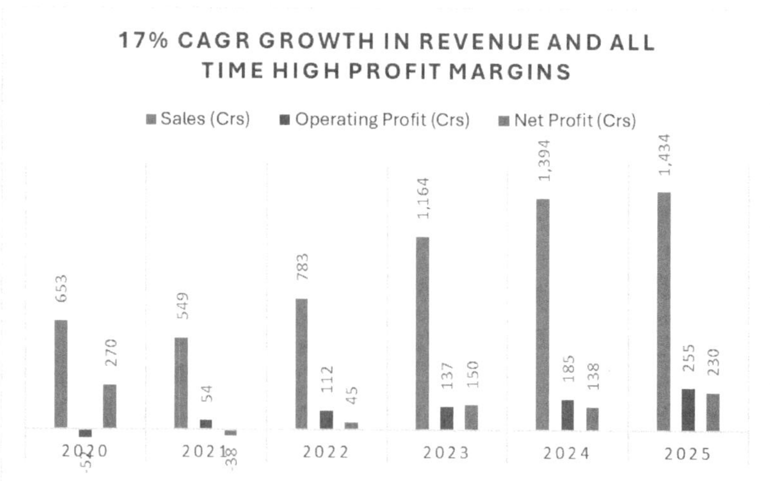

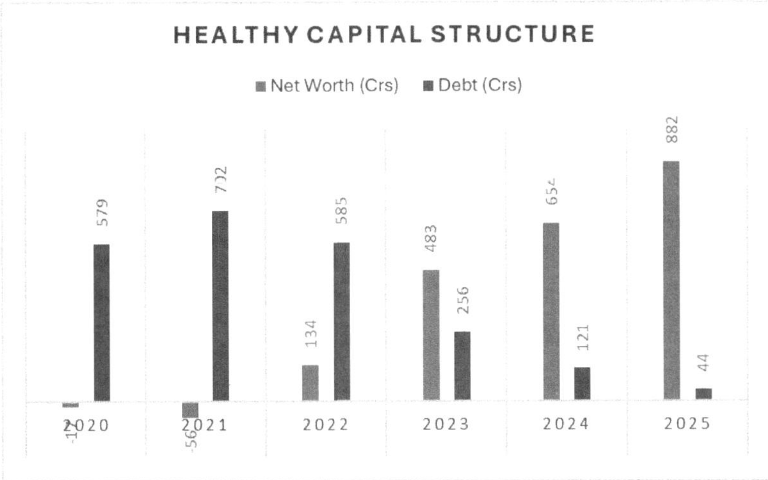

Leverage Ratios	2020	2021	2022	2023	2024	2025
D/E (X)	-33.29	-12.61	4.38	0.53	0.19	0.05
Interest Cov (X)	-0.40	0.76	1.81	3.41	6.94	20.96

WC Days	2020	2021	2022	2023	2024	2025
Debtors	136	120	110	106	110	104
Inventory	115	200	144	152	113	83
Accounts Payable	298	412	340	169	135	74

Source: Screener.in

The company has not only returned to profitability but has also demonstrated strong growth in both sales and net profit. Its borrowings have been drastically reduced, and it became net debt-free in March 2025. Leverage ratios have a lot more headroom and the working capital days have normalized.

Credit Rating Upgrade:

The significant improvement in the company's financial risk profile has been recognized by credit rating agencies. In December 2024, CRISIL Ratings revised its outlook on the long-term bank facilities of Tilaknagar Industries to 'Positive' from 'Stable' and reaffirmed its rating at 'CRISIL

A-'. This upgrade is a testament to the success of the company's turnaround efforts.

The Road Ahead: Acquisition of Imperial Blue

In a bold move that signals its renewed ambition, TIL recently announced the acquisition of the popular whisky brand Imperial Blue from Pernod Ricard. This acquisition, valued at approximately ₹4,150 crore, will be funded through a mix of equity and debt. This strategic acquisition is expected to significantly enhance TIL's product portfolio, market share, and growth prospects.

Conclusion

The turnaround of TIL is a compelling case study in corporate resilience and strategic management. By addressing its crippling debt burden through a timely restructuring and the implementation of a well-defined operational strategy, the company has not only survived a near-fatal crisis but has also emerged stronger and more competitive. The acquisition of Imperial Blue marks a new chapter in its growth story, and the company appears to be well-positioned to capitalize on the opportunities in the Indian alcoholic beverage market.

Chapter 04

Independent Business Review

"An IBR measures runway, not rhetoric."

Introduction

Every successful corporate turnaround begins with an accurate diagnosis. Much like a physician cannot treat a patient without understanding the underlying illness, a business in distress cannot be revived without a deep and honest assessment of its true condition. This is the role of the Independent Business Review (IBR), the foundation of any effective turnaround plan.

An IBR is not just a review of financial numbers, it is a multidimensional diagnostic tool that evaluates the business model, operating environment, liquidity status, organizational leadership, and strategic viability. It separates symptoms from root causes, identifies gaps between aspirations and realities, and lays down a preliminary roadmap for revival.

In the Indian context, where promoter-driven businesses often blur the lines between ownership and management, an independent and objective diagnosis becomes even more crucial. Stakeholders viz., lenders, investors, regulators, debtors, and vendors - all need clarity before they can support any revival plan. And management needs a mirror to understand what went wrong and what needs to be done.

This chapter lays out the core components of an IBR, structured around six key elements:

1. Strategic rationale for the business to exist
2. Reality gap / Cash gap

3. Causes of decline
4. Management assessment
5. High-level turnaround blueprint
6. Stakeholder alignment around facts

We explore each of these in depth in the pages below:

Strategic Rationale for Business to Exist

It may sound odd, but in every turnaround situation, it's important to assess right up front whether there is a reason for the business to exist. Does it fulfill a useful role in society and the economy? Collectively, is it the most efficient use of its assets, viz., people, machinery and supply chain networks? If not, then maybe a better solution for the business is to sell its assets or wind down the business.

Without such an exercise, any capital structuring and turnaround effort will not lead to a sustainable solution as the business may become distressed again.

Following is a summary of the kind of analysis that needs to be done to make such an assessment:

Market Analysis:

- Analyze the industry's growth potential. Does the business operate in a sustainable and growing market, or is it facing structural decline? What are the growth projections in the next 3–5 years?
- Evaluate the company's competitive position. Can the company differentiate itself from competitors, and does it have a sustainable competitive advantage?

Core Capabilities:

- Does the company have a unique value proposition, technology, intellectual property, or other assets that justify its continued existence?

- Can the business pivot or adapt to new market conditions (e.g., through product innovation or market diversification)?

Financial Viability:

- Can the company return to profitability within a reasonable time frame, given the proposed turnaround actions? Consider the financial resources required and potential returns.

Strategic Alternatives:

- If the company is not viable on its own, consider alternative strategies such as merging with a competitor, selling to a strategic buyer, or liquidating non-core assets.

Case Example

HMT Ltd — The Failure of Strategic Fit

HMT (Hindustan Machine Tools), once known as the "Timekeeper of the Nation," is a classic example of a business that lost its strategic relevance. As Indian consumers moved to quartz and digital watches, and players like Titan disrupted the industry with design, branding, and distribution innovation, HMT failed to adapt. No amount of financial restructuring or cost control could revive a business whose core offering was no longer relevant. The real issue was not liquidity, it was strategic obsolescence.

An IBR must call out such hard truths. If the business lacks a strategic rationale, stakeholders are better off considering a graceful exit or liquidation.

Reality Gap and Cash Gap: Bridging Perception with Truth

One of the most critical and often uncomfortable roles of an Independent Business Review (IBR) is exposing the reality gap: the chasm between how management or promoters perceive the business situation versus what the actual data reveals. In distressed companies, this gap is frequently wide, even dangerously so.

The Reality Gap: Denial, Optimism, and Blind Spots

Promoters and senior management, particularly in family-owned or closely-held Indian businesses, often retain a deep emotional attachment to the business. This emotional lens leads to persistent underestimation of the severity of distress. They may believe:

- "This is just a temporary liquidity issue."
- "If we get one big order or a working capital line, things will turn."
- "Market conditions are to blame, not our decisions."

This benign view is usually reinforced by selective data, legacy loyalty from employees, and a desire to maintain stakeholder confidence, especially lenders, customers, and employees.

The IBR acts as a mirror to this optimism, providing an evidence-based picture of operational underperformance, eroded customer trust, weakening vendor terms, margin compression, and liquidity shortfalls. It answers the hard question: What is the actual condition of the business today, and how far has it drifted from sustainability?

The Cash Gap: What It Takes to Get the Wheels Moving

While the "reality gap" highlights the broader disconnect between perceived and actual performance, the cash gap focuses on a more tactical yet vital question:

What is the minimum cash required to unlock the business to restart operations, pay vendors, retain employees, and get the engine running again?

Unlike a full financial restructuring plan, this is a bridge capital assessment. It seeks to answer:

- What critical payments (vendors, salaries, utilities) must be made now?
- What cash outlay is required to complete unfinished orders or replenish inventory?

- What is needed to restore vendor confidence and restart supply chains?
- How much funding is required to collect receivables stuck due to operational gaps?

This phase of the IBR does not involve a detailed 13-week rolling cash flow that comes during Crisis Management (Step 2 of the Turnaround Framework). However, a directional understanding of near-term cash requirements and working capital constraints is essential to frame the urgency and scale of the crisis.

By clarifying both the scale of the problem and the cash it takes to stabilize the situation, this section of the IBR often acts as a wake-up call. It sets the tone for realistic planning and builds the case for urgent stakeholder support or hard restructuring choices.

Case Example

A large Indian shipbuilder

In one engagement, a large Indian shipbuilder had recently secured an ₹1,500 Cr bridge finance to help complete its pending order book, which comprised both global private and Indian government orders. Prior to finalising the disbursal, the lenders appointed a Chief Restructuring Officer (CRO), a technical advisory/Lead Engineer (LE) firm to evaluate vessel costs and monitor procurement, and a commercial advisor to evaluate the commercial viability of ships being completed.

According to the management, the bridge finance was meant to be sufficient to revive the business, as it had forecast the completion of 40 ships with these funds, with each ship being net cash positive, generating additional cash for the business. Large new orders were forecast from the government.

However, the IBR conducted by the CRO and his team revealed that the cost estimates for each ship were outdated; several under-construction ships had been scavenged to show progress on other orders, and many ships were net cash negative (that is, advance payments had been received without comparable progress on the construction). A review of the order book revealed a grimmer picture, with no real customers behind several orders and no clear visibility regarding the large government orders.

In reality, the funding requirement was much larger, and even that wouldn't restore normalcy. It would merely create breathing space. This reality gap, once made visible, helped lenders reset expectations and forced the promoters to acknowledge the gravity of the situation.

Causes of Decline: What Went Wrong, and Why?

To find the best solution for turnaround, the Corporate Turnaround leader needs to understand why the business went into distress. The first and foremost objective of the IBR is to identify and understand the root causes behind the company's distress to ensure targeted and effective interventions.

A data-led analysis is definitely part of the process, but an experienced practitioner would get more insights by walking the floor, speaking to stakeholders, employees, customers and vendors, preferably in person. Experience will help distinguish between those who have an agenda to influence the analysis and those who genuinely want to help. Such conversations also provide ideas for reviving the business, an assessment of management capability and culture prevalent in the business.

Causes typically fall into four buckets:

- **Strategic Missteps:** Wrong product-market choices, poor capital allocation, ignoring competitive shifts.
- **Operational Inefficiencies:** High-cost structures, poor inventory management, weak procurement.

- **Financial Indiscipline:** Overleverage, misreporting, poor cash controls.
- **Governance Failures:** Related-party transactions, promoter interference, board inaction.

Case Example

An Indian Electrical Equipment Company

The engineering business of this large group faced operational and financial decline in the mid-2010s. Key causes included international misadventures (loss-making acquisitions in Europe), high leverage, and poor capital allocation. A forensic IBR helped isolate the root causes and led to a restructuring and sale of international assets, restoring the core India operations to health under new ownership.

The goal of this analysis is not to assign blame, but to identify what needs to change. The review must be fact-based, drawing from performance metrics, board minutes, audit reports, and stakeholder interviews.

Management Assessment

Beyond the tangible financial and operational metrics, an IBR delves into the often-intangible yet profoundly impactful qualitative factors: management capability, organizational culture, and internal politics. These elements are frequently the deepest root causes of a company's distress, influencing every aspect of its performance and its ability to adapt. It is also true that a lot of good employees leave first for better opportunities, leaving behind a weakened organization and also significant gaps across hierarchical levels of the business. Senior management is often guilty of making false promises to lenders, investors and key business stakeholders, creating a trust deficit. If there is fraud involved, it is important to have a hypothesis on who could be potential perpetrators.

All of the above assessments can be done or organized by an experienced turnaround leader. He/ she will also answer the following questions during the IBR in order to make sure that the turnaround efforts have a higher probability of success.

Leadership Review:

- Assess the current management team's ability to execute under pressure. Are they experienced in crisis management? Are they aligned with the needs of the turnaround?
- Conduct interviews with key members of the management team to gauge their vision, readiness to change, and commitment to the turnaround.

Talent Assessment:

- Identify gaps in key roles, such as finance, operations, sales, or marketing. Consider whether additional expertise or external leadership (e.g., interim managers) is needed.
- Assess the company's organizational structure—are there redundancies, silos, or inefficiencies that hinder execution

Employee Engagement and Morale:

- Gauge the overall morale of employees. Are they motivated, or has trust been eroded? Assess the culture and whether it supports the changes needed for a turnaround.
- Analyze retention risks—are critical employees at risk of leaving? Ensure retention plans are in place for key personnel.

This often becomes the trigger for a change of guard, bringing in a Chief Restructuring Officer (CRO, if not already in place), new CEO, or strengthening second-line leadership.

Case Example

IL&FS — Leadership Change as a Turning Point

The IL&FS crisis in 2018 was as much about misgovernance as it was about debt. The newly appointed board, under Uday Kotak, represented a reset in governance and credibility, which became the foundation for asset monetization, investor trust rebuilding, and resolution.

In distressed situations, rebuilding trust is half the battle, and that requires visible change at the top.

High-Level Turnaround Blueprint: Options Under Pressure

An IBR is not a substitute for a detailed turnaround plan, but it must culminate in a credible high-level blueprint, a set of actionable strategic pathways, developed at pace, under uncertainty, and often in a politically charged atmosphere.

At this stage, the seasoned turnaround professional becomes not just a diagnostician, but a rapid response architect, crafting a preliminary rescue outline in an environment where:

- Time is scarce,
- Liquidity is drying up, and
- Stakeholder patience is wearing thin.

The options developed here are directional and not detailed implementation plans, but enough to frame decisions, secure interim support, and initiate priority actions. These options are tailored to those who commissioned the IBR, since the sponsor's interests, legal rights, and risk appetite heavily influence the range of viable solutions.

A. When the IBR is Sponsored by Shareholders / Promoters

When promoters or the board initiate the IBR, often in anticipation of stress or to pre-empt pressure from lenders, the high-level blueprint focuses on preserving ownership and business continuity.

Key options may include:

- **Self-funded revival:** Infusion of promoter capital to stabilize operations and buy time for internal turnaround.
- **Equity dilution to strategic investors or PE:** Bringing in a capital partner with turnaround credentials to fund and guide recovery.
- **Operational restructuring:** Tight cost controls, rationalization of product lines, headcount optimization, renegotiation of contracts.
- **Non-core asset monetization:** Selling real estate, subsidiaries, sale-and-leaseback transactions or brand rights to fund working capital.
- **Debt restructuring through bilateral negotiation:** Pre-IBC settlement with key lenders to defer or restructure payments.
- **Management refresh:** Voluntary reconstitution of leadership with experienced turnaround talent.

The emphasis here is on retaining promoter control, minimizing reputational damage, and seeking voluntary support from stakeholders before formal action becomes unavoidable.

B. When the IBR is Commissioned by Lenders / Creditors

In cases where banks or credit funds initiate the IBR, typically after payment delays, covenant breaches, or forensic red flags, the blueprint skews toward protecting value and minimizing credit losses.

Here, the range of options includes:

- **Change in management / induction of a CRO:** Imposing governance discipline and oversight to restore lender trust.

- **Standstill arrangement:** Short-term debt moratorium in exchange for visible promoter commitment (e.g., partial repayment, equity infusion).
- **Sale of business / assets as a going concern:** Identifying strategic buyers under a controlled sale process (pre-IBC or via Swiss challenge).
- **One-time settlement (OTS):** Especially in smaller exposures, where recovery through legal action is uncertain.
- **Initiating IBC / NCLT proceedings:** Where promoter cooperation is lacking or value erosion is accelerating.
- **Converting debt to equity / quasi-equity instruments:** To de-leverage the balance sheet and facilitate fresh capital.

In these cases, the blueprint is often coupled with a viability assessment and haircut estimate critical for the credit committees and resolution teams.

Common Elements Across Blueprints

Regardless of the sponsor, a good turnaround blueprint under IBR must contain the following components:

1. Stabilization Plan

- Immediate cash need to resume operations
- Critical stakeholder communication plan
- Interim governance improvements

2. Strategic Direction

- Which businesses to retain, fix, or exit?
- Industry trends and competitive positioning
- Long-term value drivers

3. Execution Pathway

- What is required in the next 30, 90 or 180 days?
- Key decisions and who must make them
- Capital structure implications

4. Enablers and Constraints

- Dependencies on government clearances, regulators, unions, or cross-border approvals
- Legal disputes or forensic issues that may impair value realization

At the end of the IBR, the goal is not to present a single answer, but to develop a menu of plausible strategic options, aligned with the sponsor's objectives, grounded in business reality, and sensitive to time and execution constraints.

This blueprint serves as a bridge between diagnosis and action, equipping decision-makers with clarity, confidence, and direction. In India, where turnaround windows are narrow and stakeholder alignment is hard-earned, this ability to develop and communicate options with speed and judgment is often the difference between recovery and ruin.

Case Example

Shareholder-Led Independent Business Review of a Management-Developed Turnaround Plan

The shareholders of the sole distributor of the world's largest electronics brand in the Kingdom of Saudi Arabia faced a trust deficit with their senior management team. Despite operating in one of the most vibrant economies in the Middle East, this $400 million revenue business was struggling to generate profits. The shareholders had already installed a new CEO with a strong résumé in developed markets. However, two consecutive years of missed budgets and underperformance eroded confidence further.

When the CEO presented an ambitious turnaround plan projecting marked improvements in profitability and operating cash generation, the shareholders sought an objective and independent review before committing further capital. They commissioned a focused Independent Business Review (IBR).

Key Findings from the IBR

The review revealed several glaring shortcomings in the management's plan:

1. Technology Gap

The brand owner was falling behind competitors, particularly Korean companies whose products had captured consumer preference for televisions. Without technological superiority, the distributor had little chance of succeeding in its largest product category.

2. Distribution Misalignment

Consumer electronics retail in Saudi Arabia was rapidly shifting to large shopping malls and exclusive brand outlets. The distributor, however, continued to rely on main-street electronic shops with limited inventory and visibility. This structural misalignment meant they were ceding prime shelf space to competitors.

3. Unrealistic Forecasts on New Products

The plan rested heavily on aggressive sales and margin assumptions for a new Virtual Reality (VR) product. Yet, neither pricing nor margin agreements with the brand owner were finalized. Market feedback and independent research suggested that such rapid adoption in the KSA market was highly improbable.

4. No Strategic Engagement with Brand Owner

Despite sustained losses and technological disadvantages, the CEO had not initiated negotiations with the brand owner on royalty fees, credit terms, or support packages. For a business critical to the brand's Middle Eastern presence, this was a missed opportunity to secure relief or partnership.

5. Weak Cost Discipline and Operating Model Redesign

The turnaround plan lacked tough cost-cutting measures or innovative thinking on operating model restructuring. The assumptions leaned toward revenue fixes without credible efficiency initiatives.

6. Incomplete Financial Risk Assessment

The management plan forecasted only up to EBITDA, ignoring balance sheet and cash flow dynamics. Independent scenario analysis revealed a material risk of covenant breach on bank loans—an existential threat that was not even acknowledged by management.

Shareholder Takeaways and Recommendations

The IBR concluded that the CEO's turnaround plan was overly optimistic and inadequately grounded in market realities. Shareholders were presented with high-level options, including:

Cost optimization and operating model redesign to preserve margins and cash.

Realignment of retail presence toward malls and branded outlets to protect market share.

Renegotiation with the brand owner on royalties, support, and credit terms to reflect the distributor's critical market role.

Preparation for liquidity stress, including the possibility of fresh equity infusion, given the high risk of technical default on banking covenants.

Impact of the IBR

Although brief, the IBR provided shareholders with a clear, fact-based lens on management's plan. More importantly, it prepared them for the difficult possibility of capital infusion and governance changes, while highlighting that business continuity could not be taken for granted.

This case underscores how shareholder-led IBRs act as a vital reality check, especially when management's credibility is in question. It demonstrates the need to test plans against market realities, stakeholder dynamics, and balance sheet stress—not just top-line optimism.

Case Example

Lender-Led Independent Business Review of a Borrower's Cash Flow Forecast

A prominent scaffolding engineering and supply company in the UAE had enjoyed strong growth during the real estate boom. The business generated reasonable margins but was inherently capital-intensive. Customers typically paid invoices after 60 to 90 days, while operating costs like salaries, office rents, and vehicle leases had to be met monthly. Additionally, the company made significant upfront investments in scaffolding equipment.

To finance these requirements, the British owners, long-time residents of Dubai, had raised debt from a UK-based lender. Over the years, however, business concentration increased: nearly 70% of revenue came from a single quasi-government customer.

The Trigger for the IBR

This concentration risk became acute when the quasi-government customer faced significant project delays and questions over the viability of its marquee development due to macroeconomic headwinds. International media, including the Financial Times, reported extensively on the challenges facing the UAE's real estate sector. The UK lender, increasingly concerned about its loan exposure, requested a cash flow forecast from the borrower.

When the forecast presented by management appeared overly optimistic and inconsistent with external signals, the lender commissioned an Independent Business Review (IBR) to validate the company's ability to service its debt.

Key Findings from the IBR

The review uncovered critical gaps in the management's assumptions:

1. Collections Misrepresented

The forecast assumed cash inflows based on agreed credit terms with the customer. However, invoice-level analysis revealed that actual collections over the past six months were progressively delayed, reflecting the customer's tightening liquidity.

2. Rising Deductions

Deductions for performance and quality had increased as a percentage of billed amounts compared with prior years. This suggested the quasi-government client was using contractual scrutiny to contain its own costs. Given the nature of the relationship, the company had little bargaining power to contest these deductions.

3. Declining New Business

The order pipeline had weakened sharply. New contracts were scarce, and competitive intensity was rising. This meant that near-term revenues would likely decline, and margins would compress further.

Revised Cash Flow Forecast

After incorporating these findings, the revised forecast showed that without a timely equity infusion, the company would run short of liquidity within three months, rendering it unable to meet loan commitments.

Outcome and Lender Takeaways

The lender's proactive decision to commission an IBR provided crucial early visibility. Armed with objective insights, the lender gained sufficient time to engage with the shareholders, evaluate capital support options, and pre-empt a potential workout or default situation.

This case highlights how lender-led IBRs function as an early-warning tool, bridging the gap between management optimism and ground reality. By stress-testing assumptions around collections, customer behavior, and new business generation, lenders can safeguard their position while giving borrowers a chance to stabilize before insolvency looms.

Stakeholder Alignment: Getting Everyone on the Same Page

Finally, a well-crafted IBR serves as the platform for stakeholder alignment. In a turnaround, different parties (lenders, promoters, vendors, regulators) often have conflicting perceptions and expectations.

The IBR becomes the shared document of truth, helping all stakeholders:

- Agree on facts and figures
- Understand key challenges and trade-offs
- Commit to a unified recovery path or an exit plan

This step requires skillful communication. A good turnaround leader will tailor the messaging of the IBR to each stakeholder group, ensuring transparency without triggering panic.

Conclusion: The IBR as the Turnaround Trigger

In the Indian context, many turnarounds fail because stakeholders jump straight to solutions—restructuring debt, selling assets, and replacing CEOs— without understanding the problem deeply enough.

The IBR is not a checkbox exercise. It is the diagnostic core of a turnaround, rigorous, independent, and forward-looking. It ensures that revival efforts are grounded in reality, not wishful thinking.

As we proceed to the next steps in the Corporate Turnaround Framework viz., Crisis Management, Turnaround Planning, Stakeholder Engagement, Financial Restructuring, and Implementation, the insights from the IBR will guide every decision. In the end, a well-executed IBR is not just about saving a business. It's about restoring confidence in leadership, in the future, and in the possibility of redemption.

Chapter 05

Crisis Management

"If it doesn't add cash or confidence this week, it waits."

Introduction

Once an Independent Business Review (IBR) has laid bare the true condition of the business, the turnaround effort must immediately move into crisis containment mode. This is not yet the time for grand strategy or long-term capital restructuring. The first imperative is survival.

The crisis management phase is about creating breathing room, managing liquidity under extreme pressure, containing value leakage, and buying time to prepare a detailed turnaround plan. In medical terms, this is the stage of emergency care where the patient is losing blood and needs immediate stabilization before surgery can be considered.

In Indian corporate contexts, many businesses wait too long before seeking help. By the time restructuring advisors are called in, the bleeding has accelerated, trust is broken, and time is a luxury they no longer have. The crisis management phase, if executed well, helps shift the business from uncontrolled decline to controlled intervention.

This chapter explores the six critical components of crisis management:

1. Leadership
2. 13-Week Rolling Cash Flow Forecast and Full-Year Liquidity Planning
3. Quick Wins Identification and Execution

4. Stopping the Bleed / Arresting Cash Losses
5. Standstill Agreement with Creditors
6. Stakeholder Messaging

1. Leadership in Crisis: A Specialized Skill

The most important and often underestimated requirement in a crisis is the right leadership. A typical corporate CEO or business head, even a high-performing one, is usually trained to lead in a growth environment: with adequate resources, functioning systems, and time to make decisions. These capabilities, however, do not translate naturally into crisis leadership.

Leading a distressed business demands a completely different skill set:

- **Decisiveness under ambiguity:** Making tough calls with limited data
- **Cash-centric thinking:** Prioritizing liquidity over profitability
- **Calm communication:** Inspiring confidence amidst internal panic and external scrutiny
- **Urgency without chaos:** Driving results in days and weeks, not months
- **Credibility with stakeholders:** Especially lenders, investors, and regulators
- **Resilience under pressure:** Handling fatigue, internal resistance, and media glare

The Role of Interim Leaders or CROs

Because of this unique requirement, many stakeholders in developed economies appoint an interim Chief Restructuring Officer (CRO) or a turnaround CEO — a specialist leader who can manage business continuity, build trust, and lay the groundwork for a recovery.

A capable turnaround leader is part firefighter, part general, and part therapist. He or she brings method to mayhem, and knows which levers to pull and in what sequence to restore stability.

Case Example

IL&FS and the Kotak Board

After the collapse of IL&FS in 2018, the government replaced the board with a team led by Uday Kotak. The change sent a clear message of intent, and the new leadership's credibility became a stabilizing force. Its actions to isolate toxic entities, monetize assets, and communicate transparently turned what could have been a financial system contagion into a relatively contained resolution process.

2. 13-Week Rolling Cash Flow Forecast and Full-Year Liquidity View

In a distressed environment, cash is the only truth. Traditional P&L statements or budgets become irrelevant because they are based on accrual assumptions and stable operations, neither of which holds in a crisis. Therefore, the cash flow forecast becomes the single most important management tool.

The Two-Layer Approach

An effective liquidity management framework during a crisis consists of:

A. 13-Week Rolling Cash Flow Forecast (WCF)

This short-term, weekly forecast provides granular visibility over the next 13 weeks (one quarter). It allows leadership to:

- Identify cash inflows (collections, customer advances)
- Prioritize essential outflows (salaries, raw materials, electricity)
- Defer or renegotiate non-critical payments
- Trigger alerts for negative cash positions in advance
- Make funding or bridging decisions at the right time

The rolling nature means this forecast is updated weekly, always maintaining a forward-looking 13-week view. It becomes a living document and the basis of daily decision-making.

B. Monthly Full-Year Cash Flow Forecast

In parallel, a monthly forecast for the full financial year should be prepared. While the first 3 months are built using the weekly model, the remaining 9 months use monthly granularity, giving stakeholders a sense of medium-term liquidity outlook and capital requirement.

This two-layer system enables management to zoom in for control and zoom out for strategic alignment.

Best Practices in Forecasting

- **Use conservative assumptions** — overestimating inflows or underestimating costs can be fatal
- **Stress test cash flows** — simulate scenarios like customer defaults or raw material inflation
- **Build a cash waterfall** — ranking outflows by priority to decide sequencing in tight weeks
- **Validate forecast with actuals weekly** — closing the loop and building credibility

Case Example:

Marble Mining Company in Oman

A mid-sized marble mining company in Oman was facing mounting losses. Complicating matters, the company also operated two unrelated businesses, a travel agency and an IT services firm that distracted management's focus and consumed scarce resources without delivering meaningful synergies.

The Omani shareholder, concerned about the deteriorating performance, engaged a leading strategy consultant to help chart a turnaround plan. However, midway through the engagement, the consultant recognized that the business challenges extended beyond strategy and required a deeper focus on cash flow and financial viability. To address this, a restructuring advisor was brought in.

The Restructuring Advisor's Approach

The restructuring advisor began by conducting interviews with management, probing into:

- Business conditions and operational performance
- Cash flow pressures and liquidity position
- Vendor payment delays and supplier relationships
- Loan obligations and repayment timelines

Several responses raised red flags. Drawing on prior experience with distressed businesses, the advisor quickly recognized the risk of imminent financial stress. To bring clarity, he developed a 13-week cash flow forecast.

Within two weeks, the forecast revealed the stark reality:

- The business was in deep financial trouble, with cash inflows insufficient to cover immediate obligations.

- Without urgent cash-focused measures, the company would default on its loan commitments, creating a significant reputational risk for the Omani shareholder.
- Liabilities were quietly building up as management delayed vendor payments and focused only on day-to-day firefighting.
- The finance function, led by a financial controller, was limited to accounting and short-term management, lacking the strategic financial oversight required in a crisis.

Lessons and Outcome

The 13-week cash flow forecast acted as an early warning system, highlighting how quickly liquidity was deteriorating. It shifted the narrative from long-term strategy to urgent survival actions—such as vendor negotiations, working capital management, and discussions with lenders.

For the shareholder, this was a wake-up call: the company was not merely underperforming but was on the brink of default. The restructuring advisor's intervention ensured that corrective steps could be initiated before the situation spirraled into a full-blown default with reputational consequences.

This case demonstrates the critical role of short-term cash flow forecasting in distressed situations. While strategy consultants often focus on long-term competitiveness, it is the discipline of restructuring professionals grounded in liquidity management and covenant monitoring that helps prevent businesses from sliding into crisis unnoticed.

3. Quick Wins: Restoring Control and Building Momentum

In a crisis, small wins matter immensely. They create momentum, build internal morale, and show external stakeholders that the business is taking charge.

Quick wins are typically tactical interventions with high impact and low implementation complexity. Examples include:

- Clearing high-value stuck receivables with intense follow-up
- Negotiating payment deferrals with key vendors
- Stopping cash-guzzling SKUs or loss-making branches
- Tightening controls on travel, marketing, or discretionary spending
- Releasing slow-moving inventory at discounts
- Cutting off unproductive contract labor

The goal here is not transformation, but traction.

A good turnaround leader ensures these quick wins are identified in the first few weeks and executed in parallel with forecasting and crisis negotiations. They signal seriousness, especially to lenders.

4. Stopping the Bleed: Arresting Cash and Value Leakage

Beyond quick wins, every turnaround requires immediate cash conservation and loss reduction measures. These are not one-time interventions but structural controls aimed at halting further deterioration.

Common bleeding points in Indian distressed companies include:

- High procurement cost per unit
- Unmonitored plant utilities and wastage
- Excessive credit terms to distributors
- Idle staff and under-utilized shifts
- Duplicate or unnecessary vendors
- Underutilised regional offices and warehousing capacities Legacy discount schemes that erode margin
- Aggressive sales incentives disconnected from collections

Each of these requires a forensic lens not only to identify the leakages but also to triage them into what must stop immediately and what can be phased out.

Centralized Cash Control

One powerful move is to implement a cash control tower, a daily control mechanism where all cash disbursements above a certain threshold require CRO or CFO approval. This forces discipline and centralizes liquidity prioritization.

Stopping the bleed is not about saying "no" to every expense — it's about saying "yes" only to what keeps the engine running.

5. Standstill Agreement: Buying Time with Creditors

A vital aspect of crisis management is engaging with creditors, especially banks and NBFCs to secure a temporary standstill on enforcement actions.

A standstill agreement gives the company:

- Breathing space to stabilize operations
- Time to prepare a credible turnaround or resolution plan
- Protection from legal or enforcement action during the interim

In India, informal standstills are often negotiated outside court, especially in consortium lending situations. A formal standstill can also be created through Intercreditor Agreements (ICA) or under pre-IBC processes like the RBI's Prudential Framework.

Lenders may be more amenable to standstill requests when:

- They see credible cash forecasts
- There is a functioning CRO or turnaround leader

- Promoters show skin in the game (e.g., asset sales, fresh equity)
- Quick wins are already delivering visible results

6. Stakeholder Messaging

While a detailed chapter on Stakeholder Management follows later in this book, it's important to recognize that managing internal and external communications during a crisis is a crucial enabler of successful stabilization.

Key principles at this stage:

- Internal staff need clarity and reassurance, not sugar-coating
- Vendors and customers must be managed actively to avoid ecosystem collapse
- Lenders must see professionalism and transparency in every interaction

Mishandling this communication, especially if mixed signals come from promoters, consultants, and management, can erode fragile trust and sabotage even the best-laid plans.

Conclusion

Crisis Management is the most time-sensitive phase of the corporate turnaround journey. Done well, it can convert free-fall into controlled descent. Done poorly, it can close the window for any recovery.

A successful Crisis Management phase doesn't fix the business; it prepares it for revival. It preserves value, wins time, and builds the foundation on which the full turnaround can stand.

As one veteran turnaround advisor once said:

"If the IBR diagnoses the cancer, Crisis Management is the chemotherapy. It's not easy, but it's what gives the patient a fighting chance."

Chapter 06

Stakeholder Management

"Credibility is collateral."

The Human Side of Turnaround

In the midst of a corporate turnaround, it's easy to focus solely on numbers, cash flow forecasts, debt restructuring, cost cuts, and asset sales. Yet, behind these numbers lie people: lenders, employees, vendors, customers, regulators, and owners, each with their own anxieties, interests, and influence. The fate of a distressed company is often decided not just by what the plan says, but by how it is received, interpreted, and acted upon by these stakeholders.

Stakeholder management, therefore, is not a peripheral activity in turnaround strategy. It is central. Misalignment among stakeholders can derail even the best operational or financial restructuring plans. On the other hand, skilled management of relationships and expectations can unlock time, resources, and flexibility, often tipping the scales in favor of revival.

Understanding the Stakeholder Landscape

A turnaround leader must first map the full spectrum of stakeholders. These are not just the people "owed" something by the company; they include all those who can influence the outcome:

Stakeholder Group	Typical Concerns
Lenders & Creditors	Recovery of dues, future exposure, trust deficit
Employees	Job security, unpaid salaries, morale
Suppliers/Vendors	Past dues, future orders, working capital cycles
Customers	Continuity of service, product quality, warranties
Shareholders	Value erosion, dilution, strategic direction
Regulators	Compliance, systemic risk, investor protection
ARCs/Investors	Entry valuation, control rights, potential upside

In India, the stakeholder dynamic is further complicated by factors such as:

- Family-owned business cultures, where promoter reputation overrides economics
- Multiple lender consortiums with misaligned internal processes
- Heavily unionised labour forces in sectors like textiles, shipping, or steel
- Regulatory entanglements, especially in NBFCs, aviation, telecom, infrastructure, mining, or real estate

A successful turnaround leader must understand each stakeholder's motivation, pain point, and levers of influence and craft a tailored engagement strategy.

The Trust Deficit: A Slow Poison

In distressed companies, the biggest intangible, and the most toxic, is the trust deficit.

This deficit doesn't arise overnight. It builds up slowly, often through:

- Repeatedly missing deadlines and loan covenants
- Overpromising and underdelivering on revival plans
- Concealing true financial health or legal problems
- Delayed or selective information sharing

Initially, some of these missteps may stem from genuine optimism or denial. Over time, however, as stress compounds and reality sets in, stakeholders begin to discount every message, expecting spin, not substance.

The consequences of a trust deficit are severe:

- Suppliers demand cash upfront or stop supplies.
- Customers explore alternate vendors fearing disruption.
- Employees become disengaged or start exiting.
- Lenders refuse to restructure, fearing deeper exposure

Reversing this erosion is both urgent and delicate. It requires not only communication but actions that speak louder than words, transparency, humility, and reliability.

Principles of Rebuilding Trust

1. Transparency as the Bedrock of Trust in Turnarounds

Trust is the most precious currency in a turnaround. Stakeholders know that distress brings difficult news like declining revenues, liquidity shortages, covenant breaches. What they cannot tolerate is being kept in the dark or misled. Yet, transparency is not the same as naivety. A turnaround leader must carefully calibrate disclosures: enough to build credibility and mobilize support, but not so much that it causes panic or irreparable reputational damage.

This balance is difficult. Oversharing raw information without context can be disastrous. For instance, bluntly announcing "cash will run out in two weeks" to employees could accelerate resignations, even if contingency financing is in process. Similarly, disclosing every litigation or operational mishap in detail might overwhelm lenders, when what they really need is a clear picture of solvency and recovery prospects. Therefore, transparency must be coupled with tact and framing. Bad news should be acknowledged, but always alongside a roadmap for corrective action. The underlying principle is: candor without chaos.

This is why the presence of a turnaround leader or a CRO with a stellar reputation becomes so critical. A CRO brings an external credibility halo, reassuring stakeholders that disclosures are not defensive spins but hard truths backed by professional rigor. Their independence and track record in steering other distressed businesses help reset trust. When a respected CRO says, "Here's the liquidity gap, here's what we need from lenders, and here's our 13-week action plan," the message lands with far greater authority than if delivered by an internal team that may already be seen as compromised.

The contrast between Tata Motors and Future Retail illustrates this well. When Tata Motors faced setbacks with the Nano project and mounting pressures on its passenger vehicle business, its leadership did not shy away from admitting missteps whether in product positioning, pricing, or consumer acceptance. More importantly, they framed these admissions within a forward-looking narrative: stronger product pipelines, a refocus on design and safety, and eventual capital support from the parent group. This candid but solution-oriented communication allowed investors and employees to stay aligned, even during tough quarters.

Future Retail, on the other hand, exemplified the risks of opacity. As liquidity pressures mounted and debt obligations loomed, the company downplayed the scale of its problems for too long. Vendors continued supplying goods without full knowledge of the depth of liquidity challenges; lenders remained uncertain of the true exposure until defaults cascaded; employees learned more from media leaks than from management updates. By the time distress was acknowledged openly, trust had evaporated, making sustainable solutions nearly impossible.

From a financial stakeholder's perspective, transparency is not optional. It is the first test of credibility. Banks, ARCs, and private credit funds have long memories of companies that sugar-coated problems until the last minute, forcing fire-sale resolutions. When management provides timely, consistent, and fact-based updates, even if the numbers are grim, the lenders are more inclined to extend forbearance or working capital lines. They know the information they are working with is reliable, allowing them to assess recovery scenarios rationally.

In fact, seasoned lenders often say that the "quality of disclosure" is as important as the financial ratios themselves. A company that admits, "We overestimated festive season demand, and as a result our inventory days have doubled, but here are the corrective steps we're taking," is seen far more favourably than one that blames the economy or competitors without quantifying the impact. In distressed lending committees, a credible turnaround leader who presents risks and mitigants with equal candour often tips the balance in favour of giving the company breathing room.

The irony is that in distress, disclosure does not weaken a company's negotiating position; it strengthens it. Stakeholders can deal with bad news, but they cannot deal with uncertainty. When management communicates candidly and tactfully through a credible messenger, it creates space for lenders to restructure terms, for employees to rally despite salary delays, and for shareholders to inject fresh equity with conviction.

The most powerful sentence in a turnaround remains: "We got it wrong. But here's how we plan to fix it." When framed with tact, backed by data, and delivered by a leader with credibility, this admission is not a weakness. It is leadership. It is the spark that can turn suspicion into alignment, and paralysis into collective action.

2. Consistency of Messaging

In the fog of corporate distress, clarity of communication becomes as important as clarity of strategy. When different voices within a company say different things, trust unravels quickly. Promoters may reassure lenders of abundant liquidity, managers may quietly tell employees to brace for delays, and suppliers may hear yet another story altogether. Such inconsistency is not simply a communication lapse; it is a signal that leadership itself is fragmented. And in a turnaround, fragmentation can be fatal.

Consistency of messaging does not mean that every audience hears the same script. Lenders require fortnightly or monthly updates built on cash flow forecasts and covenant analysis. Employees, by contrast, look for answers on job security and salary continuity. Suppliers want to know whether their invoices will be paid, and customers need assurance about product delivery and service continuity. What unites these conversations is not identical wording but a common foundation of facts and assumptions: a single set of numbers, a shared interpretation of risks, and an aligned view of next steps. These are the anchors that prevent mixed signals from creeping in.

Structured rhythm helps. Fortnightly lender calls, monthly all-hands meetings with employees, supplier town halls, and periodic customer briefings create predictability. Stakeholders stop speculating because they know when and where they will hear from leadership. Rumours lose power in the face of disciplined cadence. Over time, this regularity builds not only trust but also calm, an undervalued asset in situations where panic can be as damaging as the underlying financial distress.

The role of the turnaround leader is central here. In many successful restructurings, the CRO or turnaround professional becomes the single authoritative voice. By leading from the front, absorbing difficult questions, and deciding when to involve promoters or senior managers, the CRO ensures that messaging does not splinter. Their independence lends credibility, while their discipline enforces coherence. The CRO's presence signals to external stakeholders, particularly lenders, that what is being said is objective, fact-based and aligned.

Indian corporate history offers instructive contrasts. The airline industry in India has seen significant business turbulence, with several large airlines becoming bankrupt, accompanied by bad publicity and media coverage. Based on media statements from shareholders, lenders and other stakeholders, it becomes evident that as debt mounted and liquidity evaporated, disclosures to stakeholders varied in tone and timing. Vendors were not fully informed of payment delays, lenders struggled to obtain a coherent picture of exposures, and employees often learned more from media reports than from internal briefings. By the time the scale of distress was communicated, trust had already drained away. Negotiations that might have been collaborative turned adversarial, entering a downward spiral that proved irreversible.

A different perspective comes from Tata Steel's acquisition of Bhushan Steel. Once the insolvency process brought Bhushan Steel into the public domain, Tata Steel's communication was deliberate and consistent. Creditors, employees, and regulators all received aligned messages: financial liabilities would be settled in a structured manner, operations would continue, and integration would proceed with clarity of purpose. The result was not only the stabilization of Bhushan Steel but also a restoration of stakeholder confidence in the combined entity.

These examples illustrate that consistency of messaging is not a cosmetic exercise. It is a structural element of a turnaround. It provides the scaffolding on which trust is rebuilt, negotiations are conducted, and collective action is mobilized. The turnaround leader's task is to ensure that no matter how complex the stakeholder landscape, the voice of the company remains steady, coherent, and believable. In the noise of distress, that steady voice often makes the difference between collapse and recovery.

3. Early Wins to Build Confidence

In the uncertain atmosphere of corporate distress, words alone seldom suffice. Stakeholders — lenders, employees, suppliers, customers — have heard many promises before. What restores belief in a turnaround is not eloquence, but evidence. Visible, tangible wins, however modest, act as proof points that the plan is not merely theoretical but already taking shape.

These early wins rarely solve the entire problem. Paying a month's delayed salaries does not cure a broken capital structure. Restarting one production line does not erase years of underinvestment. Yet their symbolic power is immense. Each small victory shows that paralysis is giving way to motion, that management is taking control of the levers that matter, and that the crisis is no longer spiralling unchecked.

Salary payments, for instance, are more than a financial transaction; they are a signal to employees that their sacrifices are recognized and their faith will not be betrayed. Restarting idle production lines demonstrates to suppliers and customers that operations have not collapsed, and the company remains a participant in the market. Securing even a small new order suggests that customers are still willing to trust the brand. Raising interim funding, perhaps through promoter infusion or asset monetization, signals to stakeholders that management has both commitment and skin in the game.

Turnaround leaders deliberately design these early victories. They look for actions that can be achieved quickly, within constrained resources, but which resonate widely. In many cases, they prioritize credibility wins over strategic wins. A modest but timely gesture that rebuilds trust may do more for momentum than a grand but delayed restructuring announcement.

From a financial stakeholder's perspective, these early wins play a vital signalling role. Banks, ARCs, and investors use them as leading indicators of whether management can execute under pressure. If payroll stabilizes, if operations show even modest improvement, if governance appears tighter, these are read as signs that the company is regaining basic control. No banker may loosen purse strings on the basis of such wins alone, but they are far less likely to harden their stance prematurely if they see evidence of discipline and progress. In a consortium, where skepticism can quickly harden into collective refusal, early wins help soften the narrative and keep lenders engaged in discussions rather than closing doors.

Indian corporate history offers telling examples. When a large technology services company reeled under the accounting scandal in 2009, the immediate task for the government-appointed board was to stabilize operations. Before addressing the complex issues of ownership and valuation, the board focused on ensuring salaries were paid on time and customer contracts remained serviced. These early steps, modest in scale, preserved the company's human capital and reassured global clients. By the time a competitor acquired them, the core business was intact precisely because the early wins had bought time and rebuilt confidence.

Another case is the revival of a reputed agro-chemical and fertilizer business in the early 2000s. Under Group leadership, management emphasized achievable operational improvements like tighter working capital cycles, improved customer responsiveness, and stabilizing cash flows. Each small success was communicated internally and externally, gradually convincing skeptical employees and suppliers that the company could indeed pull through. The final turnaround was the result of sustained effort, but its momentum was born from these early markers of progress.

The key takeaway is that in the early stages of a turnaround, perfection is not required, progress is. Stakeholders want to see that the company is moving, however cautiously, in the right direction. Each early win becomes a brick in the rebuilding of confidence. Once accumulated, they transform a fragile belief into a durable conviction that the turnaround plan is not only possible but already underway.

The Turnaround Leader: Messenger and Mediator

1. What Makes a Great Stakeholder Communicator?

In a turnaround, the leader is not only a strategist and an executioner but, above all, a bridge-builder. Strategy and financial engineering may provide the scaffolding for recovery, but it is communication that binds stakeholders together long enough for those plans to take effect. The ability to convey hard truths, inspire belief, and negotiate alignment often determines whether a turnaround gains traction or collapses under suspicion.

Several qualities define an effective communicator in times of distress.

Integrity is non-negotiable. Stakeholders will forgive misjudgements; they will not forgive deceit. A leader who acknowledges uncomfortable realities like declining revenues, missed projections, painful cost cuts will earn credibility. Without this foundation, even the most polished strategy will be dismissed as spin.

Empathy is equally vital. Distress impacts stakeholders differently: an employee worried about feeding their family, a supplier whose working capital is tied up in unpaid invoices, or a banker defending the exposure before a credit committee. Understanding these anxieties, and speaking to them sincerely, helps defuse anger and humanizes the leadership.

Clarity ensures that complex ideas are grasped quickly. Restructuring plans often involve intricate financial constructs like debt-to-equity swaps, moratoriums, and haircuts, which can alienate those unfamiliar with the jargon. The turnaround leader must distil complexity into plain language, ensuring that no stakeholder feels excluded from the conversation.

Courage is tested most visibly in public forums. Facing down a room of angry employees, or a consortium of sceptical lenders, requires a steadiness of demeanour that communicates resolve. Defensiveness weakens authority; calm candour strengthens it.

Finally, **negotiation acumen** converts communication into tangible progress. Each conversation is, in essence, a negotiation, persuading lenders to grant breathing space, convincing employees to stay the course, or encouraging suppliers to extend credit. The communicator's skill lies in framing outcomes as mutually beneficial, even when sacrifices are required.

The great stakeholder communicator moves fluidly between settings. In the boardroom, they explain the mechanics of a debt-to-equity swap with precision. On the shop floor, they listen to workers fearful of closures and offer reassurance grounded in fact. In meetings with bankers, they defend cash flow forecasts line by line, demonstrating mastery over detail. Each environment demands a different language, yet the underlying qualities remain constant.

Corporate India has seen the consequences when these qualities are absent. In several high-profile collapses, leaders withdrew from open dialogue, avoided difficult conversations, or allowed inconsistent voices to dominate. The result was mistrust, fragmentation, and ultimately, accelerated decline. Conversely, where leaders displayed integrity, empathy, clarity, courage, and negotiation skill even in the direst of circumstances, the stakeholders remained engaged long enough for recovery to take root.

In the end, great stakeholder communicators do not merely transmit information. They create belief. And in a turnaround, belief is the first step toward survival.

2. Role of the Turnaround Leader as an Information Conduit

One of the most overlooked aspects of corporate distress is the breakdown of information flow. In stable companies, data flows reasonably smoothly, viz., promoters brief the board, managers update employees, lenders receive MIS reports. But in distress, the system fractures. Promoters fear disclosure, worried that too much honesty will trigger panic or damage reputation. Employees rely on rumors, filling the silence with speculation that often proves more damaging than fact. Lenders operate on outdated MIS, sometimes receiving reports weeks or months after reality has shifted on the ground.

This asymmetry creates a vicious cycle: suspicion rises, trust erodes, and stakeholders begin to act at cross-purposes. Lenders assume the worst, employees disengage, and promoters grow defensive. In this fog of mistrust, even good news can be disbelieved.

The turnaround leader's role, therefore, is not limited to strategy and execution. They must also act as the information conduit, i.e., the central node through which reliable, timely, and relevant information flows. Their task is threefold:

i. **Curating** the right information. Not every data point matters to every stakeholder. A lender wants covenant compliance schedules, while a worker wants assurance about wages. The turnaround leader distils vast amounts of raw data into the essential insights that matter to each audience.

ii. **Verifying** the accuracy of that information. In distress, even management accounts can be unreliable. Revenues may be overstated, liabilities understated, or cash flow projections optimistic. The turnaround leader applies a forensic eye, ensuring that numbers shared externally are grounded in reality.

iii. **Distributing** the information in a form that each party can understand is essential. To lenders, this may mean a 13-week cash flow forecast with detailed assumptions. To employees, it may mean a simple assurance: "Salaries will be paid on the 7th of each month, starting this cycle." To suppliers, it could be a clear payment plan that prioritizes critical vendors.

When performed well, this role of conduit builds alignment. Lenders base their decisions on facts rather than fears. Employees reduce reliance on corridor gossip. Promoters, once shielded, can still shape the narrative — but through structured, credible channels rather than ad hoc whispers.

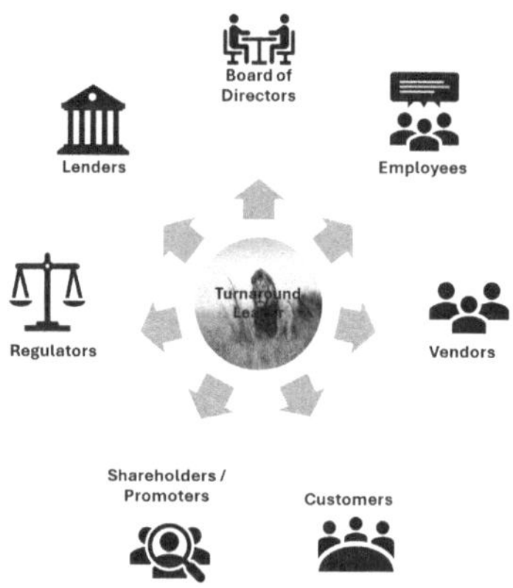

Image: Turnaround Leader as the information conduit

The Indian experience offers several reminders. In the case of a large ship-building company, employee salaries and suppliers were not paid for several months. The promoter was missing in action, asking managers to bring documents to his palatial bungalow for signatures. Vendors, especially contract labour suppliers were anxious and getting aggressive with yard heads. In an unfortunate instance, one of the suppliers took matters into his own hands and physically attacked a yard head. Lack of communication also forced some suppliers to coordinate action and to collectively barge into the head office, demanding clarity. Lenders organised forums and invited the promoter and senior management to come, to provide answers for fund infusion and progress on order book. Each time the stakeholders had to push for answers and clarity, creating an adversarial environment.

In a slightly better-managed situation, Promoter and COO of a real estate ancillary business held weekly calls with senior employees and regional heads, hoping a consistent message would percolate down. The COO met select customers regularly, following up on payments but also updating them on ongoing distress. The CFO met with lenders periodically to provide updates. However, inconsistent messages, missed commitments and lack of follow-through left room for gossip, rumors and anxiety, compounding a complex situation.

3. Intra-Lender Alignment: Herding Cats

In most Indian turnaround situations, "the lenders" are not a single entity. They are a patchwork of institutions with different mandates, incentives, and constraints. A distressed borrower might have exposure spread across public sector banks, private sector banks, NBFCs, mutual funds, bondholders and even foreign lenders or ECB providers. At first glance, they appear as a consortium. In practice, they are often a collection of competing agendas.

Each category of lender approaches distress differently. Public sector banks are guided not only by commercial logic but also by regulatory oversight and political scrutiny, often making them risk-averse and procedural. Private banks may push for quicker resolutions, but their legal teams tend to be more aggressive. NBFCs often have tighter liquidity positions themselves and therefore a lower tolerance for delay. Foreign banks bring their own compliance frameworks and can be inflexible if head office approval is required.

Differences also arise from provisioning status and risk appetite. A bank that has already provided fully against the loan may be more willing to agree to a steep haircut and move on. Another lender that has not provisioned adequately will resist any concession, preferring to delay in the hope of full recovery. These diverging positions create a combustible mix.

When such conflicts harden, decision-making slows to a crawl. Standstill agreements, meant to provide the breathing space for restructuring, may fail because some lenders refuse to sign. Negotiations over debt restructuring terms become prolonged as each lender holds out for better treatment. Fresh funding, essential for stabilizing operations, rarely materializes because no one wants to move first. In extreme cases, the stalemate pushes lenders toward fragmented enforcement actions or premature insolvency proceedings under the IBC, both of which typically destroy value for everyone.

It is here that the turnaround leader can play a critical role. Their job is part strategist, part mediator, part herder of cats. They must recognize that lender alignment cannot be achieved by appealing to goodwill alone; it requires structure, data, and imagination.

Practical tools can make the difference. Convening joint lender forums or encouraging an informal inter-creditor agreement (ICA) creates a platform where differences can be aired, but also where consensus can gradually emerge. Circulating standardized cash flow forecasts and scenario models ensures that lenders debate from a common factual base rather than their own spreadsheets. Creative financial instruments can break deadlocks: split tranches that give short-term lenders quicker recovery while rewarding long-term patience; collateral sharing arrangements that rebalance security; or tiered repayment schedules that match differing appetites. Independent third parties, like valuers, forensic accountants, and legal advisors, can provide credibility when mistrust among lenders runs high.

Above all, the turnaround leader must frame the consequences of inaction starkly. A well-prepared presentation that compares the likely recovery under collective restructuring versus piecemeal enforcement can be persuasive. Lenders do not have to love the plan; they only need to recognize that consensus, however reluctant, is better than the alternatives.

The metaphor often used is apt: herding cats. Each lender has its own instincts, incentives, and anxieties. The turnaround leader cannot change these, but by creating structure, ensuring factual debate, and presenting the costs of disunity, the leader can guide the group toward a fragile but workable alignment. In India, where consortium lending is the norm, this skill may be the single most decisive factor in whether a turnaround progresses or stalls indefinitely.

4. Engaging Equity Holders: Hope vs. Reality

Few issues are as fraught in Indian turnarounds as the role of equity holders. In many cases, equity ownership is concentrated in the hands of family promoters or long-term strategic investors. For them, control of the company is not just a financial position; it is tied to identity, legacy, and social standing. Asking them to accept dilution, loss of control, or even displacement is therefore not a simple financial negotiation, it is an emotional battle.

This tension often leads to destructive delays. Promoters stall debt resolution in the hope of a miraculous recovery that allows them to retain control. They block debt-to-equity conversions, preferring legal battles to the humiliation of dilution. In boardrooms, such misalignment frequently fractures governance and pushes companies toward IBC filings, where control is lost entirely and usually with little value salvaged for equity.

For the turnaround leader, managing this dynamic requires a mix of sensitivity and realism. Promoters must be treated with dignity, but they must also be shown the cold math of insolvency. The leader's credibility is critical: only when equity holders perceive fairness and competence do they open themselves to compromise.

Several techniques have proven effective in navigating this delicate terrain:

- **Carving out a role for promoters in the revived entity** can soften resistance. This may be through management contracts, advisory positions, or defined operational responsibilities. The message is clear: even without majority ownership, they can remain part of the company's story.
- **Upside-linked incentives** such as warrants, earn-outs, or performance-based equity tranches allow promoters to share in future success without obstructing the immediate restructuring. This preserves hope of eventual upside while creating space for fresh capital today.
- **Scenario-based discussions** can be particularly persuasive. When promoters are presented with side-by-side models such as recovery values under a consensual restructuring versus near-zero value under liquidation, the numbers often succeed where arguments fail. Data can cut through denial in a way that words cannot.
- **Reframing the idea of value** is essential. Instead of presenting dilution as a loss, it is shown as preservation. The reality is stark: some value with reduced control is better than zero value with absolute control. Leaders who can communicate this message with empathy often succeed in bringing promoters to the table.

Table below provides a perspective on resistance tactics used by promoters to delay restructuring:

Promoter Resistance Tactic	Why It Happens	Turnaround Leader Response
Delaying debt resolution (hoping for recovery without loss of control)	Emotional attachment to ownership; fear of reputational damage	Present what-if scenarios showing erosion of value from delays; emphasize speed as a value-preserving lever
Blocking debt-to-equity conversions	Fear of dilution and losing boardroom influence	Offer upside-linked instruments (warrants, earn-outs) and highlight possibility of retaining a role under new structure
Resisting new investor entry	Anxiety over loss of family legacy and influence	Explore promoter participation through management contracts or advisory roles; show benefits of strategic investor capital
Litigation and obstruction (to stall restructuring or IBC)	Buying time; betting on political or judicial relief	Highlight costs of litigation (value destruction, reputational harm); build consensus with lenders to reduce scope for unilateral stalling
Denial of financial reality	Hope, ego, or misinformation	Use independent third-party validation (valuers, auditors) to present irrefutable facts; reframe "loss of control" as "preservation of some value"

Ultimately, engaging equity holders is as much about psychology as finance. Promoters must feel respected even as their position erodes. They must be shown a path to participate in revival, even if only symbolically.

And above all, they must see that the alternatives like liquidation or hostile takeover strip them of not just control, but dignity.

Handled with dignity and grounded in data, even the most reluctant equity holders can move from denial to reluctant acceptance. And in that shift lies one of the most crucial breakthroughs of any turnaround.

5. Vendor and Employee Management

Turnarounds are not won in spreadsheets alone. They are won in the trenches with vendors who keep the supply chain alive and employees who keep the operations running. Both groups are often the most immediate casualties of distress, yet both are essential if a company is to recover. Managing them well requires empathy, discipline, and visible leadership.

A. Vendors: The Forgotten Financiers

Suppliers to distressed companies are, in effect, involuntary financiers. They continue to ship goods on credit, extend payment timelines, or absorb shocks to receivables, often without the protections enjoyed by banks. Over time, patience wears thin. Vendors shorten credit cycles, demand advance payments, or quietly disengage. In the worst cases, they cut off supply altogether, choking operations at the very moment continuity is most critical.

A thoughtful turnaround team recognizes that vendors are not a homogeneous group. The first step is to categorize them by criticality: which ones are indispensable to core operations, which are secondary but important, and which can be substituted. This segmentation allows scarce cash to be deployed strategically. For critical vendors, partial payment plans coupled with future order commitments can be enough to maintain cooperation. For others, hard negotiations on delayed payment plans and haircuts may have to be evaluated.

But beyond financial engineering, what often matters most is personal outreach by leadership. When a senior executive or turnaround leader calls a supplier, explains the situation candidly, and commits to a roadmap even when there is no immediate payment, it earns respect. Vendors, particularly in India where relationships matter deeply, are often willing to stand by a company that treats them with dignity. This human touch can keep supply chains intact when contractual rights alone cannot.

B. Employees: Culture Amidst Chaos

If vendors are the lifeblood of the supply chain, employees are the heart of the enterprise. In distress, they face uncertainty on multiple fronts: fear of layoffs, delayed salaries, stalled promotions, and reputational damage by association with a failing company. Morale deteriorates quickly, productivity collapses, and talented staff begin to leave. Left unmanaged, this spiral can accelerate decline.

The turnaround leader's task is to restore a sense of dignity and direction. Frequent communication is the starting point, even when answers are incomplete. Silence fuels rumors; regular updates, however imperfect, reduce speculation. Identifying and empowering departmental influencers, the informal leaders whom colleagues trust, helps create ripple effects of reassurance across teams.

Equally powerful are symbolic quick wins that signal recovery: repairing long-idle machinery, reinstating canteen services, or clearing a backlog of expense reimbursements. These gestures show that the company is regaining control of its environment, however modestly.

Where possible, the introduction of selective, performance-linked incentives tied to turnaround milestones provides a tangible sense of shared purpose. Even in loss-making companies, modest rewards linked to visible progress can motivate teams far beyond their monetary value.

In the end, vendors and employees are not passive stakeholders in a turnaround; they are its co-architects. Treating them as such with honesty, respect, and creativity often spells the difference between a company that limps into insolvency and one that claws its way back to viability. A leader who engages these groups directly is not only managing stakeholders but also restoring the human foundation of the enterprise.

The Stakeholder Trust Triangle

Hopefully, it should be clear to the reader that at the core of every successful turnaround lies one intangible yet indispensable asset: trust. Without it, no plan, however clever, will survive the scrutiny of lenders, employees, suppliers, or regulators. With it, even the most difficult restructuring has a chance of success. Trust, however, is not built on promises alone. It rests on three interdependent pillars, viz., Transparency, Competence, and Fairness, which together form what can be called the Stakeholder Trust Triangle.

Transparency

The first vertex of the triangle is transparency. As discussed earlier, in distressed situations, stakeholders often operate in an information vacuum. Lenders rely on outdated MIS reports, employees listen to rumours, and customers speculate in the market. The turnaround leader must pierce this fog by sharing real-time data and context, even when the numbers are uncomfortable. This includes timely updates on cash flows, operational disruptions, and realistic forecasts. Equally important is the courage to acknowledge past failures openly. In India, promoters and boards have historically hesitated to admit mistakes, preferring to attribute distress to external shocks. Yet, experience shows that credibility is earned, not lost, when leaders say: "We miscalculated, but here is how we will correct it."

Competence

Transparency, however, is insufficient if not matched by competence. Stakeholders will not trust a leader who speaks candidly but fails to deliver results. Competence is demonstrated by traction on the ground e.g., restarting a dormant plant, securing an interim funding line, closing a new customer order. It is also reinforced by the creation of cross-functional execution teams that show the organization can implement change beyond the leadership suite. In many Indian turnarounds, early operational wins, even symbolic ones, like normalizing salary payments or repairing long-idle equipment, has done more to restore credibility than elaborate PowerPoint plans. Competence reassures stakeholders that the leader not only sees the problem but also knows how to act.

Fairness

The third vertex of the triangle, fairness, is often the hardest to sustain but equally vital. In restructuring, sacrifices are inevitable. Lenders may need to accept haircuts, employees may face job losses, and promoters may see dilution. What stakeholders cannot accept is favoritism or secrecy. If one bank perceives another has been given a better deal, or if employees feel that management shields its own perks while cutting staff benefits, trust collapses. Fairness means offering balanced sacrifices across groups, guided by principles of equity and proportionality. It does not mean that every party suffers equally, but rather that no group feels singled out for undue pain or excluded from the process.

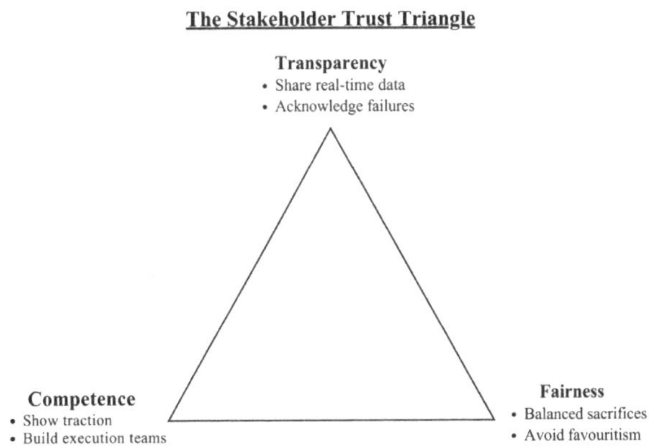

Adapted from Bain & Company's Trust Triangle concept

When all three vertices of the Trust Triangle are strong, the effect is transformative. Support begins to flow not only from lenders but also from employees, suppliers, customers, and sometimes even competitors who recognize that the company is being stabilized with integrity. Where any one side is weak, however, the triangle collapses. Transparency without competence breeds despair. Competence without fairness fuels resentment. Fairness without transparency invites suspicion. Only the balanced interplay of all three sustains confidence long enough for a turnaround to succeed.

In the Indian landscape where mistrust of distressed companies runs deep, the Trust Triangle offers a practical compass. Leaders who embed these three principles into every action find that alignment, though never easy, becomes possible. And alignment, in the end, is the soil from which revival grows.

Conclusion: The Turnaround is in the Relationships

In the end, stakeholder management is about humanizing the turnaround. It's about moving from suspicion to partnership, from silence to dialogue, from brinkmanship to shared problem-solving.

Technical fixes i.e., restructuring, refinancing, and rationalization are necessary, but not sufficient. The emotional energy, reputational equity, and human trust behind those transactions are what sustain a turnaround.

As one senior banker in a distressed case rightly observed:

"We didn't back the plan. We backed the person leading it."

And that, above all, is the power of stakeholder management.

Chapter 07

Development of a Turnaround Plan

"The new operating model that sets the foundation for survival."

Introduction: Moving from the ICU to the Operating Theatre

Crisis management stabilizes the critically ill enterprise; a Turnaround Plan charts the course to recovery and long-term health. The mindset shift is dramatic:

Crisis Management	Turnaround Plan
Minute-by-minute cash triage	Multi-year value creation roadmap
"Stop the bleeding"	"Heal, strengthen, and grow"
Decisions under war-room pressure	Cross-functional collaboration & governance
Non-negotiable speed	Speed plus analytical rigour

This phase rejects 30,000-ft theorizing. It demands practical, ground-level changes that can be executed with scant time, cash, and managerial bandwidth. In India, where promoter influence, lender consortiums, and regulatory complexity collide, the turnaround plan must be granular and credible enough to win support from battle-weary stakeholders.

Laying the Analytical Bedrock

Given below are several frameworks to analyze a business and develop a turnaround plan. Each can be used in its entirety or partly as a combination with other frameworks.

1. A Brutally Honest SWOT

SWOT (Strengths, Weaknesses, Opportunities, and Threats) analysis is a critical initial step in developing a turnaround plan for a struggling business. It provides a structured framework to assess both internal and external factors impacting the company, helping to identify the root causes of underperformance and lay the groundwork for effective recovery strategies.

Here's a breakdown of how each element of SWOT analysis is applied in the context of turnaround plan development:

- **Strengths (Internal):** These are the internal capabilities, resources, and advantages that the company possesses, which can be leveraged during the turnaround. In a crisis, identifying and leaning on existing strengths is crucial. In a turnaround, this involves pinpointing what the company still does well, its competitive advantages (e.g., strong brand, loyal customer base, unique technology, skilled workforce, efficient processes in certain areas), and valuable assets. These strengths can be the foundation upon which the recovery is built, potentially by focusing on core competencies or areas where the company still has an edge.

- **Weaknesses (Internal):** These are the internal deficiencies, limitations, and disadvantages that hinder the company's performance. Addressing these directly is vital for a successful turnaround. This involves an honest assessment of what's going wrong internally (e.g., poor financial controls, inefficient operations, high employee turnover, outdated technology, weak management, lack of market penetration). Identifying these weaknesses helps in prioritizing areas for immediate improvement, cost reduction, or restructuring.

- **Opportunities (External):** These are favorable external factors or trends in the market or industry that the company can potentially exploit to its advantage. This means looking for external shifts that could create a path to recovery (e.g., emerging market trends, new technologies, underserved customer segments, changes in regulations, competitor weaknesses, potential partnerships or acquisitions). Spotting opportunities allows the company to pivot, diversify, or reposition itself for future growth.

- **Threats (External):** These are unfavorable external factors or trends that could pose challenges or risks to the company's survival and recovery. This involves recognizing external dangers (e.g., increasing competition, economic downturns, changing consumer behavior, supply chain disruptions, new regulations, technological obsolescence). Understanding threats helps in developing mitigation strategies and contingency plans to protect the business during the turnaround process.

Strengths:	**Weaknesses**
Internal capabilities, resources and advantages (examples): • Strong brand • Monopoly in a region or market • Experienced management • Strong R&D centre with unused patents • Automated packaging line	**Internal** deficiencies, limitations, and disadvantages (examples): • Technologically outdated plants • High employee turnover • Inefficient manufacturing operations • Weak internal controls • High cost of procurement • Manual sales and operations planning
Opportunities	**Threats**
External factors or trends that can be exploited (examples): • Competition in disarray • Favourable regulatory development, like import barriers • Strong currency, making exports competitive • Supply glut of key raw material	**External** factors or trends that are unfavourable (examples): • Growing competition • Weakening currency, making imported raw material expensive • Supplier consolidation • Customer consolidation • Technology disruption

In summary, for turnaround plan development, a SWOT analysis is crucial because it:

- **Identifies Root Causes:** Helps pinpoint the underlying reasons for the business's decline, rather than just treating symptoms.

- **Informs Strategic Choices:** Provides a basis for developing strategies that capitalize on strengths and opportunities while addressing weaknesses and mitigating threats.

- **Prioritizes Actions:** Enables leadership to focus on the most critical areas for intervention and resource allocation, especially when time and resources are limited.

- **Aligns Stakeholders:** A well-executed SWOT analysis can bring management and other stakeholders (employees, creditors, investors) onto the same page regarding the current situation and the necessary steps for recovery.

- **Facilitates Realistic Goal Setting:** By understanding the internal and external landscape, companies can set achievable and impactful goals for the turnaround.

Essentially, SWOT analysis acts as a diagnostic tool, providing a comprehensive picture of the company's current state, which is indispensable for crafting a targeted and effective turnaround strategy. The turnaround SWOT is not a marketing slide. It brings the turnaround leader and the management of the company together in developing the plan. It links opportunities and threats to cash impact and time horizon, a 2x2 matrix that can help prioritize actions to be taken.

Case Example

SWOT Analysis of one of India's largest packaging company, undergoing significant distress

Strengths:	Weaknesses:
◘ Pan India manufacturing footprint ◘ Industry's most experienced management ◘ Strong customer relationships, forged over decades and an experienced sales team ◘ Considered a strong brand, even after several years of stress	◘ Poor governance practices ◘ Weak internal controls ◘ Ageing plants, with inefficient power / utility consumption ◘ Low on cash and broken banking relationships due to default ◘ Low employee morale, no salary increments in 5 years ◘ Unionised workforce, with significant labour issues at two plants ◘ High risk of accidents at plant due to poor plant maintenance historically

Opportunities:	**Threats:**
¤ Vibrant customer base, looking to innovate to create new demand ¤ Growing demand ¤ Fragmented competitors ¤ Key raw material prices peaked	¤ Lenders blocking funds for capital expenditure, both for large maintenance and new product lines ¤ Vested interests not aligned with company turnaround ¤ Non-availability of adequate quantity of a key raw material

Agreed initial actions to be taken to revive the business:

- EBITDA linked, profit sharing for employees to be paid on part monthly, part quarterly basis (upto 25% of cost to company, giving employees a significant jump in compensation)
- Regular management meetings to discuss key initiatives and KPIs and performance against budgets. Open and transparent discussions to address potential governance issues
- Selective price increases
- Cut off sales to customers, who bought products at steep discount (addressed margin and potential governance risks)
- Negotiated long-term contracts with Indian suppliers of key raw materials, to ensure competitive and transparent pricing. Ensured an adequate mix of suppliers (manufacturers and international traders), to maintain competitive intensity
- Sourcing alignment to reduce logistics costs for a raw material
- Encouraged and periodically rewarded plant, sales and procurement teams for achieving significant milestones e.g. high production efficiency, improving average price / ton, etc.

Outcome

- Company achieved a 10 year high profitability within 18 months
- Cash position improved significantly, such that lenders could collect an additional 25% recovery
- Sold the business at double the price versus what was offered by promoters as settlement to banks.

2. Porter's Five Forces for Industry Reality Check

Porter's Five Forces, developed by Michael Porter of Harvard Business School, is a framework for analyzing the competitive intensity and attractiveness of an industry. Unlike SWOT, which has internal and external aspects, Porter's Five Forces solely focuses on the external industry environment. It helps businesses understand the underlying forces that determine industry profitability and identify strategic opportunities and threats.

In the context of turnaround plan development, Porter's Five Forces helps a struggling company understand why its industry might be inherently unattractive or how its competitive position within that industry has deteriorated. This understanding is crucial for formulating a recovery strategy that addresses the systemic issues, not just the symptoms of decline.

Here's a breakdown of each of the five forces and its relevance in turnaround plan development:

- **Threat of New Entrants:** This force assesses how easy or difficult it is for new companies to enter the industry. If the threat of new entrants is high (low barriers to entry), it means that even if the struggling company improves, new competitors can quickly flood the market, putting renewed pressure on prices and market share. A turnaround plan might need to focus on creating or strengthening barriers to entry (e.g., building strong brands, securing proprietary technology, establishing strong distribution channels, achieving economies of scale) to protect future profitability. Conversely, if barriers are already high, the turnaround can focus on fixing internal issues without immediate fear of new disruptors.

- **Bargaining Power of Suppliers:** This force examines the ability of suppliers to dictate prices or terms for inputs (raw materials, components, labor, etc.). If suppliers have high bargaining power, they can squeeze the struggling company's margins, making recovery difficult. The turnaround plan might involve:

    - Diversifying suppliers: Finding alternative sources to reduce dependence on a few powerful ones.

- Negotiating better terms: Leveraging what little bargaining power the company might still have, or exploring longer-term contracts.
- Vertical integration (backward): If feasible, taking over the production of key inputs to control costs.
- Redesigning products/processes: To use less expensive or more readily available inputs.

- **Bargaining Power of Buyers:** This force analyzes the ability of customers to drive down prices or demand higher quality/more services. If buyers have high bargaining power (e.g., many sellers and few buyers, low switching costs for buyers, undifferentiated products), the company may be forced to lower prices, further eroding profitability. A turnaround strategy could involve:
    - Product differentiation: Creating unique products or services that justify higher prices and reduce buyer sensitivity.
    - Building customer loyalty: Through superior service, brand building, or loyalty programs to increase switching costs.
    - Targeting niche markets: Focusing on specific buyer segments where their bargaining power is lower.
    - Cost leadership: If differentiation isn't an option, focusing on drastically reducing costs to remain competitive on price.
- **Threat of Substitute Products or Services:** This force considers the likelihood of customers finding alternative ways to meet their needs from a different industry. If the threat of substitutes is high, the struggling company's core offering may be becoming obsolete or less valuable. The turnaround plan must address this by:
    - Innovating: Developing new products or services that offer superior value or address the underlying need more effectively.
    - Increasing perceived value: Enhancing the current offering's features, quality, or branding to make it more attractive than substitutes.

- ¤ Repositioning: Shifting the company's focus or market segment to areas less threatened by substitutes.
- ¤ Exiting non-viable segments: If the threat is too strong, it might be necessary to exit markets completely saturated by substitutes.

- **Rivalry Among Existing Competitors:** This force assesses the intensity of competition among firms already in the industry. High competitive rivalry (e.g., many competitors, slow industry growth, high fixed costs, and similar products) often leads to price wars, increased marketing spend, and reduced profitability – common causes of business decline. A turnaround strategy needs to:
    - ¤ Identify sustainable competitive advantages: Moving away from pure price competition.
    - ¤ Rationalize capacity: Reducing excess production or operations to match demand.
    - ¤ Focus on efficiency and cost reduction: To compete effectively even in a price-sensitive market.
    - ¤ Seek strategic alliances or consolidation: To reduce competitive pressure.
    - ¤ Differentiate offerings: To reduce direct head-to-head competition.

How to use Porter's Five Forces in a Turnaround Plan:

- Analyze the Current State: Conduct a thorough Five Forces analysis of the industry the struggling company operates in. This helps diagnose the external pressures contributing to its decline.
- Identify Profit Erosion Points: Determine which forces are most significantly eroding the company's profitability. Is it intense rivalry, powerful buyers, or the rise of substitutes?
- Prioritize Strategic Responses: Based on the analysis, formulate specific strategies to:

- ¤ Reduce the power of unfavorable forces: For example, by increasing switching costs for buyers or diversifying suppliers.
- ¤ Exploit opportunities: Such as entering segments with weaker competitive forces.
- ¤ Reconfigure the value chain: To create a more defensible position against the forces.

- Inform Restructuring and Resource Allocation: The insights gained from the Five Forces analysis will guide decisions on where to cut costs, where to invest, and which business units might need to be divested or shut down.
- Set Realistic Expectations: Understanding the industry's inherent attractiveness (or lack thereof) helps set realistic goals for the turnaround and determines if a full recovery is truly feasible or if a strategic exit is the better option.

In essence, Porter's Five Forces provides the external lens to complement the internal view of a SWOT analysis, giving a struggling company a holistic understanding of its challenging environment to build a robust and sustainable turnaround plan.

3. Value-Chain & Cost-Driver Mapping

Value Chain Analysis, popularized by Michael Porter, is a strategic framework that breaks down a company's activities into discrete, value-adding processes to understand where value is created and where costs are incurred. It helps a company identify its sources of competitive advantage, either through cost leadership (performing activities more cheaply) or differentiation (performing activities in a unique way that customers value).

In a turnaround, Value Chain Analysis is critical for:

- **Identifying Cost Inefficiencies:** By mapping out each activity, a struggling company can pinpoint specific areas where costs are unnecessarily high (e.g., inefficient operations, expensive inbound logistics, high marketing spend with low ROI). This granular view helps move beyond general cost-cutting to targeted cost optimization.

- **Revealing Value Gaps:** It helps understand where the company might be failing to deliver value to customers, leading to declining sales or customer dissatisfaction. Is the service poor? Is marketing failing to communicate the product's benefits?

- **Spotting Opportunities for Differentiation:** Even in a crisis, a company might have hidden strengths in certain activities that can be amplified for differentiation. For example, exceptional post-sales service could be a differentiator to rebuild customer loyalty.

- **Benchmarking:** It allows comparison of the company's activities and their costs/value contribution against competitors or industry best practices. This can highlight areas where the company is significantly underperforming.

- **Strategic Outsourcing Decisions:** Understanding which activities are core and which can be more efficiently performed externally, helps in making critical outsourcing decisions to reduce costs or improve quality.

Cost Driver Mapping (often a component of Cost Driver Analysis or Activity-Based Costing - ABC) involves identifying the underlying factors or activities that cause a cost to be incurred and then quantifying their impact. It moves beyond simply looking at total costs and drills down into what makes those costs go up or down.

Examples of cost drivers include:

- **Volume-based:** Number of units produced, number of labor hours, machine hours, number of customers served.

- **Batch-related:** Number of production setups, number of quality inspections, number of purchase orders.

- **Product-related:** Number of product designs, complexity of product, number of components.

- **Customer-related:** Number of sales calls, number of customer returns.

- **Facility-related:** Square footage, depreciation, utilities.

Cost Driver Mapping is invaluable for a turnaround because it enables precise cost management:

- **Root Cause Analysis of Costs:** Instead of just seeing "high manufacturing costs," cost driver mapping can reveal that the cost driver is actually "excessive machine setups" due to small batch sizes or "high rework" due to poor quality control. This pinpoints the exact operational issues driving costs.

- **Targeted Cost Reduction:** Once cost drivers are identified, the turnaround plan can focus on managing or reducing the activities that drive those costs. For example, if machine setups are a major cost driver, the plan might involve strategies to increase batch sizes or reduce setup times.

- **Resource Allocation Optimization:** It helps allocate resources (financial, human) more effectively. By understanding which activities consume the most resources and why, management can make informed decisions about where to cut back or where strategic investment might yield the biggest cost savings.

- **Improved Pricing Decisions:** By understanding the true cost of producing different products or serving different customer segments based on their cost drivers, the company can make more informed pricing decisions, ensuring that products are priced profitably.

- **Performance Measurement:** It provides specific metrics (the cost drivers themselves) to monitor the effectiveness of cost-cutting initiatives. For instance, tracking "number of reworks per batch" can show if quality improvements are indeed reducing costs.

In a turnaround scenario, Value Chain Analysis provides the framework for understanding all activities, and Cost Driver Mapping provides the detailed insight into what makes those activities expensive.

A company might use Value Chain Analysis to identify that "Operations" is an area with high costs and low value-add.

Then, Cost Driver Mapping within "Operations" would reveal that the high costs are driven by "number of defective units" and "machine downtime."

The turnaround plan can then focus on specific initiatives to reduce defective units (e.g., investing in new equipment, employee training) and machine downtime (e.g., preventive maintenance programs), directly targeting the identified cost drivers within the value chain.

By combining these analyses, a turnaround team can move from a general understanding of financial distress to a precise, actionable plan for operational efficiency and value creation, which is crucial for pulling a company back from the brink.

4. Pricing, Customer & Product Profitability Lenses

In the context of a turnaround plan, making optimal pricing decisions, analyzing customer profitability, and understanding product profitability are critical. They directly influence a company's revenue generation, cost structure, and ultimately, its cash flow and working capital.

4.1 Pricing Decision

Pricing decisions involve setting the monetary value at which a company sells its products or services. In a turnaround, pricing is not just about covering costs and making a profit; it's a strategic lever to stabilize the business, generate immediate cash, and signal value to the market. Following different models can be considered to determine a different price for its products:

- **Cost-Plus vs. Value-Based vs. Competitive:**
    - **Cost-plus:** Start with total costs (variable + allocated fixed) and add a desired markup. While simple, it ignores market realities and customer willingness to pay. In a turnaround, this is a baseline, ensuring you don't sell below your cost to serve.
    - **Value-based:** Price according to the perceived value to the customer. This can allow for higher margins if your product

solves a critical problem or offers significant benefits. In a turnaround, identifying and communicating unique value is key to avoiding destructive price wars.

- ¤ Competitive: Prices are based on what competitors charge. This is essential for market positioning but can be dangerous in a turnaround if it leads to unsustainable price cuts.

- **Dynamic Pricing:** Prices are adjusted based on demand, seasonality, competitor actions, or even customer segments. This can maximize revenue in varying conditions.
- **Psychological Pricing:** This involves utilizing pricing tactics like ₹9.99 instead of ₹10, or offering bundles, to influence perception and encourage purchase.
- **Consider Elasticity:** Understand how sensitive demand is to price changes. For highly elastic products, even small price increases can lead to significant drops in sales.

Impact on Cash and Working Capital:

- **Price Increases:** While tempting for immediate revenue, they can reduce sales volume. A sharp drop in sales volume can lead to excess inventory (tying up working capital) or under-utilized production capacity (increasing per-unit fixed costs), negatively impacting cash. However, if carefully managed, increased prices for stable demand can significantly boost cash flow and profitability.
- **Price Decreases (Discounts/Promotions):** They can stimulate sales volume, generating quick cash. However, if the discount is too deep, it can erode margins, leading to lower total profit and potentially negative cash flow if variable costs aren't covered. Excessive discounting can also damage brand perception and train customers to wait for sales, impacting future full price sales and, consequently, cash flow. It can also quickly deplete inventory, requiring rapid replenishment, which can strain working capital.

- **Pricing terms (e.g., net 30, net 60):** Shorter payment terms for customers (e.g., net 15) can improve cash collection and reduce accounts receivable (a component of working capital), thus boosting working capital. Conversely, offering longer terms to secure sales ties up cash in receivables.

4.2 Customer Profitability Analysis (CPA)

Customer Profitability Analysis (CPA) involves calculating the revenue generated by each customer or customer segment and subtracting all direct and indirect costs associated with serving that customer or segment over a period. This goes beyond simple sales figures to reveal which customers are truly contributing to the bottom line and which are draining resources. Costs considered include sales and marketing efforts, order processing, delivery, customer service, technical support, and even collection costs. The following can be used as a guideline to initiate analysis of customer profitability:

- **Identify Profitable vs. Unprofitable Customers:** Rank customers or segments from most to least profitable (often resulting in a "whale curve" where a small percentage of customers generate most profits, and a small percentage destroy value).

- **Understand Cost to Serve:** Break down the specific activities and resources consumed by different customer types. For example, some customers may require frequent sales visits, custom orders, expedited shipping, or extensive post-sale support, driving up their cost to serve.

- **Strategic Actions:**

  - **Nurture Profitable Customers:** Invest more in retaining and growing relationships with high-profit customers.

  - **Improve Margins on "Carriage Trade" Customers:** These are high-revenue but also high-cost customers. Can their demands be streamlined, or can they be charged more for premium services?

- **Re-evaluate "Bargain Basement" Customers:** These are low-revenue, low-cost customers. Can efficiency improvements make them more profitable, or should the company simply streamline service?
- **Address Unprofitable Customers:** Implement strategies to make them profitable (e.g., adjust pricing, reduce service levels, eliminate costly features) or, as a last resort, consider "firing" them.

Impact on Cash and Working Capital:

- **Focusing on Profitable Customers:** Prioritizing profitable customers (who pay on time, require less support, and place larger orders) leads to better quality revenue, less need for extended credit, and faster cash conversion. This directly improves cash flow and reduces the strain on accounts receivable, thus improving working capital.
- **Reducing Service to Unprofitable Customers:** Reducing the effort and resources spent on unprofitable customers frees up cash tied up in servicing them (e.g., less inventory for bespoke orders, fewer collection efforts, less marketing spend on low-ROI segments). This improves the cash conversion cycle and releases working capital.
- **Payment Terms:** Profitable customers often have better payment histories or can be persuaded to accept shorter payment terms, directly accelerating cash inflows and reducing the average days sales outstanding (DSO), which is a key component of working capital.

4.3 Product Profitability Analysis

Product Profitability Analysis assesses the profitability of individual products or product lines by comparing the revenue generated by each product with all the costs associated with its development, production, marketing, sales, and distribution. Similar to CPA, it moves beyond gross margin to a fuller understanding of true profitability. Guidelines for conducting a product profitability analysis:

- **Identify Core Products:** Determine which products are truly profitable and which are not, considering all direct and allocated indirect costs (e.g., R&D, marketing campaigns specific to a product, warranty costs).
- **Lifecycle Stage:** Consider the product's position in its lifecycle. A new product might be unprofitable initially due to high development costs, while a mature product might be facing declining demand and intense price competition.
- **Strategic Actions:**
  - **Focus on Profitable Products:** Prioritize resources (marketing, R&D, production capacity) on high-margin, high-demand products to maximize overall profitability.
  - **Streamline or Divest Unprofitable Products:** For consistently unprofitable products, explore ways to reduce their costs (e.g., simplifying designs, changing suppliers) or, if they continue to drain resources, consider discontinuing or divesting them. This can free up capital and capacity.
  - **Rationalize Product Portfolio:** Eliminate product proliferation if it leads to complexity, higher inventory costs, and diluted marketing efforts. A streamlined portfolio can reduce costs and improve focus.
  - **Innovation for Margins:** Invest in R&D for products that can command higher prices due to innovation or differentiation, thereby improving gross margins.

Impact on Cash and Working Capital:

- **Eliminating Unprofitable Products:** Discontinuing products that consume more cash than they generate (e.g., due to high production costs, slow sales leading to obsolete inventory, or significant marketing spend) directly improves cash flow. It also frees up working capital tied up in raw materials, work-in-progress, and finished goods inventory for those products.

- **Focusing on High-Margin Products:** Shifting production and sales focus towards products with higher profit margins generally leads to better cash generation per unit sold. These products often have better inventory turnover rates, reducing the amount of cash tied up in inventory (a major working capital component).
- **Inventory Management:** Product profitability analysis highlights products with slow turnover or high holding costs. Improving inventory management for these products (e.g., reducing safety stock, implementing just-in-time) reduces inventory levels, converting assets into cash faster and improving working capital.
- **Production Efficiency:** Understanding product costs drives efforts to improve production efficiency. Faster production cycles and reduced waste mean less cash tied up in work-in-progress and raw materials, enhancing working capital.

By meticulously applying these analyses, a struggling business can make data-driven decisions that not only improve its income statement (profitability) but also critically enhance its balance sheet (working capital) and cash flow statement (liquidity), laying a solid foundation for a successful turnaround.

Designing Operational Restructuring Initiatives

Operational levers precede financial engineering; otherwise, new money merely fills a leaking bucket. Financial engineering is a tool to support a sound operational plan, not a substitute for it. Without operational discipline, any financial infusion is akin to pouring water into a bucket full of holes, a futile exercise that merely delays the inevitable.

Too often, debt restructured in India under various RBI schemes has failed to survive more than a few years, leading to these businesses either being back on the table to renegotiate debt or being put through the formal bankruptcy process. Refer to the table below for sample large cases that went through debt restructuring under various RBI schemes, and subsequently, within a few years, went through formal bankruptcy.

Company	Prior RBI restructuring (year)	IBC / CIRP admission (year)
Essar Steel India	CDR (2003)	2017
Bhushan Steel (Tata Steel BSL)	5/25 flexible refinance (2015)	2017
Bhushan Power & Steel	SDR (2015)	2017
Electrosteel Steels	CDR (2013); SDR (2016)	2017
Monnet Ispat & Energy	SDR (2015)	2017
Alok Industries	CDR (2012)	2017
Amtek Auto	SDR (2015)	2017
Lanco Infratech	CDR (2013)	2017
Era Infra Engineering	CDR (2013)	2017
ABG Shipyard	CDR (2013–14); S4A (2016)	2017
Binani Cement	JLF/CAP – MRA (2014–15)	2017
Reliance Communications (RCom) / RCIL	SDR (2017)	2019
Reliance Infratel	SDR (2017)	2019
Reliance Telecom	SDR (2017)	2019
Aircel group (Aircel Ltd / Aircel Cellular / Dishnet Wireless)	SDR (2017–18)	2018
Jet Airways (India)	BLPRP under RBI Feb-12-2018 circular (2019)	2019
Future Retail	One-Time Restructuring – COVID framework (2021)	2022
DHFL (Dewan Housing Finance)	ICA under RBI June-7-2019 Prudential Framework (2019)	2019

SREI group (SEFL, SIFL)	One-Time Restructuring – COVID framework (2020)	2021
Reliance Naval & Engineering (RNEL / ex-Pipavav)	CDR (2015; exit okayed 2017)	2020
IVRCL	CDR (2014); SDR (2015)	2018
Lavasa Corporation	SDR (2017)	2018
Videocon Industries (group)	JLF/CAP restructuring attempt (2017)	2019
Nagarjuna Oil Corporation (NOCL)	CDR / recast (c. 2013–14)	2018
Ruchi Soya Industries	CDR (2011/2014)	2017
Uttam Value Steels	SDR (2016)	2017
Uttam Galva Metallics	SDR (2016)	2017
Orchid Pharma	CDR (2014)	2017
Castex Technologies (Amtek group)	SDR (2015)	2017
Murli Industries	CDR (c. 2012–13)	2017

After the lessons learned during IBR and the structured analysis listed in the previous section, it is time to formulate robust operations restructuring initiatives. These initiatives form the bedrock of any turnaround from a loss-making/cash-losing business to a profit-making/cash-generating machine. Reasons why development of an operational restructuring plan must precede a debt restructuring and simultaneous implementation (to the extent feasible) are the following:

- **Address Root Causes:** Operational levers (like those discussed in SWOT, Porter's Five Forces, Value Chain, and Cost Driver Mapping) focus on the fundamental flaws within the business model and its execution. They aim to:

- ¤ Improve efficiency (e.g., lean manufacturing, process optimization).
- ¤ Reduce costs (e.g., renegotiating supplier contracts, cutting waste).
- ¤ Enhance revenue generation (e.g., optimizing pricing, improving sales processes, focusing on profitable customers/products).
- ¤ Improve quality and customer satisfaction. These actions are about "plugging the holes" in the bucket.

- **Sustainability:** If you pump new money (through financial engineering) into a business without fixing its operational flaws, that money will simply flow out through the existing "leaks." The company might get a temporary reprieve, but it will soon be back in the same, or worse, financial distress. The root problems remain unaddressed, making any recovery unsustainable.
- **Credibility with Stakeholders:** Lenders, investors, and even employees are more willing to provide support (new money, concessions, effort) if they see a credible plan to fix the underlying operational issues. A company that only seeks new financing without a clear path to operational improvement is seen as a higher risk. They want to see that management has identified why the business is failing and has a concrete plan to make it profitable and cash-generative on its own merits.
- **Maximizing the Impact of New Capital:** When operational efficiencies are in place, any new capital brought in through financial engineering can be used much more effectively. Instead of being used to cover ongoing losses, it can be invested in strategic initiatives for growth, technology upgrades, or market expansion, truly fuelling recovery.
- **Achieving Self-Sufficiency:** The ultimate goal of a turnaround is to make the business financially self-sufficient. This means it can generate enough cash from its operations to cover its costs, service its debts, and eventually fund its own growth. Financial engineering might

provide temporary liquidity, but only operational improvements can deliver long-term solvency.

Operations restructuring initiatives can range from aggressive (but intelligent) cost reduction, working capital optimization, revenue and margin enhancement initiatives, supply chain optimisation, non-core asset sale and process reengineering. Each of the ideas must be quantified in terms of its impact on profit and cash, the investment required, implementation complexity, and time.

Core Operational Restructuring Initiatives:

1. **Aggressive (but Intelligent) Cost Reduction:**

   This goes beyond simple "across-the-board" cuts. It involves a deep dive into the cost structure (informed by Value Chain and Cost Driver Analysis) to identify non-value-added activities, redundant overhead, inefficiencies, and areas where spending provides low ROI. "Intelligent" means distinguishing between wasteful spending and essential investments (e.g., cutting marketing for unprofitable products vs. cutting R&D for future growth).

   ¤ Examples: Workforce rationalization, renegotiating vendor contracts, reducing discretionary spending (travel, entertainment), facility consolidation, outsourcing non-core functions.

2. **Working Capital Optimization:**

   This involves focusing on the efficient management of current assets (inventory, accounts receivable) and current liabilities (accounts payable) to free up cash. The goal is to minimize the cash tied up in the operating cycle.

   ¤ Examples:

   - **Inventory:** Just-in-Time (JIT) principles, reducing safety stock, improving forecasting, clearing obsolete inventory.

- **Accounts Receivable:** Tightening credit terms, aggressive collections, offering early payment discounts.
- **Accounts Payable:** Negotiating extended payment terms with suppliers, but carefully to avoid damaging relationships.

3. **Revenue and Margin Enhancement Initiatives:**

Not just cutting costs, but also strategically boosting the top line and improving profitability per sale. This involves understanding customer and product profitability.

¤ **Examples:** Strategic pricing adjustments (up or down, based on elasticity and value), focusing sales efforts on high-margin products/customers, cross-selling/up-selling, introducing new value-added services, optimizing sales channels, improving lead generation.

The Turnaround Leader can also consider applying the "Fix, Exit, Milk" grid (adapted from Boston Consulting Group or BCG Growth-Share Matrix). The framework is a simple, strategic model used in business analysis to guide a company's decisions regarding its business units or product lines. It helps to determine the best course of action based on the performance and potential of each unit.

Quadrant	Action
High Margin / Core	Fix / Invest (lean, innovate, upsell)
High Margin / Non-Core	Milk (defensive hold, no fresh CapEx)
Low Margin / Core	Fix Hard (OEE, pricing, redesign)
Low Margin / Non-Core	Exit Fast (sale, licensing, closure)

This model categorizes business units or product portfolio into three groups, each with a corresponding strategy:

- **Fix**: This category includes business units or products that have high potential but are currently underperforming due to specific issues. The strategy is to invest resources to "fix" the problems, such as operational inefficiencies or marketing shortcomings, to help the unit achieve its full potential. The goal is to turn the unit into a strong performer.

- **Milk**: This refers to established, profitable business units that are not expected to grow significantly. These units are often in a mature market. The strategy is to "milk" them for cash flow by minimizing new investments and maximizing profits. The cash generated is then used to fund the "Fix" strategies or other growth initiatives.
- **Exit**: This applies to business units or products that have consistently low performance and limited future potential. The strategy is to discontinue, sell, or divest these units. The goal is to stop the drain on company resources and reallocate them to more promising areas.

4. **Supply Chain Optimization:**

   Streamlining the entire flow of goods and services from raw materials to end customers. This encompasses procurement, manufacturing, logistics, and distribution.

   ¤ **Examples:** Supplier rationalization, strategic sourcing to reduce input costs, improving logistics efficiency (e.g., route optimization, warehouse consolidation), better demand planning to reduce stockouts or overstocking, implementing technology for visibility.

5. **Non-Core Asset Sale:**

   Divesting assets that are not central to the company's core operations or strategic future. This is a crucial way to generate immediate cash and reduce carrying costs (e.g., maintenance, depreciation).

   Examples: Selling excess real estate, unused machinery, non-strategic business units, intellectual property that isn't central to future plans.

6. **Process Reengineering:**

   Fundamentally rethinking and redesigning core business processes (e.g., order-to-cash, procure-to-pay, product development) to achieve dramatic improvements in cost, quality, service, and speed. This often involves leveraging technology.

- **Examples:** Automating manual tasks, centralizing shared services, redesigning customer service workflows, implementing new ERP systems (though the system itself is an investment, the reengineering is the process change).

The Critical Need for quantification and prioritization:

Once the initiatives are identified, it is important to quantify the potential impact and investments and costs required to generate the impact. This quantitative rigor is absolutely essential for several reasons:

1. **Prioritization**: In a turnaround, resources (time, money, people) are scarce. Quantification allows the leadership team to prioritize initiatives based on their potential impact relative to the resources required and the speed of realization. You want to identify "quick wins" (high cash and profit impact, low investment, low complexity, short time) as well as larger, more strategic bets.

2. **Decision Making:** It provides a data-driven basis for making tough choices. Should we cut 5% of the workforce or invest in a new automated system? Quantifying the impact of each helps determine the most effective path.

3. **Accountability**: Once initiatives are quantified, specific targets can be set, and performance can be tracked against these targets. This creates accountability for the teams responsible for implementation.

4. **Stakeholder Communication**: Investors, creditors, and employees need to see a clear, well-supported plan. Quantified impacts lend credibility and build confidence that the turnaround is viable and well-managed.

5. **Risk Assessment**: Understanding implementation complexity and time helps in assessing the risks involved with each initiative and developing contingency plans.

Below are some guidelines to assess each initiative in terms of quantitative impact, ability to implement, and time required to implement:

- **Profit Impact:** How much will this initiative increase revenue or decrease costs, thereby improving net profit? This is typically measured over a specific period (e.g., monthly, quarterly, annually).
    - ¤ **Example:** Reducing a specific raw material cost by 10% on 1,000 units per month, improving profit by ₹X per month.
- **Cash Impact:** How much net cash will this initiative generate or save, and when will that cash flow occur? This is often more critical in a turnaround than profit, as liquidity is paramount.
    - ¤ **Example:** Selling a non-core asset for ₹Y will generate ₹Y cash immediately. Reducing inventory by ₹Z will free up ₹Z in working capital. Delaying supplier payments by 10 days on ₹A purchases per month will improve cash by ₹A * (10/30) = ₹A/3 per month.
- **Investment Required:** What capital (CapEx) or operating expenses (OpEx) are needed to implement the initiative? This could include software, new machinery, consulting fees, training costs, or temporary staffing.
    - ¤ Example: Implementing new inventory management software might cost ₹M upfront.

Implementation Complexity: A qualitative but critical assessment of how difficult the initiative will be to execute. This considers:

- ¤ Organizational change management required.
- ¤ Technological hurdles.
- ¤ Reliance on external parties.
- ¤ Regulatory approvals.
- ¤ Risk of disruption to ongoing operations.
- ¤ Rating: Low, Medium, High (or a numerical scale).

- **Time (to Implement and Realize Impact):** How long will it take to get the initiative fully in place, and how long until the forecasted profit and cash impacts start to materialize?
    - **Example:** Negotiating new supplier contracts might take 3 months to implement, with cash savings starting in month 4. A large-scale process reengineering might take 12-18 months.

The table below provides an overview of one way to think about initiatives. Not all initiatives can be implemented immediately. There is tremendous value in capturing quick wins as it builds momentum, provides a foundation to bring the team together, and its successful implementation gives confidence to all stakeholders.

Lever	Quick Win (≤ 90 days)	Structural Fix (6–18 months)
Procurement	Reverse auction for MRO items	Consortium-buying platform with peers
Manufacturing Overheads	Idle-shift shutdown	Theory-of-Constraints debottlenecking
SG&A	Freeze travel & non-essential marketing	Shared-services or GBS migration
Energy	Tariff renegotiation with DISCOM	Solar or waste-heat co-gen CAPEX (OPEX-neutral)

By meticulously evaluating each operational restructuring initiative against these quantified metrics, a turnaround team can construct a robust, actionable, and financially sound plan that systematically addresses the company's distress and paves the way for sustainable recovery.

Lastly: The Cash-on-Cash Imperative

Turnarounds are not simply about cutting costs and squeezing liquidity. Almost every distressed business also faces years of underinvestment in people, technology, plant, and machinery. As cash dries up, maintenance is deferred, systems age, and talent leaves. By the time a turnaround begins, the enterprise is often hollowed out. The paradox is that revival demands fresh investment, yet cash is precisely what the company does not have.

The turnaround leader, therefore, lives in a constant tension: how much scarce cash should be allocated to investment needs versus immediate operational restructuring? Spend too little, and operations cannot stabilize; spend too much in the wrong place, and the company runs out of runway. In such contexts, the discipline of cash-on-cash return becomes the guiding principle. Every rupee spent must be justified by how quickly it comes back and whether it returns with a multiplier.

There are two practical ways to apply this lens.

1. Completing Work to Release Stuck Cash

Often, customers hold back large payments until the final portion of work is completed — even if 80–90% of the order has already been delivered. In such cases, it may be prudent to deploy scarce cash to finish the remaining 10–20%, thereby unlocking the full payment. Similarly, clients may withhold payment for one project because of unresolved issues in another, even unrelated, project. Addressing these issues, though painful, can release significant amounts of overdue receivables. The principle here is simple: spend ₹X today to collect a multiple of ₹X tomorrow.

2. Evaluating Products, Customers, and Markets on Cash Returns

Beyond immediate collections, cash-on-cash thinking also applies to strategic decisions. Product lines, markets, and customer segments must be evaluated not merely on revenue or margin, but on their working capital cycle and cash yield. A high-margin product that consumes disproportionate working capital may, in fact, destroy liquidity. Conversely, a lower-margin customer that pays reliably and quickly may be more valuable in a turnaround. Similarly, new projects or products should be judged on the incremental cash they generate over the incremental investment required, not on theoretical margins years into the future.

This mindset forces management to focus relentlessly on speed and the multiplier of cash returns. It reframes decision-making away from accounting profits, which may be illusory, toward hard liquidity, which is the true lifeline of a distressed company.

Indian examples repeatedly illustrate this dynamic. In construction and EPC turnarounds, many companies discovered that completing stalled projects even at low apparent profitability was often the fastest way to release withheld receivables and mobilization advances. In contrast, those who chased new bids without addressing legacy execution gaps often found themselves starved of both cash and credibility. Likewise, in manufacturing, product lines with long receivable cycles and high input stocking requirements often had to be pruned despite headline profitability, while faster-paying customer segments became the bedrock of revival.

Ultimately, cash is the kingmaker in any turnaround. The discipline of cash-on-cash return provides a simple but powerful compass: every rupee spent must either come back quickly or bring back multiples of itself. Without that filter, even the most well-intentioned investments can accelerate the slide toward insolvency. With it, scarce liquidity can be converted into momentum, credibility, and survival.

Putting it all Together: An Integrated Turnaround Plan that Acts as a Tool for Restructuring, Negotiation, and Execution

In a corporate turnaround or debt restructuring negotiations, a well-structured 3–5 year integrated financial plan is far more than a spreadsheet; it becomes the strategic anchor and negotiation platform around which all stakeholders align.

Whether the objective is to restructure debt, bring in new capital, or balance competing interests between creditors and shareholders, this plan becomes the single source of financial truth, offering transparency, feasibility, and a data-driven roadmap for revival.

1. Integrated turnaround plan as a negotiation instrument in debt restructuring

When a business is in distress, lenders demand clarity on two questions:

- Can the company service its debt going forward?
- Is it viable enough to justify restructuring rather than liquidation or sale?

An integrated turnaround plan provides the answer by:

- Projecting debt servicing ability under different scenarios (Base, Downside, Stress)
- Quantifying cash flows available for debt, including timing of shortfalls and proposed mitigation steps (e.g., moratorium, refinancing)
- Highlighting the funding gap and establishing the quantum and timing of capital infusion needed to stabilize operations

Key uses in lender negotiations:

- **Demonstrate viability:** Show a path to EBITDA recovery, positive cash flows, and debt service coverage over the plan horizon.
- **Drive debt structuring terms:** Use forecasts to justify moratorium periods, revised repayment schedules, bullet payments, or interest deferment.
- **Covenant reset:** Set realistic financial covenants (e.g., Net Debt/ EBITDA, DSCR) aligned with the recovery trajectory.
- **Contingency triggers:** Define early-warning triggers (e.g., cash burn rate, revenue threshold) that initiate pre-agreed corrective actions.

2. Integrated turnaround plan as a tool to align shareholders and new investors

For promoters and shareholders, the plan plays a dual role:

- As a mirror showing the dilution of value if corrective action is delayed
- And as a guide to the level of equity support needed to retain control or revive business value

Uses for shareholders / promoters:

- **Control vs. survival trade-off:** The model simulates outcomes under different levels of equity infusion — from promoter-led to third-party investor-led recapitalization. This helps shareholders see when bringing in external equity becomes a lesser evil than value erosion or insolvency.
- **Valuation bridge:** Demonstrates how valuation multiples (e.g., EV/ EBITDA, P/B) evolve across scenarios, helping align shareholder expectations with ground reality.
- **Cash flow alignment:** Shows how delays in equity infusion could exacerbate cash gaps and deepen dependence on creditors, strengthening the case for timely action.

Uses with new / existing equity investors:

- **Model-based valuation:** Serves as the basis for arriving at valuation and structuring (e.g., equity vs. convertible, preferred shares, warrants).
- **Use of funds mapping:** Ties every rupee of equity raised to a cash gap, turnaround initiative, or growth plan — thereby increasing investor confidence.
- **Exit visibility:** Offers clarity on potential exit routes and timelines (e.g., IPO, strategic sale), allowing new investors to model IRR and risk-adjusted returns.

3. The plan as the roadmap for turnaround execution

Once approved, the plan becomes the execution blueprint—not just for the CFO's office, but for lenders, the board, new investors, and turnaround advisors.

Execution benefits:

- **Actionable milestones:** Each quarter's performance (revenue, cost, cash flow, collections, etc.) is benchmarked against the plan. This allows early detection of slippages.
- **Granular cash flow visibility:** By modelling cash flow at a monthly or weekly level in the initial 6–12 months, the plan allows near-real-time cash monitoring, improving discipline across functions.
- **Linked to operational KPIs:** The plan incorporates performance drivers, e.g., sales per FTE, cost per unit, DSO/DPO/DIO, that track whether turnaround levers are yielding results.

4. Scenario planning to build confidence and credibility

One of the biggest sources of friction in debt and equity negotiations is the credibility of projections. A static plan with a single base case is often rejected by lenders or investors as overly optimistic.

A good model allows for:

- **Base / downside / stress scenarios:** Showing how the company will perform under volatile macro conditions, customer churn, or delay in funding.
- **Mitigation steps:** Overlay operational levers and financial backstops (e.g., standby line of credit, asset monetization, working capital relief) to show preparedness.
- **Dynamic inputs:** A "control panel" of assumptions (e.g., volume growth, gross margin, capex, interest rates) that management and stakeholders can toggle to run their own sensitivities.

This capability builds trust and buy-in, especially from cautious lenders and risk-averse boards.

5. KPI monitoring and covenant tracking

As the turnaround progresses, lenders and equity investors need a structured mechanism to monitor performance. The financial plan evolves into a live dashboard, tracking:

Financial KPIs:

- EBITDA, Gross Margin, Net Margin
- Free Cash Flow
- Net Debt / EBITDA, DSCR
- Cash Runway (months of operations left without fresh capital)

Operational KPIs:

- Collection Days (DSO)
- Payable Days (DPO)
- Inventory Days (DIO)
- Customer Retention Rate
- Revenue per Employee

Covenant Monitoring:

- Plan embeds loan covenants and calculates them for each period
- Triggers alerts when covenants are likely to be breached in the coming quarters
- Helps in initiating advanced dialogue with lenders for waiver or reset, if required

6. Governance and Transparency

To reinforce credibility and transparency:

- The plan should be shared in a board-reviewed format, preferably with scenario decks and narrative explanations.
- A monthly or quarterly performance pack should be extracted from the model, highlighting actual versus planned outcomes and key deviations.

- Updates to the plan (due to new funding, customer wins, cost overruns, etc.). should follow a structured change control process, with clear documentation of changed assumptions.

Conclusion

In a turnaround or restructuring context, a well-crafted 3–5 year integrated turnaround plan becomes more than numbers. It becomes:

- A negotiation platform to align creditors, shareholders, and new investors
- A blueprint for execution and governance
- A credibility enhancer in front of the board, banks, and capital providers

When done right, it bridges the gap between strategic vision and operational reality, enabling not just survival, but revival. Excel may be the medium, but this plan becomes the company's heartbeat during the turnaround.

Chapter 08
Financial Restructuring

"The waterfall clears the delusions of grandeur."

Before we get into what financial restructuring is and why we need it, it is important to take a step back and briefly understand how business ventures are financed, the types of financing instruments used, the right mix and what happens when the mix is lopsided.

Capital Structure

Capital structure refers to the specific mix of long-term debt and equity a company uses to finance its assets and operations. It is a fundamental concept in corporate finance that outlines how a business raises funds to support its activities and growth.

The key components of a capital structure include:

1. **Equity:** This represents ownership in the company. It includes funds raised from selling shares to investors (common stock and preferred stock) and profits that the company has retained and reinvested in the business (retained earnings). Equity holders are considered owners and have a claim on the company's assets and earnings after all debt holders have been paid. While equity doesn't carry the same repayment obligation as debt, it often has a higher cost due to the higher risk borne by investors.

2. **Debt:** This is money borrowed from external sources that the company is obligated to repay with interest. It can include bank loans, corporate bonds, and other forms of borrowing. A major benefit of

debt is that interest payments are tax-deductible, which can lower a company's overall cost of capital. However, too much debt increases a company's financial risk, as it must make fixed payments regardless of its profitability. Debt also comes with several strings attached, viz., covenants and conditions under which lenders have a say in several important decisions.

3. **Hybrid Instruments:** These are financial instruments that combine features of both debt and equity. Examples include convertible bonds, which can be converted into shares of common stock, and preferred stock, which typically provides fixed dividends like debt but has some characteristics of equity.

The goal of a company's management is to find the optimal capital structure. This is the particular mix of debt and equity that minimizes the company's weighted average cost of capital (WACC) and, in turn, maximizes the firm's market value. This optimal balance varies from company to company, depending on factors such as the industry, business risk, cash flow stability, and management's tolerance for risk.

Here is a light-hearted analogy of capital structure: Capital structure is like hosting a house party.

- **Equity** is your family and close friends — they bring snacks, music, and love. They don't expect to be paid back, but they'll definitely judge your choices and want a say in everything.
- **Debt** is like inviting your banker or neighbour — he brings expensive wine, but expects you to return the bottle, pay him interest, and stick to a 10 pm noise limit. Miss a deadline, and he might call the cops (or the NCLT).

If you invite too many bankers and not enough friends, the party becomes stressful, not fun. But if it's all friends and no wine, the party may never really take off.

Moral of the story: A good party, like a good company, needs the right balance of fun and funding.

As we learned in one of the initial chapters that the presence of debt can compound business stress and aggravate a difficult situation further. So why do companies borrow money? The simple answer is that companies borrow money to take advantage of several benefits that debt provides, which equity does not. The choice between debt and equity is often described as a trade-off, where a company weighs the advantages of one against the risks of the other.

Here are the primary reasons why companies borrow money instead of funding everything with equity:

1. Tax Advantages (The Interest Tax Shield)

Interest payments on debt are tax-deductible expenses for a company. This means that a company can subtract its interest payments from its taxable income, which reduces its overall tax liability. This tax saving is known as the "interest tax shield." Dividends paid to equity holders, on the other hand, are paid with after-tax profits and are not deductible. This makes debt a cheaper form of financing on an after-tax basis.

For example, if a company has a 25% tax rate and pays ₹1,000 in interest, it saves ₹250 in taxes. The effective cost of that debt is not ₹1,000 but rather ₹750. The ₹250 saved on taxes can be either reinvested in the business or used to pay higher dividends to equity owners.

2. Lower Cost of Capital

Historically, debt has been a less expensive source of capital than equity. This is because lenders face less risk than equity investors. Lenders have a senior claim on a company's assets and income, meaning they get paid before shareholders in the event of bankruptcy. Due to this lower risk, lenders are willing to accept a lower rate of return (interest) compared to the return that equity investors require.

By using a mix of lower-cost debt and higher-cost equity, a company can lower its Weighted Average Cost of Capital (WACC). A lower WACC makes it easier for a company to undertake new projects and investments, as it lowers the hurdle rate that must be surpassed for a project to be considered profitable.

3. Retaining Ownership and Control

When a company raises funds through equity, it sells a portion of its ownership. This dilutes the ownership stake of existing shareholders. New equity investors, especially large ones like venture capitalists, often demand a say in the company's decisions, and their goals may not always align with those of the original founders or management.

With debt financing, a company can raise capital without giving up any ownership or control. The lenders have no say in the day-to-day operations of the business (as long as the company is making its loan payments), allowing management to maintain full control over the company's direction.

4. Financial Leverage

Borrowing money can amplify the returns to shareholders. This is known as financial leverage. If a company uses borrowed funds to invest in a project that generates a return greater than the interest rate on the debt, the extra profit goes directly to the equity holders. This can lead to a significant increase in earnings per share and overall returns for shareholders.

However, leverage is a double-edged sword. If the return on the project is less than the cost of the debt, it can magnify losses for shareholders.

The reasons above highlight why a company would want to use debt. However, there are also significant risks, primarily the cost of financial distress. This includes the risk of bankruptcy, where the company might default on its loan payments, leading to legal and administrative costs, and potentially the liquidation of the business.

The Trade-Off Theory of capital structure explains this dynamic. It suggests that a company chooses its optimal capital structure by balancing the benefits of debt (like the tax shield) against the costs of financial distress. As a company adds more debt, the tax benefits increase, but so does the risk of financial distress and the cost of borrowing. The optimal capital structure is reached when the marginal benefit of adding more debt is equal to the marginal cost.

Before we move further ahead to discuss financial restructuring, we need to briefly discuss covenants and conditions that lenders impose on companies and shareholders. Covenants are clauses within a loan agreement that serve as a form of insurance (and sometimes early warning signals) for lenders. They are the conditions that the borrower must either do or refrain from doing to protect the lender's investment and ensure the company remains financially healthy enough to repay the loan. If a company violates a covenant, it can trigger a technical default, giving the lender the right to take action, such as demanding immediate repayment of the entire loan.

Covenants are generally categorized into two types:

1. Affirmative (or Positive) Covenants

These covenants require the company to perform specific actions. They are designed to ensure the borrower maintains good business practices and transparency. Examples include:

- Maintaining Financial Ratios: The company must keep certain financial ratios, such as the interest coverage ratio or debt-to-equity ratio, within a specified range.
- Providing Financial Statements: The company is required to submit regular, audited financial reports (e.g., quarterly or annually) to the lender, so it can monitor the company's performance.
- Maintaining Insurance: The company must maintain adequate insurance on its assets to protect the collateral securing the loan.

2. Negative (or Restrictive) Covenants

These covenants restrict the company from taking certain actions that could increase the risk to the lender. They are often more significant and can limit the company's operational flexibility. Examples include:

- Restrictions on Additional Debt: The company cannot take on more debt beyond a certain limit without the lender's approval. This prevents the company from becoming overleveraged and diluting the lender's claim.

- Dividend Restrictions: The company is prohibited from paying out large dividends to shareholders or repurchasing its own stock, which would reduce the cash available to repay the debt.
- Limitations on Asset Sales: The company cannot sell a significant portion of its assets without the lender's consent. This protects the lender's collateral, especially in secured loans.
- Restrictions on Mergers and Acquisitions: The company is often required to get the lender's approval before engaging in a major merger, acquisition, or restructuring, as these events can drastically change the company's financial profile.

These covenants are a key part of the negotiation process between a company and its lenders. By agreeing to certain covenants, a company can often secure a lower interest rate on its debt, as the lender's risk is reduced. For shareholders, these covenants can limit the company's ability to pay dividends or pursue certain strategies, directly impacting their returns and control over the business.

Can a Wrong Capital Structure Lead to Distress?

A wrong capital structure can absolutely lead to financial distress, and what constitutes a "wrong" structure is highly dependent on the industry. The ideal capital structure is not a one-size-fits-all solution; it must be tailored to the specific characteristics, risks, and cash flow patterns of a particular industry.

The core of this principle lies in a company's ability to reliably service its debt. Industries with stable, predictable cash flows can safely take on more debt than those with volatile or cyclical cash flows. The nature of a company's assets, its business cycle, and its vulnerability to external factors like commodity prices are all crucial determinants.

Here's a breakdown of how capital structures differ by industry:

Industries that Can Leverage Debt Heavily

Certain industries are inherently suited for high debt levels due to the nature of their operations, assets, and cash flows.

- **Infrastructure, Utilities, and Real Estate:** These sectors are often characterized by significant, long-term asset investments (e.g., roads, power plants, office buildings) that generate highly stable, predictable cash flows. For example, a toll road or a regulated utility will have a consistent revenue stream that is less susceptible to economic downturns. This stability makes them a low-risk borrower in the eyes of lenders. They often use large amounts of long-term debt to finance these capital-intensive projects, as the predictable cash flows are sufficient to cover the fixed interest payments. The assets themselves also serve as valuable collateral for lenders.

- **Engineering, Procurement, and Construction (EPC) and Shipbuilding:** These industries undertake large, multi-year projects that require massive upfront capital. Debt is a necessary tool to fund these projects before a company can receive final payment. Because the projects are often backed by contracts and involve tangible assets being built, lenders are willing to provide significant financing.

Industries that Require Lower Leverage

In contrast, other industries face higher business risk and a greater degree of uncertainty, making heavy reliance on debt a dangerous strategy.

- **Industries with cyclical demand:** Companies that produce goods or services with highly cyclical demand, such as automotive manufacturers, consumer durables, or luxury goods, should maintain lower leverage. During an economic boom, their revenues are high, and they can comfortably service debt. However, during a recession, demand plummets, and their cash flows can dry up completely. In such a scenario, a company with a high debt burden could easily default, even if it was profitable just a few quarters earlier. A low-leverage structure provides a crucial buffer during these lean times.

- **Sectors with excessive influence of changing commodity prices:** Companies in industries like mining, oil and gas, or agriculture are highly exposed to volatile commodity prices. A sudden drop in the price of their core product can drastically reduce revenue and profitability, making it difficult to service debt. While these companies often require capital for exploration and development, they must be cautious with their debt levels. A lower-leverage structure allows them to survive periods of low commodity prices without succumbing to financial distress.

- **Technology and R&D-intensive companies:** These businesses often have intangible assets (patents, software, intellectual property) and highly uncertain future cash flows. They are not well-suited for debt financing. The value of their assets can be difficult for lenders to assess, and their success is dependent on innovation and market adoption, which are inherently risky. These companies typically rely more on equity financing (e.g., from venture capitalists and public markets) to fund their growth, as it does not come with the rigid repayment obligations of debt.

In conclusion, the decision of how to structure a company's capital is not a simple choice between debt and equity. It is a strategic one that requires a deep understanding of the industry's specific risks and opportunities. A company with the "wrong" capital structure, for instance, a cyclical business with an infrastructure-level debt load, is operating with an unnecessary and potentially fatal level of risk. The best-run companies align their financing strategy with the fundamental economics and risk profile of their business to ensure long-term stability and success.

What is Financial Restructuring?

Financial restructuring (often also called Debt Restructuring) is the comprehensive process of reorganizing a company's capital structure to improve its financial health, address liquidity problems, and ensure long-term viability. It is typically undertaken when a company is in financial distress and unable to meet its existing debt obligations, but it can also be a proactive strategy to optimize a company's capital structure and position it for growth.

It is a critical component of our six-step Turnaround Framework to which we referred in an earlier chapter. Without this, no amount of operational turnaround can lead to a sustainable solution and the business will end up in bankruptcy or worse, in liquidation. All the prior steps in the Turnaround Framework, viz., IBR, crisis management, stakeholder management, development of a turnaround plan, are all in preparation for a financial restructuring. Without a suitably revised capital structure that is aligned with forecast cash flows, developed as part of the integrated turnaround plan, the business will not recover from distress. The lenders' and equity shareholders' requests have to be addressed, and any trust issues that have developed inter se need to be addressed as well through the financial restructuring process.

For MSME businesses, the financial restructuring is usually simple (from a structuring perspective, not necessarily from a process perspective), as the business will have only one or two domestic lenders. The restructuring process becomes considerably complicated as the debt stack becomes larger, multi-layered and involves several lenders, at times both domestic and foreign.

Understand Each Lender's Perspective

In India, scheduled commercial banks still provide a large majority of credit to corporates and own a dominant share of the outstanding credit. Banks have fulfilled corporate India's credit requirements through a variety of long-term and short-term debt instruments, including non-fund-based facilities. Over the years, the corporate bond market has evolved to become an ₹54 lakh crore market as per RBI's Financial Stability Report of June 2025, growing at high single digits year on year. Further, Non-Bank Financial Companies, Debt Mutual Funds, AIFs and even family offices have become a meaningful and fast-growing source of corporate credit over the years. Indian companies have also leveraged external commercial borrowings, which as of September 2024, in aggregate stand at $190bn as per RBI. Further, lenders often sell down the loans to other lenders, adding to the number of debt owners in a company. If a debt default has occurred (referred to as a Non-Performing Asset (NPA)), lenders often sell the debt at a discount to Asset Reconstruction Companies (ARCs) or AIFs.

Clearly, when a large company is in distress, the turnaround leader has his / her task cut out to understand the complex debt instruments used, covenants, pricing, security and each lender's perspective on how they would want to handle the distress. A failure to do so is a common reason why restructurings fail, become protracted, or lead to formal bankruptcy. In a scenario where a company is already in default and faces the imminent threat of a formal bankruptcy filing under the Insolvency and Bankruptcy Code (IBC), the urgency, stakes, and required approach for a turnaround leader intensify dramatically. The execution must be far more strategic, swift, and legally precise.

Here's a breakdown of why this understanding is crucial and how a turnaround leader should strategically go about it to build consensus and expedite the process:

- **Establish credibility and trust:** A turnaround leader must immediately demonstrate that he or she understands the company's financial obligations and the lenders' specific claims. Arriving at the table with a thorough grasp of the loan documents shows competence and signals a serious intent to solve the problem, not just to buy time. This is the first step in rebuilding the trust that has likely been eroded by the company's distress.

- **Identify the "pecking order":** Not all debt is created equal. Lenders have different levels of seniority and security.

    - ¤ **Secured creditors:** Those with a lien on specific company assets (e.g., property, machinery, inventory) have a higher claim on those assets.

    - ¤ **Unsecured creditors:** Those without a specific lien (e.g., bondholders, some suppliers) have a lower claim. A turnaround leader must know who gets paid first and from which assets. This "pecking order" is the foundation of any negotiation, as it dictates each lender's leverage and its minimum acceptable recovery.

- **Predict lender behavior and motivations:** A lender's willingness to compromise is directly tied to its potential recovery. A bank with a secured loan against a highly valuable, liquid asset may be less willing to take a "haircut" than an unsecured bondholder. By understanding each lender's specific position, a turnaround leader can anticipate their demands, craft proposals that appeal to their self-interest, and avoid presenting a one-size-fits-all plan that is destined to fail.

- **Develop a realistic and fair restructuring plan:** Any viable restructuring plan must be grounded in the legal reality of the company's obligations. An attempt to propose a plan that ignores or unfairly treats a specific creditor's security or seniority will be immediately rejected and destroy any chance of a consensual agreement.

  The importance of understanding each lender's position is magnified by the default. The focus shifts from proactive management to reactive crisis management, with the goal of avoiding or managing a formal IBC process.

- **Managing secured creditors' rights:** In a default scenario, secured creditors have the right to enforce their security interests and take possession of the collateral. A turnaround leader must know exactly which assets are at risk and engage these creditors to secure a standstill agreement (a temporary moratorium on legal action) to buy time for a consensual resolution.
- **Identifying "problem" covenants:** Covenants that have been breached are no longer a future risk; they are the reason for the default. The leader must meticulously identify every breached covenant and its implications, as this will be the basis for all lender conversations. The focus is no longer on preventing a breach but on managing its consequences.

Financial Restructuring Outside IBC

When a business in India enters financial distress, the fear of being dragged into the Insolvency and Bankruptcy Code (IBC) process looms large. For promoters, this is often the last resort: it implies loss of control, reputational damage, and compressed timelines for resolution.

Yet, IBC is not the only way. India's financial architecture provides several alternative pathways to restructure debt outside IBC. These include frameworks prescribed by the Reserve Bank of India (RBI), schemes under the Companies Act, 2013, negotiated settlements, and transfers of stressed loans to specialized investors such as Asset Reconstruction Companies (ARCs) or Alternative Investment Funds (AIFs).

From the perspective of a corporate borrower, navigating this landscape requires clarity on the rules, timelines, regulatory guardrails, and trade-offs. Below are the restructuring options outside IBC that a promoter, turnaround leader, or Chief Restructuring Officer (CRO) must be familiar with:

RBI's Prudential Framework for Resolution of Stressed Assets (June 7, 2019)

This RBI circular applies to all Scheduled Commercial Banks (excluding Regional Rural Banks (RRB), Primary Cooperative Banks, and State Cooperative Banks, which follow a separate prudential framework), all-India financial institutions, small finance banks and NBFCs. The circular applies to the debt of all "borrowers". However, it has different levels of stringent conditions depending on "aggregate exposure" to "lenders", as follows:

- Aggregate exposure below ₹100 Crores – Restructuring can be completed without an Independent Credit Evaluation (ICE), by an RBI-approved credit rating agency;

- Aggregate exposure between ₹100 Crores and ₹1500 Crores - Restructuring can be completed with one ICE, by an RBI-approved credit rating agency; and

- Aggregate exposure above ₹1500 Crores - Restructuring can be completed after the Restructuring plan evaluation by two ICEs, by an RBI-approved credit rating agency. In addition, the lenders must disclose the restructuring in their financial statements.

"Borrowers" mean legal entities including individuals, proprietorships, partnerships, companies, trusts, etc., who have availed fund-based and/or non-fund-based credit facilities from any of the "lenders". It is important to remember:

- It is entity-agnostic i.e., an individual, partnership firm, LLP, private/public company, trust, etc.
- The definition is linked to exposure: anyone who has availed credit facilities (fund-based such as term loans, CC/OD, working capital; or non-fund based such as guarantees, LCs) from lenders regulated under the circular.
- Group companies / connected entities: The framework applies per borrower, but in practice, RBI expects lenders to consider connected exposure within a group (to avoid "evergreening" by shifting debt across affiliates).

The above "Borrower" definition has important implications for a turnaround leader or CRO, namely:

- If a company alone has borrowings above thresholds, the rules apply directly.
- If a group structure spreads debt across multiple entities, technically each entity is a "borrower." However, lenders (especially PSU banks) often club exposures at a group level when deciding whether to invoke the framework, because cash flows are fungible and promoter control is common. Hence, the CRO should anticipate that lenders will treat the economic group as one borrower for resolution purposes, even if the RBI definition technically refers to a legal entity. When preparing an integrated financial plan for financial restructuring, it would be prudent to prepare both a standalone and a group-integrated plan for the debt restructuring negotiations with the lenders.

"Aggregate exposure" is defined as the sum of all fund-based and non-fund-based exposures of all lenders to the borrower. The catch here is the definition of "lenders". "Lenders" mean scheduled commercial banks and NBFCs regulated by the RBI. In addition to the RRBs and Cooperative banks mentioned above, the following are also not covered in the definition of "Lender" under this circular:

- Bondholders
- Foreign lenders
- Mutual Funds & AIFs
- Non-PSB providers of External Commercial Borrowings (ECB)

Therefore, while computing the applicability of ICE (and disclosure in financials) as mentioned earlier, it will apply as per the "aggregate exposure", only to lenders supervised by the RBI (even if the total debt owed by the borrower is higher).

One key takeaway for a turnaround leader / the CRO is that having a mixed set of lenders complicates matters. CRO will have to negotiate a deal bilaterally with the lenders not covered by this circular and the nuances of such a deal will be influenced by lenders covered by the circular. This unfortunately, creates a circular loop that stalls overall debt restructuring and wastes precious time in a distressed situation.

The June 7, 2019 circular is generally seen by the practitioners as a marked improvement from the earlier prescriptive RBI schemes. The circular offers plenty of room to negotiate the restructuring of the debt, while ensuring adequate checks and balances during the process. It also encourages the lenders to identify stress early (or at least immediately when the default happens), take proactive steps to address it as a group and creates disincentives for lenders, if the restructuring is delayed. In this book, we will not be going through all the practical nuances of debt restructuring under this circular, but broadly identify important steps in the process:

- Once a borrower defaults, lenders must review the account within 30 days (the "Review Period").
- If resolution (restructuring) is possible, lenders enter into an Inter-Creditor Agreement (ICA). The ICA bears some similarities to standstill agreements referred to in this book earlier. The signatories to the ICA do not take Suo motu enforcement actions, while restructuring negotiations are underway as part of this process.

- The resolution plan must be approved by lenders holding at least 75% of aggregate exposure by value and 60% by number of lenders.
- Resolution (Restructuring) Plan (RP) must be implemented within 180 days from the end of the review period.
- Debt restructuring will typically consider the following different options:
    - ¤ Rescheduling the repayment schedule.
    - ¤ Granting moratoriums.
    - ¤ Lowering interest rates.
    - ¤ Converting a portion of debt into equity or compulsorily convertible instruments.
    - ¤ Bringing in a new promoter through "change in ownership."
- Once a draft restructuring plan is ready, the same will be sent for Independent Credit Evaluation (ICE) by RBI-approved credit rating agency (one or two, depending on "aggregate exposure").

Note on ICE process:

The Independent Credit Evaluation (ICE) is a regulatory safeguard: an external test of whether the restructuring plan is viable. For borrowers, it is both a hurdle and an opportunity: pass it with a solid, well-prepared plan, and you build credibility with lenders and regulators; fail it, and restructuring may collapse, pushing you closer to IBC.

RBI has authorised a list of rating agencies to carry out ICE, the same as the SEBI-registered credit rating agencies (CRISIL, ICRA, CARE Ratings, India Ratings, Brickwork, etc.), provided they are specifically empanelled for ICE assignments.

The ICE agency evaluates the viability of the Resolution Plan and assigns a viability grade:

- Resolution Plan must be assessed as "RP4" or better (where RP1 = highest viability, RP7 = lowest viability). So, if the plan gets RP1 to RP4, the plan is considered viable.

- If the plan is graded worse than RP4, lenders cannot upgrade the asset classification and must make higher provisions.

- If the ICE rating is below RP4, the restructuring process is unsuccessful unless changes are made to the restructuring plan such as increased promoter contribution or change in control (i.e., bringing in a new shareholder that infuses capital and brings new management). If these changes are not made to the plan, the lenders will most likely push the borrower into IBC.

- As mentioned earlier, the circular has built-in disincentives for lenders to ensure the restructuring happens within a time-bound manner. If the restructuring plan is not implemented within 180 days from default, lenders must:

    - Make additional provisions of 20% (over and above existing provisions).

    - If still unresolved by 365 days from the default date, they must make a total additional provision of 35%.

One-time Settlements (OTS) and Compromise Settlements

On June 8, 2023, approximately 4 years after the circular discussed earlier, the RBI issued a Circular: Prudential Framework for Compromise Settlements and Technical Write-offs (DOR.STR. REC.32/21.04.048/2022-23, dated June 8, 2023). This circular applies to all RBI regulated lenders (Regulated Entity, RE) i.e.,

- Commercial Banks (including Small Finance Banks and Regional Rural Banks)

- All India Financial Institutions

- Primary (Urban) Co-operative Banks, State Co-operative Banks and Central Co-operative Banks
- Non-Banking Financial Companies (including Housing Finance Companies)

One of the key objectives of this circular is to encourage the Board of each RE to develop policies that enable the RE "to maximize the possible recovery from a distressed borrower at minimum expense, in the best interest of the RE." The distressed borrower can make a one-time settlement (OTS) offer to the lenders, at a discount versus its total borrowing. The entire negotiated amount of the OTS is to be settled either in a single payment or in installments over a maximum period of 3 months from the date of approval by the lenders.

The turnaround leader / CRO, while developing an OTS offer, must ensure that the offer is more attractive than a restructuring under the June 7, 2019 circular, a recovery under IBC or a potential liquidation. The offer must also comply with each lender's Board-approved policy. The borrower will have to raise funds to settle the OTS amount, which means the investor (promoter, new investor, ARC or private credit) must believe in the greater potential of the business. The new funds are almost always more expensive than bank lending, and it's a fine balance to try to explain to the existing lenders as to why the borrower cannot offer a higher OTS amount.

One of the key tasks for a CRO is to find an investor that is compatible with the promoter and aligns with the future potential of the business. Here, the CRO's objective assessment of the business, robustness of the turnaround plan (including implementation) and the CRO's network of investors will hold him/her in good stead. Investing in a distressed business is risky and hence any new investor wants to be suitably compensated for the higher risk.

The OTS could also be a time-consuming process, but lenders are generally more amenable to cash settlements (subject to their internal policies and multi-layered approval process) as it allows them to recover capital, at a lower cost of recovery.

Additional points to note:

- Post the OTS, there is a cooling-off period of 12 months, i.e. the borrower cannot borrow fresh funds from the same RE / lenders with whom it did the OTS. While the circular is silent on whether other RE/lenders can lend money within this cooling-off period, most RE/lenders practically do not lend during the cooling-off period.
- As part of the OTS, the borrower and lenders can agree to contingent recovery, provided the lenders do not recognize the amount in their books until actual recovery happens. This exception helps settle cases where there are potential recoveries in the form of disputed customer claims, disputed land sales, etc.

Sale of loans to Asset Reconstruction Companies (ARCs)

Asset Reconstruction Companies (ARCs) are governed by the Securitisation and Reconstruction of Financial Assets and Enforcement of Security Interest Act, 2002 (SARFAESI) and the RBI Master Directions on Transfer of Loan Exposure, 2021. All ARCs must register with the RBI.

The SARFAESI was promulgated to empower banks and financial institutions to recover non-performing assets (NPAs) by seizing and auctioning a borrower's collateral without needing to go through lengthy court proceedings. There are three key objectives of this law:

- **Securitisation:** The process of converting an illiquid loan into a liquid security.
- **Reconstruction of Financial Assets:** This refers to the reconstruction of financial assets to enable financial institutions to realize their dues from borrowers.
- **Enforcement of Security Interest:** This refers to the legal framework for lenders to take possession of a borrower's secured assets (like property) to recover the outstanding loan amount if the borrower defaults.

Lenders can sell their loan exposures to ARCs either in cash as complete settlement or cash plus security receipts (SRs). SRs are settled against future recoveries from the borrower. Post the acquisition of the debt, the ARCs negotiate restructuring, settlement or enforcement with the borrower. The initial objective of the SARFAESI Act was to encourage banks to sell their loans to ARCs, which were set up as specialized institutions for debt restructuring and recovery, and to enable the banks to clean up their balance sheets, recoup capital for further lending, and focus on their core operations.

From a borrower / turnaround leader / CRO perspective, bringing in an ARC enables consolidation of debt with one institution that is privately held and can be more flexible in debt restructuring. ARCs are specifically useful in situations where the borrower has a large consortium of lenders and some lenders that are outside the RBI supervision. Several ARCs are part of larger financial institutions that can provide new money for working capital, capital expenditure, and growth generally. They can become a one-stop solution to bring the distressed borrower out of trouble and to become a healthy, thriving business again.

A skilled turnaround leader or CRO can use the ARC option strategically:

- to break banking stalemates,
- to consolidate debt,
- to inject fresh capital, and
- to design flexible, innovative restructuring plans.

The ARC route, when orchestrated thoughtfully, can transform from a perceived threat into a tool of survival and revival, a bridge that allows businesses to avoid the destructive spiral of IBC and chart a path back to viability.

Sale of Loans to AIFs / Special Situation Funds (SSFs)

Sale of loans to Alternative Investment Funds (AIFs) and Special Situation Funds (SSFs) is governed by SEBI (Alternative Investment Funds)

Regulations, 2012 (as amended in 2022 to create Special Situation Funds) and RBI's Transfer of Loan Exposures Directions, 2021 (Clause 58 permits transfer of stressed loans to "permitted transferees," including AIFs).

AIFs pool capital from sophisticated investors (HNIs, family offices, institutions) and invest in alternative assets (private equity, venture capital, hedge strategies, debt, distressed assets, etc.). Special Situation Funds (SSFs) were introduced by SEBI amendment in January 2022 as a Category I AIF sub-category. The mandate of SSFs is to invest specifically in "special situation assets", including:

- Stressed loans (as defined under RBI's Transfer of Loan Exposures Directions, 2021 – clause 58),
- Security Receipts issued by ARCs,
- Equity or debt instruments of companies undergoing stress or turnaround.
- SSFs can also act as resolution applicants under IBC.

Unlike traditional lenders, AIFs and SSFs are private pools of patient capital. They:

- Buy distressed debt from banks/NBFCs at negotiated discounts.
- Provide fresh capital to fund operations, capex, or working capital.
- Take equity exposure, sharing in the upside in a turnaround.
- Negotiate flexibly, unlike PSU banks tied up in committee structures.

For a turnaround leader or CRO, this means a new set of allies with an appetite for risk and revival. They can use an AIF/SSF for:

Debt Acquisition

- CRO encourages lenders to sell stressed loans to an SSF under RBI's Transfer of Loan Exposures (2021) framework.

- Once debt is consolidated with the SSF, negotiations become easier.

Co-Investment with Promoter

- Promoter (through group/family) can co-invest in the SSF alongside institutional investors.
- Aligns promoter and SSF interests in maximizing turnaround value.
- This reduces the risk of the promoter being sidelined.

Fresh Money Injection

- SSFs can provide priority working capital (structured as super-senior debt, NCDs, or preference shares).
- This addresses the classic problem: banks often refuse to lend "new money" once default occurs.

Partnering with ARCs

- Many SSFs work in partnership with ARCs:
  - ARC acquires the debt,
  - SSF subscribes to the Security Receipts (SRs) or funds an ARC-managed trust,
  - Together, they restructure the borrower.
- CRO can use this ARC-SSF partnership to bring both regulatory legitimacy (ARC) and capital flexibility (SSF) into the deal.

Structured Resolution Plans

- CRO can design creative plans with SSFs:
  - Convertible instruments (debt that turns into equity upon turnaround),

- Revenue-linked repayments,
- Exit waterfalls where SSF recovers first, and then the promoter regains upside.

Similar to the ARC structure, there are advantages and risks of partnering with an AIF / SSF:

Advantages:

- Breaks consortium deadlock.
- Provides new money, unlike banks post-default.
- Flexible structures (hybrids of debt + equity).
- Patient capital with higher risk tolerance.

Risks:

- Dilution: SSFs often demand significant equity stakes.
- Aggressive return expectations: SSFs target IRRs of 18–25%+, which can be onerous.
- Control Issues: Some SSFs push for board control or management rights.
- Regulatory complexity: Must comply with RBI/SEBI rules; improper structuring may face objections.

For a turnaround leader, AIFs and Special Situation Funds represent a new era of distressed resolution in India. Unlike traditional banks, these investors bring flexibility, risk appetite, and capital infusion capacity.

The CRO's job is to bridge the gap between conservative banks wanting to exit and opportunistic investors seeking upside, by designing a win-win structure: lenders get a clean exit, investors get high-return exposure, and the company gets a fresh lease of life.

If orchestrated well, an SSF-backed restructuring can transform a distressed company from the brink of insolvency into a successful turnaround story outside the IBC, with minimal disruption to operations.

Schemes of Arrangement under Companies Act, 2013

Section 230 of the Companies Act, 2013, provides a formal, court-supervised mechanism for a company to propose a "compromise or arrangement" with its creditors and/or members. The key advantage of using Section 230 is that once a scheme is approved by the required majority and sanctioned by the National Company Law Tribunal (NCLT), it becomes binding on all creditors, including those who dissented.

Key Steps to use Section 230

- **Develop a Restructuring Scheme:** The turnaround leader / CRO first works with the company's management and advisors to draft a comprehensive scheme of arrangement. This scheme must address how the company's financial distress will be resolved. Common elements of such a scheme include:
  - Debt Haircut: A reduction of the principal amount of debt.
  - Debt-to-Equity Conversion: Converting a portion of the debt into shares of the company, which reduces the debt burden and gives creditors a stake in the company's future.
  - Changes in Repayment Terms: Extending the repayment period, reducing interest rates, or changing the payment schedule to make it more manageable for the company.
- **File an Application with NCLT:** The company files an application with the NCLT. The application must be supported by a detailed affidavit that discloses all material facts about the company, including its latest financial position, an auditor's report, and a valuation report from a registered valuer. This step demonstrates transparency and

provides the NCLT with the necessary information to assess the fairness of the proposed scheme.

- **Convene Creditors' Meetings:** Once the NCLT is satisfied with the application, it orders meetings of the company's creditors (and/or members, if applicable). The turnaround leader / CRO can play a critical role in this stage by preparing and sending out notices to all creditors, which must include the proposed scheme, a valuation report, and a statement explaining its effect on various stakeholders. The notices are also sent to regulatory bodies like the RBI and SEBI, ensuring broad oversight.

- **Secure the Majority Vote:** For the scheme to be approved, it must be voted on and passed by a majority of persons representing three-fourths in value of the creditors present and voting at the meeting. The CRO's job is to negotiate with and persuade a large enough portion of creditors to vote in favor of the scheme. This is often the most challenging part, requiring strong communication, financial analysis, and negotiation skills. The CRO must demonstrate that the proposed scheme is a better alternative for creditors than liquidation.

- **Obtain NCLT Sanction:** After the scheme is approved by the creditors, the CRO files a petition with the NCLT to seek final sanction. The NCLT reviews the entire process to ensure the scheme is fair, equitable, and in compliance with the law. Once the NCLT sanctions the scheme, it becomes legally binding on all creditors, regardless of whether they voted for or against it. This "cramdown" effect prevents a few dissenting creditors from derailing a viable restructuring plan.

Advantages of using Section 230 versus other methods:

- **Binding on All Creditors:** This is the most significant benefit. Unlike informal settlements, a Section 230 scheme, once sanctioned, legally binds all creditors, providing a clean slate for the company.

- **Avoids Liquidation:** It's a powerful tool to prevent a company from heading into insolvency proceedings under the Insolvency and

Bankruptcy Code (IBC), which often leads to the sale of assets and may result in lower recovery for creditors.

- **Flexibility:** It allows for a wide range of restructuring arrangements, including a combination of debt reduction, debt-to-equity conversions, and changes to repayment terms.

- **Legal Protection:** The NCLT's sanction provides a layer of legal protection and certainty to the restructuring, making the new capital structure enforceable and attracting new investors more easily.

While Section 230 of the Companies Act, 2013, offers a powerful tool for corporate restructuring, companies often hesitate to use it, especially in the context of debt distress. This reluctance stems from several significant disadvantages and practical challenges that have been amplified by the introduction of the Insolvency and Bankruptcy Code (IBC), 2016. Some of the key reasons why companies don't prefer the Section 230 route:

- **Lengthy process with an uncertain outcome:** Legal processes in India can take a very long time to reach closure. This can be very detrimental for a distressed business that is short of cash and struggling for survival. Even if the stakeholders have given their approval, NCLT can order changes to the approved scheme. The final NCLT order can be challenged in higher courts, which again take time to close.

- **Strict voting threshold:** To pass a scheme under Section 230, the company needs to secure approval from a "majority of persons representing three-fourths in value" of the creditors. While this "cramdown" provision is a key benefit, achieving this high threshold, especially with multiple and diverse creditor classes (e.g., banks, bondholders, operational creditors), can be extremely difficult.

- **Prioritization of IBC:** The NCLT and appellate courts have repeatedly emphasized that the IBC takes precedence over the Companies Act in cases of conflict. If a Corporate Insolvency

Resolution Process (CIRP) under IBC is initiated, it can effectively put a stop to a pending Section 230 scheme. This makes the Section 230 route less certain and more risky for both the company and its creditors.

Summary: Practical Timelines and Complexity

Mechanism	Typical Timeline	Complexity	Promoter Dilution	Cash Requirement
RBI Prudential Framework	6–12 months	High (ICA, viability studies)	Moderate to High	Moderate (equity infusion)
OTS / Compromise	3–6 months	Medium	None	High (lump sum)
ARC Sale	3–6 months (sale) + negotiation	High	Moderate	Negotiated
AIF/SSF Sale	3–6 months	High	High	Negotiated
Section 230 Scheme	9–18 months	Very High (court process)	Moderate	Flexible

Role of the Promoter and the CRO

The promoter and the Chief Restructuring Officer (CRO) play distinct yet complementary roles in a smooth corporate restructuring, with the CRO acting as an independent expert who guides the process and the promoter serving as the key decision-maker and long-term steward. The promoter's role is to demonstrate a commitment to the company's revival and provide strategic direction, while the CRO's role is to develop and execute a credible plan with operational rigor and stakeholder trust.

The promoter is the company's founder or the person who has control over its affairs. The promoter's role in a restructuring is primarily about commitment, credibility, and long-term vision.

- **Show Commitment:** Lenders and creditors need to see that the promoter is personally invested in the company's survival. Even a modest equity infusion, or offering personal assets as collateral, can build significant trust and demonstrate a genuine commitment to the turnaround. This action signals that the promoter is not just seeking to offload debt but is ready to take a financial hit for the company's future.

- **Provide Strategic Direction:** The promoter has an intimate understanding of the company's history, core business, and industry dynamics. He or she works with the CRO to articulate a credible business plan that goes beyond just financial projections. This plan must identify the company's sustainable and unsustainable parts, focusing on core strengths and divesting non-performing assets.

- **Build Relationships:** The promoter's existing relationships with key stakeholders—employees, vendors, and customers—are crucial. A promoter's direct and honest communication can assure these groups of stability, which is vital for maintaining business operations during a crisis.

The CRO is a specialized, often interim, executive brought in to manage the restructuring process. Their role is to provide unbiased expertise, operational rigor, and a clear path to resolution.

- **Objective Assessment:** Unlike a promoter, the CRO is an outsider with no emotional or historical baggage. They can conduct an impartial stakeholder mapping, identifying all creditors and their legal standing (e.g., those under RBI rules, like banks, versus others). This objective view is crucial for formulating a fair and legally sound restructuring plan.

- **Operational Control:** A CRO's first priority is to stabilize the company's operations and manage cash flow. They implement strict controls, identify areas for cost-cutting, and ensure that the company can continue to function while negotiations are ongoing. They are the "firefighters" who put out the immediate liquidity crisis.

- **Execution and Forum Selection:** The CRO is responsible for choosing the right legal and financial forum for the restructuring. Based on a detailed analysis, they will recommend:
  - OTS (One-Time Settlement) if the company has cash to pay a significant portion of its debt.
  - RBI's Prudential Framework for Compromise Settlements if the lenders are a small, aligned group.
  - Section 230 of the Companies Act, 2013 for complex restructurings with a large number of fragmented creditors.
  - An ARC/AIF Sale is an option if the lenders are looking for a clean exit and are unwilling to participate in a longer restructuring.
- **Anticipate Delays:** The CRO, with its experience in complex restructurings, anticipates the slow and multi-layered processes of institutional lenders, especially PSU banks. It prepares detailed board notes and ensures all documentation is in place to account for multiple levels of sanction, mitigating delays.
- **Manage Communication:** The CRO acts as an honest broker between the company's management and its creditors. It is the primary contact for lenders, building trust through transparency and consistent, data-driven communication. This independent voice is often more credible to creditors than that of the promoter.

The Synergy Between Promoter and CRO

A successful restructuring relies on a strong partnership between the promoter and the CRO. The promoter provides the vision and commitment, while the CRO provides the expertise and execution.

The promoter's willingness to step back and cede control to the CRO demonstrates a clear commitment to the company's survival and a focus on long-term value creation.

Conclusion

Restructuring debt outside IBC is possible but requires navigating regulatory frameworks, lender expectations, and legal routes. For promoters, the key lies in showing commitment, preparing a viable business plan, and choosing the right restructuring path given their cash availability, willingness to dilute, and stakeholder alignment.

A CRO with a firm grasp of RBI circulars, Companies Act provisions, and lender processes can orchestrate a restructuring that is the least disruptive, maximizes turnaround chances, and avoids the value-destructive route of IBC.

Financial restructuring Using IBC: Voluntary IBC Filing as a Restructuring Strategy

India's Insolvency and Bankruptcy Code, 2016 (IBC), gives a corporate debtor the ability to self-initiate insolvency when in default. This "voluntary" route, technically an application by the corporate applicant under Section 10, can be a deliberate way to restructure liabilities within a court-supervised, time-bound process, rather than being dragged in by creditors under Sections 7 or 9. Used judiciously (and ethically), it can stop the enforcement free-for-all, create a single negotiating table, and deliver a binding outcome across all debt classes. Used casually, it can cost promoters control of the company, invite investigations into past transactions, and still end in liquidation.

Where a default has occurred, the corporate debtor may file an application in Form-6 to the NCLT with specified documents (including a shareholders' special resolution approving the filing) and a proposed Interim Resolution Professional (IRP). If the application is complete and the debtor is not barred by Section 11, the NCLT must admit it. Admission triggers the moratorium under Section 14, appointment of the IRP, and handing over of control to the IRP/RP and the Committee of Creditors (CoC). A few important points to keep in mind:

- Threshold of default to trigger IBC is ₹1 crore (since 24 March 2020).
- Section 11 bars a debtor from refiling if it is already in CIRP/PPIRP, completed CIRP in the last 12 months, violated an approved plan in the last 12 months, or is in liquidation.
- The moratorium does not shield personal guarantors and does not bar invocation of unconditional bank guarantees, two critical frictions for promoters.

Why a Voluntary Filing Can be a Restructuring Tool

- Admission under Section 10 immediately imposes a standstill i.e., no fresh suits, no enforcement, and no continuation of proceedings against the corporate debtor, while the business is kept as a going concern under the RP. This concentrates negotiations within the CoC and enables a cram-down via an approved plan under Section 31 that binds all stakeholders.
- Promoters (or the company's board before admission) often pursue one (or a combination) of these routes:
    - **Settle and exit using Section 12A**

      If a global settlement/OTS with creditors can be stitched together after admission, CIRP can be withdrawn with 90% CoC approval. The Supreme Court has recognized the breadth of CoC's commercial discretion to allow such withdrawals.
    - **Bring in a white-knight / investor plan**

      If the existing promoter is eligible under Section 29A, they (alone or with a new investor) may propose a plan; if ineligible, the investor can lead, and the promoter may participate only if the 29A disqualification is cured (e.g., by clearing NPAs linked to connected persons).

- If resolution fails: promoters can attempt to acquire the business through the liquidator under the approved liquidation process.

Constraints and Risks Promoters Must Weigh

- Loss of control from Day 1 (CIRP): The day the application is admitted, the board is suspended and the Interim Resolution Professional (IRP) takes control of the business. Post the first CoC meeting within 30 days, it becomes the de facto board, which runs the business via the Resolution Professional (RP).
- Section 29A ineligibility: If the promoter is ineligible to bid for the business according to Section 29A of the IBC, then the ineligibility needs to be cured prior to submitting the plan.
- No stay for guarantors and bank guarantees: Creditors can proceed against personal guarantors and invoke performance BGs, despite the moratorium—often painful for promoters.
- Scrutiny of past transactions: IBC mandates the RPs to conduct a review of past transactions under Sections 43/45/50 and Section 66 for preferential, undervalued, fraudulent or extortionate transactions, findings of which could create potential liabilities for the promoters.
- Section 65 (misuse): Frivolous or malicious filings can attract penalties—don't use Section 10 merely to stall one creditor.
- Timeline slippages: Though IBC targets a time-bound process, large cases can overrun despite statutory caps.

When Voluntary IBC May Make Sense:

- Multi-front enforcement risk (SARFAESI, arbitrations, suits) where a single forum and moratorium are needed to stabilize the business.
- Fragmented creditor base where a binding plan (Section 31) is required to cram down dissent.

- Need to ring-fence a going concern while seeking new capital or a strategic sale supervised by CoC/RP.

In conclusion, a voluntary filing under the IBC is a double-edged sword. For promoters, it is a powerful tool to shield their company from aggressive creditors and force a comprehensive debt restructuring. However, it requires them to cede control and place the ultimate fate of their company in the hands of their lenders, with the ever-present risk of complete loss through liquidation or a takeover. It is a strategic path that should only be trodden with careful consideration and expert guidance.

Kesoram Industries: A Case Study in Strategic Debt Restructuring

(Based on publicly available information)

This case study examines the critical debt restructuring undertaken by Kesoram Industries Limited in 2021. It outlines the company's business overview, the factors leading to its financial distress, the multi-pronged resolution strategy, and the subsequent outcomes that have reshaped the company's future.

An Overview of Kesoram Industries

Kesoram Industries Limited, a flagship company of the B.K. Birla Group, has a history of over a century. Over the years, the company has diversified its operations, but its primary focus in recent times has been on two main segments and other smaller businesses:

Cement: Operating under the well-recognized brand "Birla Shakti," Kesoram's cement division has been the cornerstone of its business. The company has 2 cement manufacturing plants with captive limestone mines in Karnataka and Telangana. Its cement portfolio comprises Portland Pozzolana Cement (PPC) and Ordinary Portland Cement (OPC).

Tyre: The company has an integrated tyre manufacturing facility in East India that sells a wide range of SKUs catering to Commercial (trucks, buses) and consumer segments (2 & 3 wheelers)

Other (Transparent Paper and Chemicals): This segment, while smaller in terms of revenue, represents another facet of Kesoram's diversified portfolio.

A snapshot of the company's financial health, based on data from Screener.in, reveals a company that went through a long period of declining revenue and profitability. Poor sales and profitability led to negative net worth, debt default, high leverage and delayed payment of creditor dues.

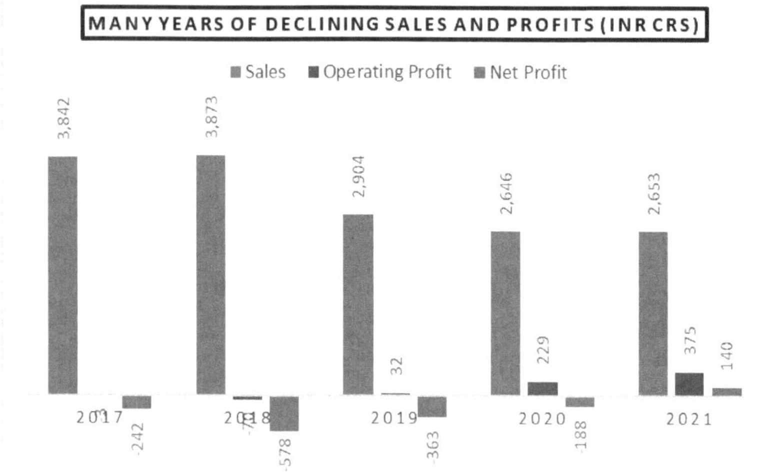

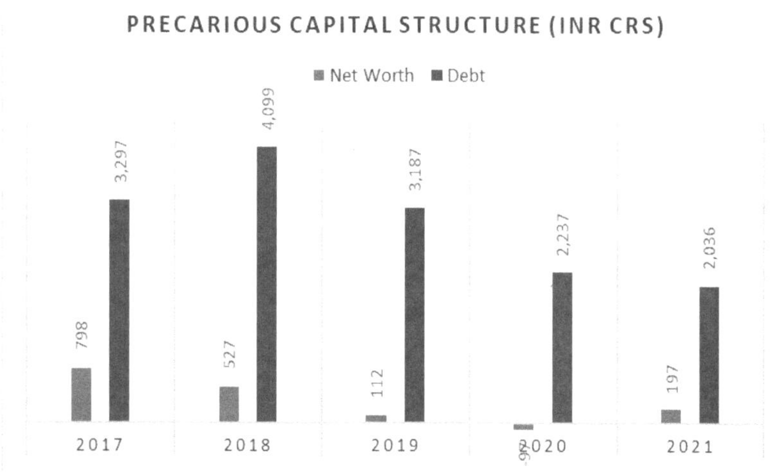

Leverage Ratios	2017	2018	2019	2020	2021
D/E (X)	4.13	7.77	28.39	-23.00	10.31
Interest Cov (X)	-0.01	-0.16	0.09	0.67	1.36

WC Days	2017	2018	2019	2020	2021
Debtors	50	54	74	27	42
Inventory	122	127	324	161	140
Accounts Payable	141	200	806	619	593

The Anatomy of Distress: A Company Burdened by Debt

By 2021, Kesoram Industries was facing severe financial stress, a culmination of several factors:

- **Continued losses from tyre business** due to lower sales volumes and low margins; the company faced stiff competition from market leaders like MRF, Apollo etc..

- **Unsustainable Debt Overhang:** The most significant challenge was a massive debt burden. Past expansionary projects, mainly ₹750 Crores or more spent on a passenger car radial tyre unit that never operationalized due to technological issues. This large debt became an overhang on the cash flows of the business leaving no cushion for setbacks in other businesses.

- **Operational Inefficiencies:** While the cement division had a strong brand, its operational efficiency was not on par with industry leaders, making it uncompetitive and inflexible especially when input prices hardened or demand reduced. High coal prices in 2017 – 18 led to contraction of already low cement margins, leading to losses.

- **Deteriorating Financial Performance:** As can be seen from the charts above, the years leading up to the restructuring were characterized by a consistent decline in key financial metrics. The company was reporting eroding revenues and persistent net losses, making it increasingly difficult to service its debt obligations.

- **Liquidity Squeeze:** The combination of these factors resulted in a severe liquidity crisis. The company struggled to meet its day-to-day operational and financial commitments, leading to stretched trade creditors and delayed statutory dues (refer to high accounts payable days in table earlier). Low margins, high debt service burden led to low cash generation and a default.

The Restructuring Blueprint: A Path to Resolution

To address the crisis, Kesoram Industries embarked on a comprehensive debt restructuring plan in March 2021. This multi-faceted approach aimed not only to avert an immediate crisis but also to create a sustainable financial and operational framework for the future.

Phase 1: Immediate Financial Stabilization

The first priority was to address the acute liquidity crunch and rationalize the existing debt structure. This was achieved through:

- **One-Time Settlement (OTS) with Lenders:** In the fourth quarter of fiscal year 2021, a crucial one-time settlement was negotiated with a consortium of lenders. The consortium, comprising more than 10 banks, had a strong secured position against the assets of the company. The company convinced the consortium to separate the debt between the cement and tyre businesses and settle the cement business debt first. Lender-approved Resolution Plan under RBI's June 7, 2019, Prudential Framework culminated in a Settlement Agreement dated Feb 20, 2021 (amended Mar 15, 2021). The settlement addressed gross debt of ₹2,181.81 crore (as of Jan 31, 2021) through three legs:
    - Upfront cash repayment: ₹1,670.94 crore to lenders;
    - Equity to lenders: 2,22,21,262 equity shares (₹10 FV) issued on Mar 8, 2021 at ₹65 per share (incl. premium);
    - Zero-Coupon OCRPS to lenders: 4,48,97,195 Zero-Coupon Optionally Convertible Redeemable Preference Shares (₹100 FV), convertible with consent within 18 months; if not converted, redeemable at par in five equal tranches starting Mar 31, 2028.
- Financing the settlement and infusion of high-yield debt: To fund the OTS and meet other pressing financial needs, Kesoram raised approximately ₹2,100 crore in March 2021. This was structured through the issuance of high-yield Non-Convertible Debentures

(NCDs) and Optionally Convertible Debentures (OCDs) with a target IRR of 20.75%, including an initial (and later step up) coupon rate of 9%. The structured debt was provided by Goldman Sachs India AIF, Cerberus (Sarvara Investment Fund/Promontoria) and Edelweiss (incl. EISSF/ECL Finance). The debt was secured against a first-ranking exclusive charge on fixed assets (including mining leases), real property and current assets. The overall debt term was 5 years but with a lock-in period of 18 months. While this move may seem counterintuitive, it was a strategic necessity to clean up the existing convoluted debt structure and provide a single, albeit expensive, line of credit. This was a calculated risk, contingent on the successful implementation of the subsequent phases of the restructuring plan.

Phase 2: Lightening the balance sheet and paving the way for growth

With the immediate crisis averted, the focus shifted to strengthening the company's balance sheet and creating a more sustainable financial architecture:

- **Rights Issue:** In September 2021, Kesoram successfully launched a rights issue, which was oversubscribed, raising crucial equity capital of ₹400 Crores. According to ICRA March 2022 rating report, "Of the rights issue proceeds, ₹55 crore was used to repay non-convertible debentures (NCDs) in November 2021 and ₹293.9 crore to prepay optionally convertible debentures (OCDs) in January 2022."
- **Strategic Divestment of Non-Core Assets:** A key part of the turnaround strategy was to identify and monetize non-core assets to further reduce debt. This process, initiated after the 2021 restructuring, was aimed at sharpening the company's focus on its core cement business.

The Aftermath and the Path Forward

The debt restructuring of 2021 was a pivotal moment for Kesoram Industries. It provided a temporary relief from potential shutdown due to losses and bank defaults. Further, the OTS helped the company avoid any enforcement action by the earlier lenders and loss of control for the promoters. However, the interest cost and debt repayment obligations weighed on the company's profitability and balance sheet. After a brief uplift in revenue, profitability and net worth, the company sank into losses again. This was a classic example of a capital structure not suitable for the realities of the business.

High accounts payable days, even after the restructuring, show that the company was unable to pay its suppliers on time due to cash constraints.

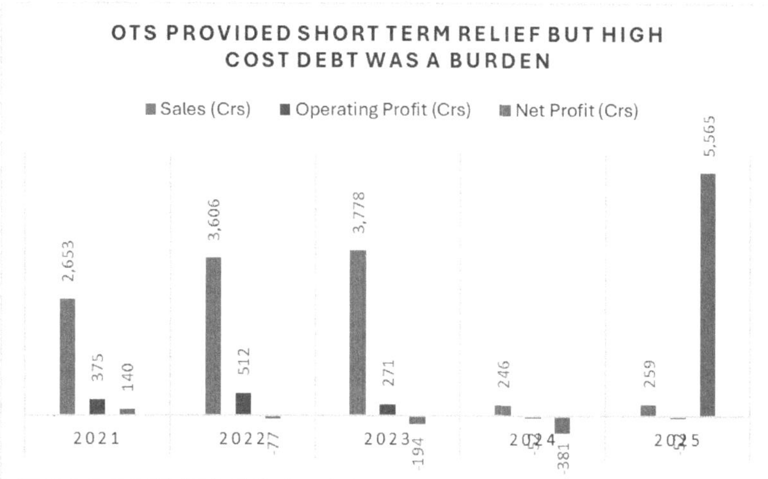

Leverage Ratios	2021	2022	2023	2024	2025
D/E (X)	10.31	3.72	4.10	23.94	0.44
Interest Cov (X)	1.36	1.02	0.60	-1.94	-1.86

WC Days	2021	2022	2023	2024	2025
Debtors	42	32	36	693	46
Inventory	140	174	197	1,006	111
Accounts Payable	593	568	463	2,186	105

Some industry analysts note that Kesoram plants were inefficient and required significant capex in order to improve their competitiveness and profitability. However, the distress caused by high leverage in 2017 – 2020, wrong investment decisions and high input costs in cement, led to a precarious financial situation. Subsequent restructuring provided

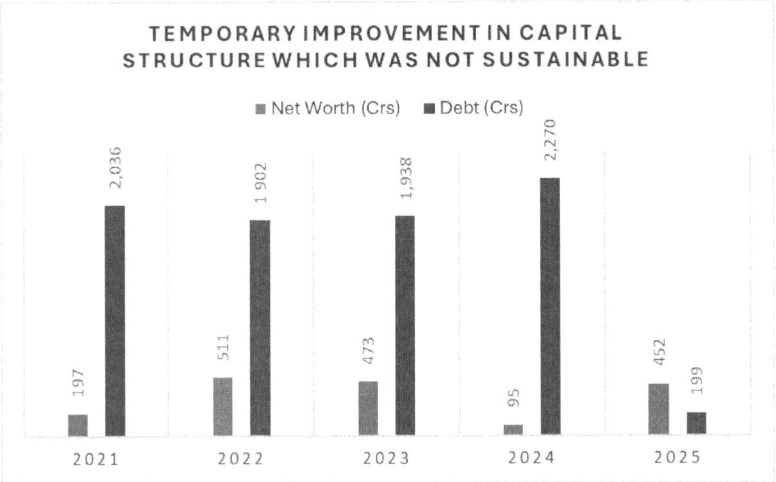

temporary relief but its high-risk nature and perhaps the promoter's reluctance to dilute, led to a high cost of debt. The high-cost debt didn't allow the business to invest in efficiency improvement projects, making the turnaround unsustainable.

As a result, Kesoram promoters ended up selling the business to UltraTech Cement. On Nov 30, 2023, the boards of Kesoram and UltraTech Cement approved a Composite Scheme of Arrangement to merge Kesoram's cement business into UltraTech with a share-swap of 1 UltraTech share for every 52 Kesoram shares. The scheme's appointed date was April 1, 2024 and it became effective Mar 1, 2025 after requisite approvals.

There are many takeaways from this case, regarding early intervention, especially around managing crisis, operational restructuring initiatives, bringing in a CRO and how promoters could have handled capital structuring differently.

Chapter 09

Implementing the Turnaround Plan

"Teamwork forges resilience; accountability turns it into momentum."

Introduction

The development of a turnaround plan is only the halfway mark in a corporate rescue. A carefully prepared document with elegant charts and projections has no value unless it is converted into consistent, visible results on the ground. In fact, the most difficult and high-risk phase of any turnaround is not the diagnosis, not even the negotiation of debt restructuring terms, but the implementation of the plan. This is the point where strategic intent meets operational reality, where entrenched habits clash with the urgency of change, and where stakeholders' patience wears thin.

Implementation is also the phase with the greatest risk of failure. Many companies in India have emerged from bank-led restructuring schemes such as CDR or S4A with plans that looked robust on paper but failed in execution. The reasons are depressingly familiar: over-ambitious timelines, inadequate management bandwidth, weak follow-through on cost savings, stakeholder disputes, and a tendency to declare "mission accomplished" after the first signs of improvement. In such cases, companies often relapse into distress, sometimes within months, and creditors' losses deepen.

This is why execution discipline is not just a project-management issue; it is the very essence of a turnaround leader's job. A credible turnaround plan is a living instrument — not a static file in someone's laptop. In a well-run process, the plan evolves month by month, with actual performance replacing assumptions, and new challenges feeding into revised actions. The integrated financial plan we spoke of earlier becomes the "single source of truth" for all parties — lenders, shareholders, board members, employees, and advisors. It is both a roadmap and a scorecard.

Translating the Plan into Action

Once the plan is approved by the board and key stakeholders, the next task is to break it down into a set of actionable, manageable workstreams. This is often where the first signs of trouble emerge: the plan is usually written in broad strategic strokes: "reduce costs by 15%," "increase market share in the premium segment," "restructure debt over 8 years." None of these statements are self-executing. They must be decomposed into specific actions, assigned to individuals or teams, with timelines, budgets, and measurable outputs.

For example, "reduce costs by 15%" could actually consist of five separate sub-projects: renegotiating supplier contracts, consolidating manufacturing locations, reducing workforce layers, implementing an energy-efficiency program, and cutting travel and discretionary spending. Each of these has different owners, timelines, and complexity levels. Without this decomposition, cost savings will remain aspirational.

Prioritisation is equally important. In a turnaround, not all tasks are equal; some have an immediate survival impact, others are long-term enablers. I often use a simple impact–urgency matrix: plot each initiative by the size of its cash or profit impact and the speed at which it can be implemented. "High-impact, short-term" items (such as renegotiating a key raw material contract or collecting a large overdue receivable) should dominate the early months.

"High-impact, long-term" projects (like setting up a new distribution network) can run in parallel, but they must not divert scarce management attention from survival-critical measures.

Assigning responsibilities is another delicate matter. A turnaround leader may be tempted to keep control of every lever, but this is neither feasible nor healthy. The chief restructuring officer (CRO) or turnaround CEO must set the direction and hold the overall picture, but operational execution must rest with functional heads, viz. production, sales, procurement, finance, each of whom is accountable for his or her slice of the plan. At the same time, these leaders need to be coached to think differently; the growth-era mindset must shift to a cash-focused, efficiency-driven mode.

A governance structure is essential. A turnaround steering committee, typically consisting of the CEO/CRO, CFO, COO, key functional heads, and sometimes a lender representative, should meet weekly or fortnightly in the early months. A project management office (PMO) can coordinate workstreams, track milestones, and prepare progress dashboards. Decision-making protocols must be clear: what can be approved at the workstream level, what needs escalation, and how to resolve conflicts quickly.

Building Momentum in the Early Phase

The first 90 days of implementation are psychologically the most important. Stakeholders viz., lenders, investors, employees, even customers, are watching closely to see whether the company can translate words into action. The turnaround leader's initial goal should be to deliver quick wins that boost credibility, generate cash, and prove that change is possible.

Quick wins could be as simple as securing a large overdue payment from a customer, shutting down an obviously loss-making branch, or fixing a chronic quality issue that has been hurting sales. The point is not the size of the gain, but the visibility and speed. When a supplier sees that the company has suddenly started paying on time because collections improved, confidence goes up. When employees see that a wasteful practice has been eliminated, they sense a shift in seriousness.

Rebuilding trust and morale is closely tied to these early wins. Internal communication is critical: employees need to know not just what changes are being made, but why. I have often found that sharing the broad outline of the financial situation (without breaching confidentiality) helps people understand the urgency. Equally important is the visible presence of leadership i.e., walking the shop floor, visiting branches, speaking directly to teams.

Operational continuity must be preserved during change. This may sound obvious, but in the excitement of implementing reforms, management can disrupt the very processes that keep the lights on. For example, changing procurement procedures overnight without training staff can lead to stockouts. The early phase must balance "surgery" with "life support" — you cannot afford to alienate customers or lose key suppliers at this stage.

Execution of Core Turnaround Levers

This is the "heavy lifting" stage of implementation, where the strategic levers identified in the plan are pulled in earnest.

Operational restructuring often starts with intelligent cost reduction. This is not the crude "cut 20% across the board" approach that demoralizes teams and damages capabilities. Instead, it is a forensic review of cost lines, identifying waste, inefficiency, and misalignment with strategy. In manufacturing businesses, this may involve renegotiating raw material contracts, consolidating production into fewer plants, or automating certain processes. In service businesses, it could mean optimizing branch networks, reducing layers of management, or outsourcing non-core functions.

Process reengineering is a more complex but high-impact lever. Here, you are redesigning workflows from scratch to remove bottlenecks, reduce cycle times, and improve quality. For example, a mid-sized Indian engineering company in distress cut its order-to-delivery time by 30% by integrating design, procurement, and production teams into a single workflow, supported by an upgraded ERP system.

Working capital optimisation is another critical lever. In distress situations, cash is oxygen, and too much of it is often trapped in receivables or inventory. Aggressive collection drives, tighter credit terms, just-in-time inventory practices, and better demand forecasting can release substantial liquidity. Supplier relationships must be managed carefully. Extending payables without damaging supply continuity is a delicate balance.

On the revenue side, margin improvement initiatives may include revisiting pricing strategy, focusing on high-margin products, or exiting unprofitable customer segments. Sales channel development, especially through digital platforms, is increasingly important in India's rapidly changing consumer landscape.

Financial restructuring usually happens in parallel. Once debt restructuring terms are agreed upon, they must be operationalised: loan documentation executed, repayment schedules loaded into the accounting system, interest serviced on time, and covenant compliance tracked. If equity infusion is part of the plan, negotiations with investors must be closed, funds brought in, and usage monitored to ensure they plug the intended gaps.

Talent and culture cannot be neglected. Turnarounds often require changes in senior leadership, either to bring in turnaround expertise or to remove blockers. Retaining key talent is vital; these are the people who will execute the change on the ground. Incentives should be aligned with turnaround milestones, not just annual profit targets. A culture of performance, transparency, and accountability must be cultivated, often a sharp departure from the pre-distress environment.

Tools for Tracking and Controlling Progress

An integrated financial plan, when linked to actual performance data, becomes the execution dashboard. Monthly (or in the early phase, weekly) updates of P&L, balance sheet, and cash flow forecasts allow management to see whether they are on track. Variance analysis, i.e., comparing actuals to plan, is a powerful tool to spot issues early. For example, if receivables are not coming in as projected, the next month's cash flow can be protected by adjusting payables or drawing on contingency lines.

Key performance indicators (KPIs) must go beyond financials. Operational metrics like on-time delivery rates, machine utilization, defect rates, customer churn are equally important. These are often the leading indicators of financial outcomes. Early warning signals should be built into the dashboard: For example, if the debt service coverage ratio (DSCR) is projected to fall below covenant level in two quarters, corrective actions can be triggered now.

Technology can greatly enhance tracking. Even a simple project-management tool can keep workstreams aligned, flag overdue tasks, and provide visibility to the steering committee. In larger companies, ERP systems can be configured to produce near-real-time dashboards.

Sample Dashboard: Executive Summary

Metric	Plan	Actual	Variance	Variance %	RAG* Status	Commentary
Revenue	120.0	112.5	-7.5	-6.3%	Red	Delay in dispatch due to raw material shortage
EBITDA	18.0	16.2	-1.8	-10.0%	Amber	Lower gross margin, partial offset by cost savings
Operating Cash Flow	12.0	9.5	-2.5	-20.8%	Red	Receivable collections slower than planned
Closing Cash	15.0	14.8	-0.2	-1.3%	Green	Close to plan
Net Debt / EBITDA (TTM)	4.2x	4.3x	0.1x	2.4%	Amber	Covenant at risk if EBITDA drops further

*RAG = Red / Amber / Green indicator for quick visual status

Sample Dashboard: Financial KPIs

KPI	Plan	Actual	Variance	Commentary
Gross Margin %	32%	31%	-1%	Higher input costs not fully passed on
SG&A as % of Revenue	14%	13%	-1%	Travel & marketing cuts implemented
DSCR	1.25x	1.20x	-0.05x	Just above covenant threshold
Interest Coverage	2.5x	2.4x	-0.1x	Stable, but dependent on Q2 recovery
Free Cash Flow	10.0	8.2	-1.8	Delay in asset sale proceeds

Sample Dashboard: Operational KPIs

KPI	Plan	Actual	Variance	Commentary
Production Output (units)	50,000	47,500	-2,500	Supplier delivery delays
On-Time Delivery %	95%	91%	-4%	Logistics bottlenecks in South region
DSO (Days)	60	72	+12	Large customer payment delayed
DPO (Days)	45	50	+5	Supplier terms renegotiated successfully
Inventory Days	55	60	+5	Build-up for festive season orders
Employee Turnover % (quarterly)	3%	4.5%	+1.5%	Attrition in mid-level sales team

Sample Dashboard: Strategic Initiatives Progress

Initiative	Target Date	Status	Commentary
Asset sale – non-core land parcel	Aug 2025	Amber	Buyer identified, due diligence underway
ERP upgrade for order tracking	Oct 2025	Green	Vendor contracted, Phase 1 complete
Vendor contract renegotiation	Sep 2025	Green	Achieved average 8% cost reduction
Launch of premium product line	Dec 2025	Red	Design delays due to vendor issues

Sample Dashboard: Covenant Monitoring

Covenant	Threshold	Actual	Status	Risk Level
DSCR	≥ 1.20x	1.20x	Amber	Medium
Net Debt / EBITDA	≤ 4.25x	4.30x	Amber	Medium
EBITDA Minimum (Quarterly)	≥ ₹45 Cr	₹44 Cr	Red	High
Interest Payment Timeliness	100%	100%	Green	Low

Sample Dashboard: Risk Register (top 3 for the month)

Risk	Potential Impact	Mitigation
Customer default – Top 3 account	₹8 Cr receivable at risk	Engage directly with customer CEO; staggered payment plan
Raw material price spike	Margin erosion	Hedge 50% of requirement for next 3 months
Attrition in skilled technicians	Project delays	Retention bonus + targeted hiring

Next Month Focus

- Accelerate receivable collections (target: reduce DSO from 72 to 65 days)
- Close non-core asset sale to generate ₹15 Cr liquidity
- Maintain EBITDA margin ≥ 15% despite raw material price pressures
- Complete phase 2 of ERP rollout for logistics tracking

Stakeholder Engagement During Implementation

No turnaround can be implemented in a vacuum; stakeholder management is an ongoing effort.

Lenders and creditors require regular updates, not just on covenant compliance but on operational progress. In India, under RBI's prudential norms, lenders have to classify accounts based on timeliness of repayment and other risk factors. Proactive communication can help maintain a more favorable classification, buying time and goodwill.

Shareholders and investors must be kept informed, even when the news is not positive. The worst mistake is to surprise equity owners with sudden cash calls or dilution events. If further equity infusion is likely, preparing the ground with regular updates and clear explanations of need and impact increases the chance of a smooth process.

Employees, often the most overlooked stakeholder group, need consistent communication. They are both the agents and subjects of change. Periodic town halls, newsletters, and visible recognition of good performance can keep morale from collapsing.

Customers and vendors require special attention. In distress situations, competitors will try to poach your customers, and vendors may tighten terms. Personal outreach by senior leaders, assurance of continuity, and on-time fulfillment of commitments can help retain their trust.

Here's a Stakeholder Meeting Calendar and a set of sample templates that can be plugged straight into a turnaround implementation process.

Stakeholder Meeting Calendar – Turnaround Implementation Phase

Week	Stakeholder Group	Meeting Type	Frequency	Duration	Key Purpose
Week 1	Internal – Steering Committee	Progress Review	Weekly (first 6 months), then fortnightly	90 mins	Review plan milestones, financial/ operational KPIs, unblock decisions
Week 2	Lenders Consortium / Key Creditor	Covenant & Performance Review	Monthly (first year)	60–90 mins	Update on covenants, cash flow, risk mitigations, and liquidity status

Week 3	Board of Directors	Board Meeting (Turnaround Focus)	Monthly or Bi-Monthly	2–3 hrs	Strategic direction, approve deviations, stakeholder updates
Week 3	Employees – All Hands	Town Hall	Monthly (first 6 months), then quarterly	45–60 mins	Communicate wins, acknowledge challenges, maintain morale
Week 4	Key Customers / Vendors	Relationship Meetings	Monthly/ Quarterly	45–60 mins	Assure continuity, address concerns, deepen engagement
As needed	Equity Shareholders / Potential Investors	Capital & Strategic Discussion	As required	Variable	Secure equity support or negotiate fresh infusion

B. First 100 Days – More Intensive Cadence

- Weekly lender check-ins (even if brief) to maintain confidence.
- Weekly PMO updates are provided to the CRO/CEO on each workstream's progress.
- Daily internal huddles (15 mins) will be held in the first month for crisis-response items like cash flow, supplier issues, or customer complaints.

Meeting Templates

1. Internal Steering Committee – Weekly Progress Review

Objective: Drive accountability for plan execution, track variances, and unblock issues.

Agenda Template:

i. **Opening & Previous Action Review** (10 mins)

  - Status of action items from last meeting

ii. **Financial Dashboard Review** (15 mins)

  - Actual vs. planned P&L, cash flow, covenants

iii. **Operational KPIs Review** (15 mins)

  - Production, sales, service, quality metrics

iv. **Strategic Initiatives Update** (20 mins)

  - Progress on asset sales, product launches, cost-reduction projects

v. **Risk & Issue Log** (15 mins)

  - New risks, mitigation status, escalation needs

vi. **Decisions & Approvals** (10 mins)

  - Urgent funding, supplier changes, leadership moves

vii. **Action Summary & Close** (5 mins)

  - Confirm ownership, deadlines, and next meeting

Pre-Read Pack:

- Monthly Dashboard
- Updated Risk Register
- Workstream status tracker

2. Lender Performance Review – Monthly

Objective: Maintain transparency, pre-empt covenant breaches, and reinforce viability.

Agenda Template:

i. **Opening Remarks** – CRO/CEO sets context

ii. **Financial Performance**

- P&L, Balance Sheet, Cash Flow (Actual vs. Plan)
- Covenant status and projections

iii. **Liquidity Position**

- Cash on hand, undrawn facilities, near-term cash requirements

iv. **Key Operational Updates**

- Cost initiatives, sales pipeline, supply chain status

v. **Strategic Initiatives Progress**

- Asset sales, debt restructuring milestones

vi. **Risks and Mitigation Actions**

vii. **Requests/Approvals from Lenders**

viii. **Next Steps & Calendar**

Pre-Read Pack:

- Executive Summary Dashboard
- Covenant Tracker
- Cash Flow Forecast (3–6 months ahead)
- Scenario Sensitivity (if key assumptions shift)

3. Board Meeting – Turnaround Focus

Objective: Align strategic direction, approve deviations, and ensure governance compliance.

Agenda Template:

i. **Chairperson's Opening Remarks**

ii. **Management Turnaround Progress Report**

iii. **Financial Update**

- YTD results, forecast updates, covenant compliance

iv. **Strategic Decisions**

- Changes to plan, M&A discussions, equity-raise strategy

v. **Operational Performance**

- Highlights and concerns in key functions

vi. **Risk Oversight**

- Compliance, legal, reputational, market risks

vii. **HR & Culture Update**

- Talent retention, leadership changes

viii. **Board Resolutions**

ix. **Action Items & Close**

4. Employee Town Hall – Monthly

Objective: Maintain morale, reinforce trust, and ensure alignment.

Agenda Template:

i. **CEO/CRO Update**

- Honest view of progress and challenges

ii. **Celebrating Wins**

- Recognise teams or individuals who delivered results

iii. **Key Priorities for Next Month**

iv. **Open Q&A**

- Pre-submitted and live questions

5. Key Customer / Vendor Meeting

Objective: Maintain relationship capital during disruption.

Agenda Template:

i. **Status Update**

- Operations, delivery, payments

ii. **Address Concerns**

iii. **Explore Opportunities**

- New orders, extended contracts

iv. **Next Steps**

Best Practices for Stakeholder Meetings in Turnaround

- **No surprises** – Pre-read packs should go 48–72 hours in advance.
- **Consistent metrics** – Use the same definitions and data cuts in every meeting.
- **Clear owners** – Every action item has a named owner and deadline.
- **Follow-through** – Actions are reviewed at the start of the next meeting.
- **Minutes distribution** – Send minutes within 48 hours to all attendees.

Managing Risks and Setbacks

Setbacks are inevitable in a turnaround. A major customer may be lost, a cost-cutting measure may backfire, or a market downturn may wipe out projected gains. The implementation plan must anticipate such risks and include contingency actions.

Common pitfalls include over-ambitious timelines (leading to missed targets and credibility loss), lack of stakeholder buy-in (causing passive resistance), and execution fatigue (teams losing steam after the initial push). Contingency planning involves defining trigger points — for example, if sales fall 10% below plan for two consecutive months, marketing spend is redirected, or a new product launch is accelerated.

Resilience is as much about leadership mindset as about process. The turnaround leader must maintain composure, avoid blame games, and focus on solutions. Celebrating small wins, even in the midst of setbacks, helps keep teams motivated.

Transitioning from Turnaround to Transformation

At some point, often 18 to 36 months into the process, the company moves from firefighting to a more stable footing. Debt is under control, cash flows are positive, and operational metrics are trending in the right direction. This is the time to shift the narrative from "survival" to "growth."

Growth investments can resume, whether in new product development, market expansion, or capacity upgrades. The brand, which may have been tarnished during the distress period, needs rebuilding through marketing and customer engagement.

Institutionalizing improvements is critical. Many companies, having recovered, slide back into old habits. The governance mechanisms, performance dashboards, and cultural shifts introduced during the turnaround should be embedded into "business as usual." Talent development should focus on building future leaders who can sustain the new way of working.

For stakeholders, this phase may include exit planning. Lenders may refinance or sell down their exposure; private equity investors may prepare for an IPO or strategic sale; promoters may seek to regain majority control if their control is diluted.

Conclusion

Implementing a turnaround plan is as much about psychology and leadership as it is about strategy and finance. The best-designed plan will fail if it is not translated into disciplined, transparent, and adaptive execution. The integrated financial plan serves as the roadmap, the scoreboard, and the common language between lenders, shareholders, management, and employees. In the messy reality of distressed business recovery, the leader who can keep all these elements in harmony has the best chance of steering the company not just back to stability, but toward sustainable growth.

Case Example

Real estate ancillary business, India

The company, a leader in fire detection and suppression, alarms and building management systems in India, was respected for its quality and integrity of its leadership. A reputed global private equity invested in the business for a significant minority stake to catalyze growth and capture the real estate boom in India and the Middle East. Fresh funds for working capital encouraged the company to go all out and win deals across the country.

The crisis

Within 18 months, the company experienced a significant working capital shortage and progress on its projects started to stall. Simultaneously, employee attrition increased and bank working capital lines were fully utilized. Senior management and PE team worked hard to stall the decline, but lack of working capital and stalled projects led to precipitous fall in revenue and order book. First vendor payments started getting delayed, then salaries, and finally the company defaulted on statutory payments due and bank loans.

The IBR

The PE investor brought in a CRO with a limited scope to manage the crisis and improve liquidity. Within 2 weeks, it was evident that this was a case of mismanaged growth, where:

- In pursuit of revenue, the company didn't make adequate efforts to strengthen the business "enablers", viz., processes, finance function, IT systems, HR, and quality. While revenue scaled, the support functions didn't.
- With more than 1500 projects in India and the Middle East, the company had tied itself in knots where performance issues in one

project were holding back payments from the same customers for other projects.

- As employees left without proper handover, the organization struggled with project status.
- Inadequate documentation and processes led to 3 different versions for accounts receivable – clients, accounts, and sales team. There was no single source of truth!
- Senior management bandwidth was getting choked on resolving internal issues, with no time left to provide quality attention to client complaints and strategic thinking on how to resolve the situation of distress

Crisis management & stakeholder management

By the time the CRO and his team stepped in, cash inflows had dropped to a trickle, employee salaries and allowances had not been paid for more than 4 to 6 months (different by region and levels), discussions were in advanced stages for a debt restructuring and additional loan facilities and investments into building automation research were stalled. Employee morale had hit rock bottom and vendors were refusing to engage. CRO and his team:

- A method was introduced to understand and summarize what the issues ailing receivables were from each project, e.g., internal reconciliation, client reconciliation, material shortage, other project issues, legal, etc.
- A cash-on-cash analysis was developed for projects with receivables above a certain threshold, to understand where some quick gains can be made.
- Books of account were made the single source of truth. A message was sent across all teams, that if it wasn't in the books, it didn't exist. Internal reconciliation between sales teams and accounting

teams was resolved as a top priority, so the focus could then shift to reconciliation with clients.

- A 13-week cash flow forecast was prepared to create visibility and transparency into flows and prioritize payments.
- Employee town halls were held to provide transparency and also allow employees to vent their fears and concerns. FAQs were prepared prior to calls to ensure message consistency and minimize confusion.
- Mid-senior management was taken into confidence and briefed on what messages to communicate to external stakeholders viz., suppliers and customers.
- Customer meeting plan was prepared with FAQs and the identification of who would attend such meetings, including clients whom the CEO would meet in person.
- Weekly briefing was provided to the PE investors.
- Cost reduction initiatives were identified across the board, including shutting down regions where RE activity had stalled (and the regional team required significant strengthening, including replacement of leadership), re-negotiating lease agreements and moving into smaller regional offices and freezing further investment into the building automation project.

With the above efforts, CRO and his team created breathing room and released some management bandwidth for the promoter to focus on strategic matters. Within 3 months, weekly cash inflows had doubled and momentum improved. By 5th month, 3 months of overdue salary and allowances were paid and statutory overdues were trending lower. Quick wins on some project handovers, salary payments and cost reduction reduced stress within the system.

Turnaround plan development and Financial restructuring

Senior management worked on developing an integrated turnaround plan along with the PE investors. A 5-year plan showed significant erosion in value, need for fresh capital and deferral of debt repayment obligations.

The promoter and PE investor brought in additional equity capital necessary to complete the stalled projects, unclog the working capital jam and give confidence to customers that the company can take on new projects. This gave the banks the required confidence to restructure the debt into a long-term repayment plan.

However, without new working capital lines from banks, the growth prospects remained limited. Finally, 2.5 years after the initial crisis, the promoter and PE investor significantly diluted their share and brought in a strategic investor. The strategic investor brought their global expatriates to address the process gaps, set up new IT systems, strengthened finance and HR functions and overhauled the product portfolio. With a global major now in the driving seat, the company could attract the best of industry talent and, combined with the knowledge of the promoter and his credibility, it laid a solid foundation for a sustainable business.

Learnings:

- Sudden influx of capital into a business to drive growth can act like a high adrenaline rush that leads to unsustainable growth. Strengthening the enabler functions to support a larger organisation (higher revenue or higher level of activity) is akin to laying a solid foundation and must be prioritised.

- Absorption of PE capital into the business and continuously high working capital line utilisation should have rung the bells to slow down the pace. There is a saying among turnaround experts, "distress whispers in working capital long before it screams in the P&L". High receivables and their analysis should have rung the emergency bells!

- Bringing in turnaround experts earlier, though it may have cost some additional fees, would have saved on equity dilution (overall much cheaper). They would have brought structure to the operational restructuring initiatives and supported the senior management in developing more solutions to come out of stress earlier versus focusing only on crisis management and managing liquidity.

Case Example

Indian packaging materials company

The company with ₹2000 Crores+ annual revenue is one of India's largest manufacturers of packaging material with a pan-India manufacturing footprint. The company had a dominant share in a large growing segment, with the ability to lead pricing in the country. Between 2000 and 2014, the company's customer landscape changed drastically from traditional Indian promoter-owned and -led to MNC-owned and professionally-led. This had significant implications for the company:

- With MNC owners with deep pockets, there was consensus that customer segment growth rate would accelerate and demand for company products would be much higher.
- Partnering with customers on innovation would be key, requiring closer partnership, investment in R&D, moulds and equipment.
- Key account management had to become more robust as a professionally run client with decentralised decision making required relationships to be strengthened across client's supply chain.

In anticipation of higher demand, the promoters of the company went ahead and invested in two large plants, one organic and the other via acquisition. The latter plant gave the company a footprint in a region it didn't have a presence in but it came with significant unionised labour issues. These investments added significant debt on the balance sheet. One unique aspect about the company was that even though it had a large market share, solid revenue and pricing power, it never declared profits. The promoters were infamous in the industry for their idiosyncratic behaviour (bordering on arrogance) and their penchant for importing a key raw material that was available in plenty in India.

Onset of Stress

The anticipated demand growth didn't materialize and the business, saddled with additional debt and inefficient procurement practices, started facing financial difficulties. Liquidity crisis led to the deferral of maintenance of equipment that was critical for efficient production and power consumption. Operating margins that were in low-to-mid teens started to decline to mid-single digits.

Transition to Distress

Accounts payable started to accumulate as the company started delaying payment to vendors and soon enough it also defaulted on its debt. A planned expansion in a new market had to be stopped, even though only last-mile capex was required. Lack of maintenance of key equipment led to plant shutdowns and a 20% reduction in available capacity. Promoters' way of working and liquidity challenges encouraged the customers to develop new sources of supply, including providing capital to a competitor to set up a plant.

Appointment of Restructuring Advisors

A few years after the onset of stress, the company appointed advisors to help restructure the debt under the June 7, 2019, Prudential Framework. Complete erosion of net worth, accumulated liabilities, lower production capacity, lower market share and inefficient operations required significant infusion of capital to make it convincing for lenders to do a restructuring. Multiple promises were made by the promoters regarding cash infusion (including bringing in PE investors) but none of the promises were kept. Market rumors suggested that new investors wanted a much higher equity stake and change in management i.e., bring in professional management, neither of which was acceptable to the promoters.

Bankruptcy Filing

Finally, the lender consortium lost patience and filed a petition with the NCLT to admit the company into bankruptcy. This opened up the company to be acquired by other interested bidders as well.

The Turnaround During Bankruptcy

The company had a history of never declaring profits over the last 10 years, so when the company was admitted into bankruptcy, it was in a precarious position:

- Employee morale was low as they had not received a pay increase for more than 5 years.
- The company was losing more than ₹20 crores per month.
- Average inventory across plants was less than 3 days and for some items, lower than half a day. Plant heads were spending more time chasing the head office procurement team to organize material and chasing supplier trucks than ensuring efficient production or quality product delivery.
- Plant maintenance and worker safety were a big risk, given the nature of production.
- Labour issues at the acquired plant had led to a lockout and the plant was now being run by staff and contract labour. Efficiency metrics were one of the lowest among all plants and monthly losses were the highest.
- Procurement choices were made more due to cash constraints and supplier rotation, compromising margins.
- Monthly cash collections were shrinking as losses grew, constraining the company's ability to produce more.

The turnaround experts accompanying the Resolution Professional immediately got onto the job and took the following key steps:

- Took control of cash flow prioritization and introduced a monthly cash budgeting, where targets were set for collection and payments were prioritized, balancing multiple demands each month viz., statutory dues, agreements with suppliers, maintenance needs, salaries, etc.

- Worked with the plant heads and head office procurement team to improve the inventory levels across plants for each key item to reduce chaos at each plant. This released plant heads' bandwidth to focus more on aligning production with sales and improving production efficiency.

- Developed an innovative incentive scheme for all permanent employees (management, staff and workers) where up to 20% of monthly reported EBITDA would be distributed among all employees subject to a cap of 25% of their CTC. Payment of the incentive was staggered as follows: 50% at the end of the month, subject to EBITDA-to-Cash reconciliation and the balance 50% at the end of the quarter, subject to auditors' limited review.

- Initiated monthly management meetings to discuss prior month performance, current month budgets, profit improvement and working capital initiatives and plant safety issues. These monthly management meetings also helped improve transparency and introduced checks and balances in the business. Cross-questioning on differential pricing for raw materials across plants, buildup of customer inventory and plant efficiency metrics, led to healthy competition and better governance.

- Simultaneously, a number of steps were taken to reduce cost of raw materials:

  - Met Indian manufacturers of key raw materials and negotiated long-term supply contracts, committing annual and monthly volumes to secure their commitment for supply. Price was kept in check by ensuring the right mix of manufacturers and traders.

  - Sourcing changes were made to reduce transportation costs and supply lead time.

- New suppliers were added to the mix for almost every raw material and transportation to break nexus, prevent leakage, and lower input prices.

- Worked with the experienced sales team, conducted a quick pricing study and demand-supply analysis that led to the decision to implement price increases for all key customers.

- As margins improved and profitability returned, money was made available for preventive maintenance and improving worker safety.

Within 3 months of initiating the above changes, the business became profitable and for the first time declared profits for a full year. Over the course of the CIRP, the net cash in the business increased 4X, allowing lenders to recover a significant portion of their dues via cash sweep at the time of handover.

The Resolution

After long legal battles, the company was sold to a strategic buyer, at twice the Section 12A offer made by the promoters during early months of CIRP. Of their claims against the company, the lenders recovered about 60% via the sale of business and 15% from cash sweep, making total recovery approximately 75%, a handsome recovery compared to an average of 33% from all CIRPs since the inception of IBC.

Key Learnings

1. Promoter Myopia

- Refusal to dilute stake or infuse capital during stress resulted in complete loss of ownership.

- Early acceptance of professional investors could have preserved some value.

2. **Role of Lenders**

    - A CRO/IBR appointment at default could have diagnosed root causes and created a turnaround roadmap.
    - Delay in filing for IBC meant lenders faced a weaker, value-eroded business.

3. **IBC Discipline**

    - Entertaining Section 12A withdrawals during CIRP undermines bidder confidence, especially for foreign strategic investors.
    - In this case, several global suppliers to MNC clients withdrew interest after learning of parallel 12A talks.

4. **Operational Fixes Matter**

    - Even deeply distressed companies can generate cash flow improvements through disciplined procurement, governance, and employee incentives.
    - Profitability during CIRP significantly boosted resolution value.

Chapter 10
Leadership Style to Lead a Turnaround

"Tell the hardest truth first, then keep every small promise."

Introduction – Leadership in the Eye of the Storm

A corporate turnaround represents one of the most complex and high-stakes tests of leadership in the business world. It is fundamentally different from managing a company in stable times, where decisions can be carefully sequenced, risks spread across longer horizons, and resources allocated with relative certainty. In a turnaround, conditions are already dire: the organisation may be on the brink of insolvency, cash flow is strained, stakeholder trust is eroded, and morale is low. External pressures intensify as creditors grow impatient, customers waver, and competitors sense opportunity. The leader is handed an organisation that has already drifted dangerously close to the rocks and is expected to bring it to safe harbour, often with fewer resources, less time, and higher scrutiny than in any other leadership situation.

The role of a turnaround leader demands the capacity to operate simultaneously as a crisis manager, strategist, motivator, diplomat, and builder. Immediate survival must be ensured, even as the foundations for long-term recovery are laid. Decisions taken in the first weeks can determine whether the organisation regains stability, is forced into liquidation, or is sold under duress. In the Indian context, where the Insolvency and Bankruptcy Code sets hard timelines and creditors hold significant sway, the demands on a turnaround leader are particularly acute.

Making an Entrance – Setting the Tone Before a Word is Spoken

The first encounter between the turnaround leader and the organisation is not merely procedural; it is symbolic. The entrance is a moment of high signalling value, when employees, lenders, customers, and the wider market form rapid judgements about capability, intent, and style. In distressed companies, people have often endured a parade of leaders and consultants, each promising change but leaving little behind. Scepticism is high, and body language, tone, and initial actions are studied as closely as any formal announcement.

A leader entering a turnaround situation must convey calm urgency, i.e., acknowledging the seriousness of the crisis without triggering panic. There is a fine balance between projecting authority and appearing arrogant, between being approachable and being overly familiar. The optics matter: the way the leader walks the floor, the time taken to engage with frontline staff, the decision to meet lenders early or to first speak to employees, all send signals about priorities. In some environments, formality reinforces credibility; in others, an overly formal demeanour may create distance. The key is congruence between the culture of the organisation and the personal presence of the leader. The first impression is not about delivering a detailed plan, but about establishing that there is competent, focused leadership in place.

Preparing for Day One – Building the Information Arsenal

The effectiveness of the first days in charge is determined largely by the preparation that occurs before formally taking the role. A turnaround leader who arrives without a working map of the terrain risks squandering valuable time in orientation while the organisation continues to haemorrhage resources and stakeholder confidence.

Pre-entry preparation involves intensive intelligence gathering. This includes understanding the liquidity position, debt maturities, contingent liabilities, operational chokepoints, and the status of key customer and supplier relationships. Stakeholder mapping is essential, identifying who holds influence over critical decisions and where alliances or resistance may lie. It is equally important to distinguish between verified facts and assumptions that require rapid testing once on the ground.

Scenario sketches help anticipate the early decision landscape. If a major creditor withdraws support, if a key supplier halts deliveries, or if regulatory action looms, the leader must have at least preliminary responses in mind. A central "war room" function, whether physical or virtual, should be in place to ensure a single source of truth for data and communications. Even the first internal and external statements should be carefully drafted before arrival, to ensure control of the narrative from the outset. This preparatory work does not replace the need to listen and learn after taking charge, but it ensures that early listening is informed by context rather than conducted in a vacuum.

Leading through the Initial Days – The First 100 Hours

The earliest phase of a turnaround is dominated by signaling, stabilization, and the establishment of rhythm. In politics, the concept of a "first 100 days" is often used to measure a leader's early momentum; in a turnaround, this window is often compressed to the first 100 hours. In that period, the organization's nervous system recalibrates to the presence of new leadership.

Listening is the first act, but it must be visible listening, often conducted on the shop floor, in operational control rooms, and in small group discussions with mid-level managers. Employees need to see that the new leadership is engaging directly with the realities of the business. Alongside listening, decisive but measured early actions can create credibility. Addressing a long-ignored operational bottleneck, announcing a sensible cost-containment step that does not damage morale, or restoring a critical customer relationship can demonstrate the capacity to act.

Reporting rhythms must be quickly established, with regular internal briefings and consistent communication to key external stakeholders. These rhythms provide structure in a period of uncertainty and signal that information will flow in a predictable manner. Crucially, grand strategies should not be announced before facts have been validated. In this early phase, over-promising can be fatal to credibility.

The Context of Turnaround Leadership

Turnarounds do not occur in a vacuum; they arise from specific triggers, and these shape the leadership challenge. Some are financial in origin, such as overleverage, mismanaged working capital, or failed refinancing. Others are market-driven, such as the arrival of a disruptive competitor or the collapse of a key customer segment. Still others stem from governance failures, regulatory sanctions, reputational crises, or external shocks like commodity price swings or pandemics.

The ownership context adds another layer of complexity. In promoter-led businesses, legacy loyalties, family dynamics, and reputational concerns influence decision-making. In private equity-owned companies, performance metrics and exit timelines dominate the agenda. In lender-controlled restructurings, consensus among multiple creditors must be maintained, often under formal frameworks. In public sector enterprises, bureaucratic processes, political oversight, and union influence must be navigated. A leader's style, pace, and communication approach must be calibrated to these contextual realities.

Core Attributes of the Turnaround Leader

Turnaround leadership demands certain non-negotiable qualities. Decisiveness is essential, as critical choices must be made on incomplete information and under time pressure. Financial and operational literacy allows the leader to interrogate numbers and operational reports with equal fluency, ensuring that strategic decisions are grounded in reality. The ability to build trust among skeptical stakeholders, often with conflicting objectives, is central to creating the space in which change can occur.

A high bias for action is required to maintain momentum, while moral courage enables the leader to take unpopular decisions that are necessary for survival. Above all, resilience—physical, emotional, and reputational—is the underpinning that sustains performance over what is often a 12- to 18-month grind of high-intensity work.

An Adaptive, Hands-on, Crisis-calm Style

Among the many schools of leadership, i.e., transactional, transformational, servant, command-and-control, the style most suited to a turnaround is adaptive leadership. This approach allows for rapid shifts in posture depending on the phase of the turnaround. During stabilisation, the style leans toward directive control, as speed is critical and ambiguity cannot be allowed to paralyse action. As the organisation pivots toward strategic renewal, the style becomes more collaborative, drawing on the knowledge and creativity of teams to co-create solutions. In the growth readiness phase, the emphasis shifts to empowerment, ensuring the organisation can function effectively without constant top-down intervention.

Hands-on involvement is particularly important in the early stages, but must be targeted. Leaders who attempt to micromanage all aspects of the business risk burnout and alienating competent managers. The art lies in identifying the few areas where deep personal involvement will have a disproportionate impact, while delegating effectively elsewhere.

Stakeholder Alignment as a Core Leadership Function

In a turnaround, stakeholders often pull in different directions. Creditors prioritize debt recovery; equity holders seek to preserve control and upside potential; employees want job security; customers need continuity; suppliers demand payment assurance. Misalignment among these groups can quickly derail a recovery.

The leader's role is to mediate these differences, sequence actions so that no critical constituency withdraws support prematurely, and translate the needs and constraints of one group into terms others can accept. This requires both negotiation skills and the ability to maintain credibility across diverse audiences.

Decision-making Under Pressure

Turnaround decision-making favors the principle that an action that is 80 percent right today is often better than one that is 100 percent right but delivered too late. This does not license recklessness; it is a recognition that perfect information rarely exists in crisis situations, and that delay can close off options permanently. Scenario thinking is a critical discipline, ensuring that each decision is accompanied by contingency plans should the chosen path prove unviable.

Communication as a Leadership Tool

In distressed environments, the absence of communication is quickly filled by rumor and speculation. Effective turnaround communication is frequent, honest, and consistent across channels. It acknowledges the challenges without destroying morale, reports progress without exaggeration, and keeps both internal and external audiences aligned. The narrative must be coherent: what is said to employees should not contradict messages given to creditors or the market.

Building and Leading the Turnaround Team

No single leader can execute a turnaround alone. The supporting team must be a carefully constructed blend of loyal insiders who understand the company's workings, new hires who bring fresh thinking, and external specialists with experience in restructuring, operations, or finance. The leader must integrate these diverse elements into a unified team, align them on a small set of immediate priorities, and shield them from the political crossfire that often erupts in distressed organizations.

Ethics and Integrity in Turnarounds

The temptation to resort to cosmetic fixes in order to create the appearance of progress is high in turnarounds. Cutting maintenance to improve short-term cash flow, deferring necessary quality investments, or inflating receivables can temporarily improve optics but undermine long-term viability. Ethical leadership not only avoids such practices but actively works to strengthen governance, recognizing that the credibility required to attract new investment is built on trust as much as on numbers.

Personal Attributes for Sustained Performance

The demands of a turnaround require physical stamina for long hours and sustained intensity, emotional intelligence to read people under stress, and self-awareness to recognise personal blind spots and the need for external support. Without these attributes, even technically competent leaders can falter under the prolonged strain of the role.

Common Pitfalls

Common errors in turnaround leadership include over-reliance on cost-cutting without addressing revenue generation, over-promising in early communications, neglecting organisational culture, and focusing so heavily on internal crises that market conditions are ignored. Each of these can erode momentum and credibility.

The Evolution of Leadership through the Turnaround Phases

Leadership style evolves through three broad phases. In stabilisation, it is directive and urgent, aimed at halting the decline. In the strategic pivot, it becomes more analytical and collaborative, focused on identifying and executing the shifts that will make the business viable. In the growth readiness phase, it shifts again to mentoring and delegating, institutionalising processes and ensuring the organisation can sustain progress without constant top-level intervention.

Exiting Gracefully – Leaving the Organisation on Higher Ground

A successful turnaround leader does not make themselves indispensable; they build a team and systems that can thrive without their presence. Exiting gracefully means choosing a departure point when the recovery has momentum but before the leader's style becomes misaligned with the needs of a growth phase. It involves ensuring that a capable successor, whether internal or external, is in place and aligned with the strategic direction. It also requires a formal transfer of knowledge and relationships, and often, a period of advisory support to provide continuity. Public endorsement of the new leadership helps reinforce confidence among stakeholders and protects the legacy of the turnaround.

Conclusion

Turnaround leadership is not about dramatic heroics. It is a discipline that combines urgency with patience, authority with humility, and strategic vision with relentless execution. It demands adaptability across phases, from the intense command of stabilization to the empowering mentorship of growth readiness. Above all, it requires the ability to enter with presence and purpose, to guide the organization through the turbulence of crisis, and to leave it not just afloat, but sailing towards greater horizons.

Section II

Chapter 11

Why Early Identification of Stress is Critical?

"Diagnose early, spare the surgery."

Early identification of stress in a business is not just critical; it's the single most important factor determining the success rate of a turnaround. The later the distress is recognized and acted upon, the fewer options remain, the higher the costs, and the lower the probability of survival.

Think of it like a medical condition: catching cancer in Stage 1 dramatically increases the chances of a full recovery with less invasive treatment. Waiting until Stage 4 often means palliative care and a grim prognosis. Business distress works similarly.

Here's why early identification is critical, highlighting the consequences of delay:

1. More Options & Flexibility:

- **Early**: When stress is minimal, management has a wide array of options. If they correctly and objectively diagnose the reason for the stress buildup, the proactive actions would be limited to minor operational tweaks, product portfolio adjustments, negotiations with customers or key suppliers or changing their go-to-market strategy. At an early stress stage, they will have access to capital, both debt and equity. In terms of debt, they may have access to full range of lenders viz., public sector banks, private sector banks, NBFCs, debt mutual funds and private credit. Even with their other stakeholders, they may have better negotiating power to drive operational change.

- **Late**: As stress builds up and moves into distress zone, options dwindle rapidly. Management is forced into taking drastic measures like forced asset sales, large layoffs or delaying salary payments. Access to capital becomes restricted. While earlier, the management had access to commercial banks, now only high-yield private credit funds or NBFCs may be interested. If the leverage is high or liabilities are substantial, raising equity becomes difficult. Management will find itself in a weak negotiating position with suppliers who may demand cash upfront, customers may seek alternatives, and talented employees may leave.

2. Lower Cost of Turnaround:

- **Early**: Cost of incremental capital is lower in stress situations versus distress as the perceived risk to a lender is lower. Survival is still not at stake, so both operational costs and opportunity costs are lower. Business does not have to forgo growth opportunities that may require capital or resources.

- **Late**: During distress, cost of additional capital skyrockets due to higher risk, potentially requiring expensive mezzanine or distressed debt. Survival itself is at stake, so the business has to pause investment in any growth opportunities, losing out vis-à-vis competition. Operational costs far exceed any benchmarks during normal times. Due to lower negotiating power, product may have to be sold at a significant discount, incur higher distribution costs or pay more for raw materials if bought on credit. Hiring good talent becomes a challenge, and at times, they may demand higher compensation if they bring specific skill sets that are critical for the business.

3. Greater Control & Less Dilution:

- **Early**: Management and existing shareholders retain control over the turnaround process and the future direction of the company. Any equity infusion is less dilutive and possibly doesn't require a change in the board or management.

- **Late**: Lenders or new investors (like ARCs, distressed PE funds in India) will demand significant equity stakes or debt-to-equity conversions to compensate for their high risk. Promoters often lose substantial control, sometimes even their majority stake. Management loses managerial discretion as lenders may impose stringent covenants, dictate decisions, or even replace management. In India, under IBC, control shifts entirely to the Resolution Professional and Committee of Creditors. Outside of IBC, many lenders impose cash control and have an agency prioritising the use of cash.

4. Preservation of Relationships & Reputation:

- **Early**: Suppliers, customers, and employees are less likely to be aware of the internal stress, or at least see management taking proactive steps. Relationships can be preserved.

- **Late**: Delayed payments lead to suppliers cutting credit terms or halting supplies, crippling operations. Quality issues, product shortages, or negative market rumours drive customers away. Key employees, sensing instability, jump ship, leaving the company with a weakened workforce. News of financial distress spreads quickly, severely damaging the company's brand and making recovery harder. So across the board, a business relationship and reputation suffer due to late identification and handling of stress.

5. Increased Likelihood of Success:

- **Early**: The underlying problems are often less complex and more manageable. The turnaround involves optimization rather than resuscitation.
- **Late**: Problems become deeply entrenched, multifaceted, and often systemic. Multiple issues (operational, financial, governance, human capital) intertwine, making disentanglement incredibly difficult. The company might be "clinically dead" even before a formal process begins.

Earlier in the book, in chapter 2, we have gone into the details of how to recognise stress early. Despite the above, Indian promoters and banks delay resolving the stress build-up.

The delay in addressing symptoms of stress by both Indian promoters and Public Sector Banks (PSBs) has been a long-standing systemic issue in India, contributing significantly to the NPA (Non-Performing Asset) crisis. This delay is a complex interplay of cultural, political, regulatory, and systemic factors.

Reasons for Delay by Indian Promoters:

1. Emotional Attachment & Entrepreneurial Hubris:

- **"My Baby" Syndrome:** Many Indian businesses are family-owned and run by first or second-generation promoters. There's a deep emotional attachment to the business, often making it difficult to accept that it's in trouble or to make hard decisions like selling assets, reducing the workforce, or diluting ownership.
- **Overconfidence:** Promoters, having successfully built businesses in the past, often believe they can "turn it around themselves" without external intervention, or that the market will eventually recover and fix their problems. This leads to them "throwing good money after bad" in the initial stages.

2. Fear of Losing Control & Dilution:

- **Control Aversion:** Indian promoters typically have a strong desire to retain majority control and operational oversight. They fear that bringing in external investors (equity) or involving turnaround professionals will lead to loss of control, management interference, and ultimately, dilution of their stake.

- **Dilution Avoidance:** Accepting new equity, especially at a distressed valuation, means significant dilution of their ownership. They often prefer to take on more debt (even expensive debt) to avoid this.

3. Reputational Stigma & Social Pressure:

- **"Failure is Taboo":** Acknowledging financial distress is often seen as a sign of personal failure and can carry significant social stigma within business circles and society. This discourages early disclosure or seeking help.

- **Impact on Group Companies:** For large business houses, distress in one company might negatively impact the reputation and financing ability of other group entities, leading to efforts to hide or delay recognizing problems.

4. "Evergreening" of Loans (Collusion with Banks):

- **Mutual Benefit (Short-term):** Historically, there was often a tacit understanding with banks to "evergreen" loans. This means providing new loans to repay old ones, or restructuring terms without truly addressing the underlying viability. This suited promoters as it delayed public recognition of distress and bought them time, and it suited banks as it prevented the loan from becoming an NPA on their books immediately.

- **Pre-IBC Weakness:** Before the IBC, the lack of a strong, time-bound resolution mechanism meant promoters faced fewer immediate consequences for not repaying.

5. Lack of Professional Management & Governance:

- **Owner-Manager Syndrome:** In many promoter-driven businesses, there's less separation between ownership and management. Decisions are often centralized with the promoter, who may lack the specific skills for crisis management or the willingness to delegate to professional turnaround experts.
- **Weak Boards:** Independent directors on boards might not have sufficient power or willingness to challenge promoters, leading to delayed corrective actions.

Reasons for Delay by Indian Public Sector Banks (PSBs):

1. Fear of Vigilance and Accountability:

- **"3 Cs" Fear:** Public sector bank officials (especially at senior levels) have historically been very risk-averse due to the fear of investigation by the CBI (Central Bureau of Investigation), CVC (Central Vigilance Commission), and CAG (Comptroller and Auditor General).
- **Decision Paralysis:** Making tough decisions in a distressed situation (e.g., taking a haircut on a loan, converting debt to equity, initiating IBC) carries the risk of being accused of wrongdoing later, even if the decision was in the bank's best interest. This leads to decision paralysis and a preference for "kicking the can down the road."
- **Blame Game:** There's an incentive to delay NPA recognition to avoid it falling on a particular official's watch or performance cycle.

2. Lack of Incentives for Early Resolution:

- **Absence of Strong Turnaround Culture:** PSBs historically lacked dedicated, skilled turnaround teams. Their focus was more on lending and recovery, not on deep operational restructuring.

- **Limited Autonomy:** Bureaucratic structures and government ownership often limit the autonomy of PSB management to make quick, commercial decisions, especially in complex and distressed situations.

3. Regulatory Forbearance (Historical):

- **"Extend and Pretend":** For a long time, RBI allowed various forms of regulatory forbearance (e.g., CDR, 5/25 scheme) where banks could restructure stressed assets without immediately classifying them as NPAs and without requiring full provisioning. This inadvertently incentivized banks to delay recognition and resolution, as it masked the true extent of bad loans on their balance sheets. While these measures have largely been withdrawn with the advent of IBC and AQR, their legacy impacted behavior.

4. Information Asymmetry & Monitoring Gaps:

- **Weak Credit Appraisal & Monitoring:** Historically, PSBs have been criticized for weak initial credit appraisals and insufficient post-disbursement monitoring, making it difficult to detect early signs of stress in borrowers.

- **Political Interference:** In the past, there were instances of political pressure influencing lending decisions, sometimes leading to loans being granted to unviable projects or entities with weak fundamentals, making subsequent recovery difficult and leading to delayed action.

5. Resource Constraints & Overburdened Staff:

- **Workload:** PSB employees, from branch level to senior management, are often overburdened with multiple responsibilities (sales targets, recovery, compliance, digital initiatives). This can lead to a lack of dedicated time and resources for complex stress identification and resolution.

- **Skill Gaps:** While improving, there can still be a shortage of specialized skills in areas like forensic auditing, advanced credit analysis, and complex legal restructuring within PSBs compared to private banks or dedicated distressed asset firms.

Impact of Delay:

The combined delay from both promoters and PSBs has several severe consequences:

- **Value Erosion:** The most significant impact. Every day of delay means further erosion of the company's value (assets, market share, brand, talent), making eventual recovery more difficult and resulting in larger haircuts for lenders and greater losses for shareholders.
- **Increased Complexity:** Simple problems become complex, multi-layered crises involving multiple creditors, legal challenges, and operational decay.
- **Higher Costs:** Turnaround costs (professional fees, restructuring costs, higher cost of new capital) skyrocket.
- **Systemic Risk:** A large number of delayed NPAs on bank balance sheets choked credit flow to healthy businesses, impacting overall economic growth.
- **Forced IBC:** The IBC, while a positive step, often becomes the last resort due to these delays. By the time a company enters IBC, its value is significantly eroded, leading to lower recovery rates for creditors than if proactive restructuring had occurred earlier.

The IBC has significantly shifted the landscape by imposing strict timelines and consequences, acting as a "nudge" for both promoters and lenders to address stress earlier. However, the cultural and systemic factors that drove the historical delays are deeply ingrained and continue to influence behavior to some extent.

Chapter 12

Turnaround as a Profession in India and the Missing CRO

"The missing CRO is the most expensive vacancy in Indian distress."

Throughout the book, there are references to the CRO as the turnaround leader; however, the fact on the ground in India is different.

This chapter examines why the CRO as a profession has not taken root in India, the cultural and structural barriers that hinder its adoption, and the consequences of continuing with promoter-led turnaround efforts that often leave significant value on the table.

Introduction

In global turnaround practice, the Chief Restructuring Officer (CRO) has become a critical figure in rescuing distressed businesses. Appointed by either promoters or lenders, the CRO serves as a bridge between management, creditors, and other stakeholders, bringing in both operational and financial expertise to steer companies away from insolvency. In the Indian context, however, the CRO remains largely absent. Despite the increasing number of stressed corporates and the growing sophistication of India's financial ecosystem, promoters rarely appoint external turnaround professionals to lead crisis management, and lenders have avoided insisting on them.

Why Promoters Resist External Turnaround Leadership

Promoters in India are deeply entrenched in their businesses, often seeing the company as an extension of family, identity, and legacy. In such an environment, the idea of bringing in an outsider to take charge, even temporarily, is perceived as:

- **Loss of Control and Face** – For most Indian promoters, agreeing to a CRO appointment feels like a public admission of failure. It signals weakness both internally (to employees and family) and externally (to customers, vendors, regulators).
- **Fear of Displacement** – A CRO by definition has sweeping powers over cash, operations, and strategy. Promoters worry that once a CRO takes charge, lenders may use them as a stepping stone to marginalize promoter influence.
- **Trust Deficit** – Many Indian promoters have limited experience working with external operating professionals. While financial advisors and investment bankers are seen as "neutral" facilitators for debt negotiations, an operating CRO is perceived as an intruder who may question long-standing practices, related-party transactions, and promoter lifestyles.
- **Perception of Cost** – Professional CROs, especially those with international experience, command fees that appear high in relation to a company already strapped for cash. Promoters often justify not appointing one on grounds of affordability, even though the cost of not bringing in expertise is far higher.

Why Lenders Avoid Appointing CROs

On the other side, lenders in India, particularly public sector banks (PSBs), have also resisted pushing for CROs despite repeated debt restructurings that fail to hold. The reasons are structural and political:

- **Fear of Accountability** — A bank insisting on a CRO appointment risks being accused later of "interference" or "management takeover."

This is especially risky for PSB executives, who work under the shadow of vigilance inquiries. By contrast, hiring a financial advisor for a debt restructuring is seen as advisory, not managerial interference.

- **Regulatory Vacuum** — RBI circulars and frameworks (from CDR, SDR, S4A to the June 7, 2019 circular) have placed emphasis on Resolution Plans, Independent Business Reviews (IBRs), and debt aggregation, but never explicitly created a role for CROs. In the absence of regulatory backing, lenders shy away from pushing for it.
- **Short-termism** – Lenders often prefer a financial restructuring that postpones recognition of loss rather than a deep operational turnaround that requires time, patience, and management change. The CRO model, by design, calls for confronting hard truths quickly, something lenders often avoid.

How Turnarounds Are Managed in India Today

Given this dual reluctance from promoters and lenders, turnaround situations in India are usually managed in one of three ways:

- **Promoter-led Crisis Management** – The default model. Promoters continue to lead, cutting costs, negotiating with creditors, and firefighting cash crises. While this preserves promoter pride, most lack the objectivity and professional toolkit to implement difficult changes.
- **Management Team Adjustments** – Occasionally, promoters bring in a new CEO, CFO, or COO. However, these appointments are often made from within the promoter's network, carrying the same limitations of loyalty and lack of independence.
- **Advisory-driven Financial Restructuring** – Lenders engage rating agencies, accounting firms, or boutique advisors for debt restructuring. These efforts focus on balance sheet engineering, tenor extensions, interest reductions, or haircuts but rarely address underlying operational inefficiencies.

The result is a cycle of "cosmetic restructuring" followed by relapse into stress. Value erosion continues, employees lose confidence, vendors tighten credit, and ultimately, many such companies slide into the Insolvency and Bankruptcy Code (IBC) process, where value destruction is steep.

The Value Lost Without CROs

The absence of professional CROs in India leads to systemic value loss:

- **Delayed Action** – Promoters wait too long to acknowledge distress. A CRO would enforce immediate triage through tools like a 13-week cash flow and crisis dashboards.
- **Ineffective Stakeholder Management** – CROs excel at balancing the conflicting interests of lenders, suppliers, employees, and regulators. Promoter-led efforts are usually biased and mistrusted.
- **Operational Blind Spots** – CROs bring industry benchmarks, procurement renegotiation, working capital optimization, and turnaround playbooks. These are missing when promoters rely only on internal teams.
- **Loss of Confidence** – For lenders and investors, the presence of a CRO signals seriousness and credibility. Its absence often leads to harsher terms or even premature liquidation proceedings.

International experience (e.g., US Chapter 11 processes, European special situations) shows that independent CROs preserve far more enterprise value. In India, by contrast, reluctance to adopt this model has meant suboptimal recoveries for lenders and lost equity value for promoters.

Emerging Possibilities

Despite current limitations, a few trends suggest that CROs may find greater acceptance in the future:

- **Private Credit Funds & ARCs** – Unlike PSBs, these investors have more flexibility and may insist on CRO-like leadership as a condition for funding or asset acquisition.
- **Evolving Governance** – As Indian corporates access global capital markets, external stakeholders may demand more professional crisis management.
- **Professional Services Ecosystem** – With more Indian professionals gaining global turnaround experience, a credible talent pool is slowly emerging.

Conclusion

Turnaround in India today is still largely promoter-led, advisory-supported, and lender-hesitant. The missing CRO is not just an academic gap, it represents a lost opportunity for Indian businesses to professionalize crisis management, preserve jobs, and safeguard enterprise value. Until promoters overcome pride and lenders overcome fear, India will continue to manage turnarounds reactively rather than proactively.

The profession of turnaround management in India will only come of age when the CRO is accepted as a neutral, professional, and value-maximizing force, not as a threat to promoters or a liability to lenders. Until then, India's corporate distress will remain more about restructuring debt than restructuring businesses.

Chapter 13

Turnaround Specialist or a Transformation Expert?

"When an accident happens, you call the paramedic and the surgeon, not the gym trainer."

Context for most corporate turnaround situations is a steep drop in operational performance, which with the presence of leverage, manifests itself as an overwhelming liquidity crisis. There is a deep trust deficit, with lenders losing confidence in the management's ability to turn around business performance and meet their obligations.

Crisis management forms an integral part of the turnaround process. This is the phase where the turnaround leadership does for the distressed businesses what paramedics and critical healthcare professionals do for individual medical emergencies. Quick diagnosis, cash generation / infusion, stabilization initiatives and asking lenders to step back are some of the steps taken during this phase.

Given the steep decline in enterprise value of the business and presence of debt, turnarounds involve deep haircuts for equity and a restructuring of the debt. Resetting expectations regarding enterprise value and negotiations between equity and lenders is a critical component of the process. For a financial restructuring to be successful and sustainable, a robust business plan that is executed well is absolutely essential.

Leadership skills to drive a turnaround are very different from typical growth CEO or Transformation CEO roles. Firm, decisive, passionate about winning, objective, detail-oriented, excellent stakeholder management, etc. are some of the key attributes of good turnaround leaders. Once the business is stabilized and has a sound capital structure in place, turnaround leaders hand over the reins of the business to the growth CEO/leader and move on to the next challenge.

Differences in Common Symptoms for a Corporate Turnaround and a Transformation Situation

		Turnaround	Transformation
Common Symptoms	Revenue trend	Mostly moderate to severe decline	Mostly below industry growth to moderate decline
	Profitability trend	Mostly moderate to severe decline	Mostly below industry growth to moderate decline
	Operating cash generation	Inadequate to negative	Inadequate to negative
	ROCE	Below WACC to negative	Around WACC to negative
	Availability of Cash	Severe crisis	Mild crisis
	People	Significant concerns regarding future Loss of good talent	Low morale Difficult to acquire good talent
	Trust deficit	Deep trust deficit across organisation and between stakeholders. Often, lenders have lost confidence in management ability to run the business	Loss of confidence amongst employees, often accompanied by politicking
	Leverage	Mostly highly leveraged	Nil to acceptable leverage

Contextual setting for a Transformation is usually a mature business that has been struggling to increase revenue and / or profitability but is still many quarters away from a cash crisis. Often, the revenue and market share are declining for several years and the business may be incurring losses. It helps if the business is not heavily leveraged as the level of urgency is alleviated and there are fewer stakeholder issues to deal with.

Given the absence of an immediate or ongoing cash crisis, there is a longer time horizon available to address the business challenges and a longer perspective can be taken when developing solutions. E.g., developing new products / markets and / or new marketing campaigns with longer lead times are solutions that work well in Transformations but will not be pursued in Turnaround situations due to cash / resource constraints. Similarly, disposal of non-core business can be done at a measured pace and time taken to find a buyer at the right price, whereas in a Turnaround situation, often, sales happen at distress valuations due to paucity of time.

Key stakeholders pushing for a transformation of a business are usually the Board of Directors and large shareholders. The new CEO driving the Transformation will have to actively engage with these stakeholders and manage the expectations. However, unlike a Turnaround, the Transformation leader most likely would not have to deal with a large group of lenders with conflicting agendas and vendors / employees who have not been paid for months.

Having successfully led a transformation, the Board of Directors would like the leader to continue to lead the organization to maintain continuity of vision.

Differences in Action Required to Resolve Stress

		Turnaround	Transformation
Action to resolve stress	Crisis Management	Yes	Mostly no
	Operations restructuring	Focus on immediately effective and high impact initiatives	Longer time horizon allows focus on a comprehensive solution
	Stakeholder management	Significant time spent on resetting enterprise value expectations, negotiations between capital providers and rebuilding trust with lenders	Significant time spent on managing expectations of large shareholders and Board of Directors
	Leadership	Mostly Creditor led. Could be Debtor led as well	Almost always, Debtor led.
		New leadership brought in like a Turnaround CEO, CRO or Interim CFO/COO etc.	Mostly, led by a new CEO, who at times, may, bring in a new leadership team.
		Once turnaround is complete transition to a Growth CEO	If transformation is successful, new leadership continues.
	Financial Restructuring	Yes	May be

Turnaround Leadership Question in the Indian Context

Creditor-led restructuring in India still happens only under the regulatory cover provided by the Bankruptcy Code. There again, the state of the business by the time admission happens, lack of interim finance, and mostly L1-based selection of insolvency professionals, leave little hope to drive a turnaround. Except for a few situations, most bankruptcies in India have been run as a process of recovery, unfortunately.

Even outside an IBC situation, for example, under RBI's June 7 2019 Circular, Lenders have shied away from appointing a Chief Restructuring Officer, who can play a critical role in driving an operational turnaround and a robust / sustainable restructuring. There are several reasons for it: promoters' influence, unwillingness to try something different, inter-creditor disputes, etc. Public sector banks still dominate corporate lending and form a large majority of the debt held by a stressed corporate. As has been my personal experience, it often boils down to the GM / CGM leading the stressed resolution at the largest bank in the JLF.

Promoters are yet to warm up to the idea of using turnaround experts. More often than not, they do not want any interference in running the business and are content with advisors to help with financial restructuring or raise new debt. One of the reasons that Promoters are reluctant to bring in turnaround expertise is fear of exposing the poor governance practices that are rampant in many businesses.

ARCs and credit funds have been warm to the idea of bringing in turnaround expertise and have benefited from it in a few situations. In some instances, their efforts have been handicapped by the NBFC crisis (inability to raise working capital), inter-creditor disputes and inability to influence the promoters, leading to suboptimal outcomes.

Stressed-assets resolution in India has come a long way and evolved significantly, especially after the implementation of IBC. It's only a matter of time until we see proper turnaround solutions developed and implemented by professionals.

(This article was published on the author's LinkedIn Profile in April 2021)

Chapter 14

Evolution of Creditor Rights in India and the Impact of the IBC (2000–2025)

"With IBC, creditor rights grew a spine."

In barely a decade, India went from double-digit bad-loan ratios and sluggish, litigation-heavy enforcement to one of the most creditor-friendly, time-bound insolvency regimes in emerging markets. The centrepiece is the Insolvency and Bankruptcy Code, 2016 (IBC). But the IBC sits atop two decades of reforms from Sick Industrial Companies Act (SICA)/ Board of Industrial and Financial Reconstruction (BIFR) and Debt Recovery Tribunals (DRTs) to Securitisation and Reconstruction of Financial Assets and Enforcement of Security Interest Act, 2002 (SARFAESI) and RBI's pre-IBC restructuring playbooks that collectively rewired incentives for borrowers, lenders, and courts.

The results show up starkly in asset quality: gross NPAs peaked at ~11.2% in FY2018 and have since fallen to multi-decade lows near ~2.3–2.6% by March–September 2025.

The Pre-IBC Era: A Fragmented and Debtor-Centric System

SICA was designed to revive sick industrial companies by referring them to the Board for Industrial and Financial Reconstruction (BIFR). However, this framework was largely a failure. It was characterized by:

- **Protracted Delays:** The process was incredibly slow, often taking years or even decades to resolve a case.
- **Debtor-in-Possession Model:** The existing management, which had driven the company into the ground, was allowed to stay in control, often with little incentive to cooperate.
- **Low Recovery Rates:** By the time a decision was reached, the company's assets would have eroded in value, leading to dismal recovery for creditors.
- **Moral Hazard:** Promoters used SICA to delay loan repayments, knowing that the process would shield them from coercive action.

The Recovery of Debts Due to Banks and Financial Institutions Act, 1993 (now the Recovery of Debts and Bankruptcy Act) created DRTs to expedite lender recoveries, but case backlogs grew. SICA was finally repealed effective December 1, 2016, paving the way for the IBC's unified design; DRTs continue under the updated 1993 law.

SARFAESI Act, 2002

SARFAESI armed secured creditors with an out-of-court enforcement: taking possession/sale of secured assets upon default, without first obtaining a court decree (subject to borrower remedies before DRT). Over time, RBI and Parliament refined rules for Asset Reconstruction Companies (ARCs), display of possessed assets, and other safeguards. SARFAESI became the primary retail and SME recovery workhorse, but it struggled for speed in large, complex corporate cases where operational restructuring and going-concern sales were required.

RBI's Pre-IBC Restructuring Toolkit (2001–2016)

To address the burgeoning NPA problem, the Reserve Bank of India (RBI) introduced a series of restructuring schemes:

Corporate Debt Restructuring (CDR) mechanism (2001)

CDR was a debt restructuring mechanism introduced by the Reserve Bank of India (RBI) in 2001. It was introduced to provide a more formalized and coordinated approach to debt restructuring than the ad-hoc, bilateral negotiations that were common before 2001. It aimed to save viable businesses that were facing temporary financial difficulties by giving them a chance to turn around. The key features of CDR are as follows.

- **Voluntary and Non-statutory:** Unlike a legal process, CDR was a voluntary scheme. It was not binding on creditors unless they chose to be a part of it.
- **Supermajority Rule:** For a restructuring plan to be approved, at least 75% of creditors by value had to agree to it. Once this supermajority was reached, the plan was binding on all lenders within the CDR cell. This was a key difference from other informal restructurings, as it prevented a small minority of creditors from derailing a viable plan.
- **Debtor-in-Possession:** A significant feature of CDR was that the existing management (promoter) remained in control of the company while the restructuring was being implemented. The plan would include a standstill period during which lenders would not take any legal or coercive action against the company.

CDR mechanism suffered from several weaknesses:

- **Time-Consuming:** The process was lengthy, often taking months or even years to finalize a plan, which led to a further erosion of the company's value.
- **Lack of Consensus:** Despite the supermajority rule, getting a large, diverse group of creditors to agree was a major challenge. Banks often had different levels of exposure and varying appetites for risk, making a collective decision difficult.

- **Moral Hazard:** The "debtor-in-possession" model created a moral hazard. Promoters could use the CDR mechanism to delay payments and avoid any real consequences for their financial mismanagement.
- **No Legal Backing:** Since it was a non-statutory framework, a CDR plan lacked legal enforceability against a dissenting creditor who was not part of the CDR Cell. This could lead to legal disputes and a breakdown of the entire restructuring process.

Post the 2008-2010 Global Financial Crisis, Indian banking non-performing loans spiked to more than 10%, forcing the RBI to come up with several schemes for debt restructuring to resolve the problem that threatened to break the Indian banking system:

Joint Lenders' Forum (JLF) and Corrective Action Plan (CAP) (2014)

The RBI introduced the JLF framework to ensure the early identification of stressed assets and prompt, coordinated action by all lenders. The idea was to bring all creditors to a single table to formulate a Corrective Action Plan (CAP) for the borrower. The JLF was triggered when a borrower's account showed signs of stress (categorized as Special Mention Account or SMA), even before it became an NPA.

Weaknesses: The JLF framework was plagued by a lack of consensus among lenders. Despite a majority voting rule, banks, particularly public sector banks, often had conflicting interests and were hesitant to take a haircut on their loans. The process was slow, leading to delays that eroded the value of the underlying assets. Furthermore, it did not have the legal enforceability to "cram down" a decision on a dissenting minority of lenders, often leading to a stalemate.

Flexible Structuring of Long-Term Project Loans (5:25 Scheme) (2015)

The 5:25 scheme was designed to address the asset-liability mismatch in the infrastructure sector. It allowed banks to extend the loan tenure of long-term project loans up to 25 years, while allowing the interest rate and other terms to be reset every 5 or 7 years. This was meant to align the loan's repayment schedule with the long-term cash flows of the project, preventing it from becoming an NPA.

Weaknesses: This scheme was widely criticized for being a form of "evergreening" of loans. Instead of a genuine restructuring, it simply kicked the can down the road by extending the loan's life. It did not address the fundamental problems of a stressed company, and its provisions were often misused to hide stress and avoid NPA classification.

Strategic Debt Restructuring (SDR) (2015)

The SDR scheme was a more aggressive attempt to shift control from a defaulting promoter to the lenders. It allowed a Joint Lenders' Forum (JLF) to convert a portion of the company's debt into a majority (51% or more) equity stake. The goal was to take over the company's management, turn it around, and then sell it to a new promoter.

Weaknesses: The scheme faced major operational challenges. Banks were not equipped to run businesses and had neither the expertise nor the incentive to do so. Finding a new promoter to buy a distressed company within the stipulated time was often difficult. The lack of a clear legal framework for transferring management control and the complexities of valuing the equity made the scheme largely ineffective. Only a handful of cases were successfully resolved under this scheme.

Scheme for Sustainable Structuring of Stressed Assets (S4A) (2016)

The S4A scheme was introduced to provide a framework for the "deep restructuring" of large stressed accounts. The core idea was to split a company's total debt into two parts: a sustainable part, which the company could service based on its current and future cash flows, and an unsustainable part, which could be converted into equity or other securities. This scheme allowed for a genuine haircut on the debt, unlike the 5:25 scheme.

Weaknesses: S4A was too complex to implement and had very strict eligibility criteria, making it applicable to only a few large companies. It also faced issues with the valuation of the unsustainable debt component and the conversion into equity. Like other schemes, it still lacked the legal power to bind all creditors, especially if they were not part of the initial forum. The IBC, introduced around the same time, was a more comprehensive and powerful solution, which ultimately rendered S4A and other schemes obsolete.

These schemes aimed to buy time and share pain but suffered coordination failures, evergreening risks, and weak promoter discipline. Their replacement with a principles-based Prudential Framework for Resolution of Stressed Assets (June 7, 2019) signalled a pivot to early default recognition, strict timelines, and IBC as the credible threat behind negotiations.

The IBC Revolution: A Paradigm Shift

The IBC, enacted in 2016, was a game-changer. It consolidated India's insolvency laws into a single, comprehensive, and time-bound framework. The core principle of the IBC is a radical departure from the past: it shifted the control of the resolution process from the defaulting debtor to the creditors.

How IBC Empowered Creditors

- Creditor-in-Control Model: Once a company is admitted into bankruptcy, the control of its management is immediately taken over by an Interim Resolution Professional (IRP) identified by the Committee of Creditors (CoC). This ends the "promoter raj" and ensures that creditors are in the driver's seat.

- Time-Bound Resolution: The IBC mandates a strict timeline for the resolution process (initially 180 days, extendable to a total of 330 days). This reduces asset value erosion and provides certainty.
- Value Maximization: The primary objective of the IBC is to maximize the value of the company's assets, not just recover debt. The Resolution Professional works with the CoC to find a suitable buyer for the business. Well-run sale process will drive competitive bidding, minimize information asymmetry and reduce uncertainty, driving a higher valuation for the business.
- Deterrent for Promoters: The threat of losing control of their company and the possibility of being disqualified from bidding for their own assets (under Section 29A) have created a strong deterrent. This has prompted many promoters to settle their dues before a company is admitted for insolvency.

The Impact on India's Credit Ecosystem

The IBC's impact has been profound and far-reaching, fundamentally reshaping the credit culture in India.

- Decline in NPAs: The fear of losing control under the IBC, coupled with the resolution of large corporate defaults, has led to a significant and sustained decline in Gross NPAs in the Indian banking system. Gross NPAs, which had peaked at 11.2% in 2018, have now dropped to 2.5% in June 2025, the lowest levels in over a decade.
- Behavioral Change: The "threat of the IBC" has instilled greater financial discipline in corporate borrowers. Promoters are now more proactive in monitoring their finances, managing debt, and seeking to restructure early to avoid the insolvency process. By Dec 2024, ~30,000 cases with ₹13.8 trillion in defaults were settled before admission, catalysed by the credible threat of IBC admission and promoter ineligibility under Section 29A. This "shadow effect" has materially strengthened creditor bargaining power outside of court.

- Improved Credit Flow: With cleaner balance sheets, banks are more confident in lending. This has led to an improvement in credit flow to the economy and lower borrowing costs for good-quality borrowers.
- Growth of the Market: The IBC has also spurred the growth of a new ecosystem, including a class of qualified insolvency professionals and a secondary market for stressed assets.

Complementary Reforms that Reinforced IBC and Changed the Credit Culture:

- **National Asset Reconstruction Company** (NARCL aka "bad bank") was set up by the GoI to take over large legacy cases that were proving difficult to resolve. Asset purchase by NARCL gave comfort to lenders about recovery amounts, improved capital flow and strengthened balance sheets.
- **IBC regulatory upgrades:** Insolvency and Bankruptcy Board of India (IBBI) under the aegis of the Ministry of Corporate Affairs (MCA) has been proactive in listening to the market participants and delivered multiple amendments and 100+ regulation tweaks since 2016 to streamline timelines, voting, homebuyer treatment, and real-estate cases.
- **Judicial capacity:** Number of benches and competent judges has been one of the biggest bane of the IBC process and the associated timelines. The Government has taken multiple steps to expand the number of NCLT/NCLAT benches and related infrastructure to improve timelines.
- **RBI supervision & prudence:** The RBI has been one of the best central banks in the world. The prudential framework under the June 7, 2019 circular, one-time restructuring during COVID, and the one-time settlement circular in June 2023 all provide a variety of tools to Indian lenders to identify stress early, take collective action and apply commercial wisdom.

In summary, a lot has changed since 2016, which led to a drastic reduction in banking system stress and a decadal low in system NPAs:

- **Clear, credible threat of loss of control (Section 29A + auction during CIRP):** Promoters now face credible risk of losing the family jewel compared to earlier debtor-in-control regime, where they could let the restructuring drag for years.
- **Collective action is solved via CoC super-majority:** IBC being a court-driven process, forces lenders to come together and take collective action.
- **Early recognition and provisioning under RBI's frameworks:** The recent RBI circulars emphasize early stress recognition, collective action and prudent provisioning, including using accelerated provisioning norms to drive faster debt restructuring.
- **Scale and signalling:** Large marquee companies like DHFL, Essar Steel, Bhushan Steel, etc., changed hands during IBC, sending a clear message to promoters about losing control.
- **Multiple routes for restructuring and resolution:** Lenders today have multiple tools in their armoury to resolve stress: SARFAESI for collateral enforcement; IBC for going-concern sales; prudential framework, OTS, pre-pack, or IBC 12A withdrawals for negotiated outcomes.

In conclusion, the evolution of creditor rights in India is a story of moving from a system of fragmentation and inefficiency to one of coherence and discipline. The IBC has been the central catalyst in this transformation, turning the tide on India's NPA crisis, empowering creditors with decisive control, and, most importantly, instilling a new culture of credit responsibility.

Afterword

By Eshwar Karra
Deputy MD – Kotak Alternate Asset Managers & CEO – Kotak Special Situations Fund

As I look back at the last three decades of India's corporate credit landscape, it feels like a story that can be shared in phases, each defined by its own legal frameworks, regulatory approaches, and the shifting balance between lenders, promoters, and the broader financial ecosystem. Having had the privilege of working across commercial banking, asset reconstruction, and private credit, I have witnessed both the missteps and the milestones that shaped India's turnaround journey. This book captures that narrative with authenticity and I am glad to share a few reflections that may complement its core message.

1990s: SICA and the search for solutions

In the 1990s, India relied heavily on the Sick Industrial Companies Act (SICA) and the Board for Industrial and Financial Reconstruction (BIFR) to deal with distressed companies. The intent was noble; i.e., rescue sick units, preserve jobs and revive productive capacity. Yet, the process often turned into a graveyard of failed efforts. The emphasis was on protecting borrowers, not creating accountability or urgency. Endless delays, inadequate monitoring, and limited teeth for creditors meant that by the time decisions were made, value had already eroded beyond repair.

This period taught the ecosystem an important lesson: time is the most precious currency in distressed situations. Every month of delay eats away at the enterprise value, making recovery harder for lenders and survival tougher for companies. Unfortunately, under SICA, early diagnosis and quick corrective action rarely happened.

2000 – 2014: CDR, structured but still inefficient

With the introduction of the Corporate Debt Restructuring (CDR) mechanism in 2001, RBI tried to create a coordinated platform for consortium lenders. As a banker, I saw the optimism with which CDR was launched. It allowed restructuring of debt with moratoriums, extended tenors, and reduced interest rates.

But over time, CDR became synonymous with "evergreening." Instead of using restructuring as an opportunity to truly revive operations, many promoters saw it as a chance to postpone pain. Lenders, too, wary of recognizing NPAs and driven by provisioning pressures, often chose to "extend and pretend." Operational restructuring, management changes, and governance improvements were seldom insisted upon. Predictably, success rates were abysmally low.

Yet, CDR was not without merit. It brought banks together at one table, introduced concepts like viability studies and monitoring committees, and created awareness that collective action was possible. It was an important bridge from SICA to the more structured frameworks that followed.

2014–2019: SDR, S4A, and the limits of innovation

By the mid-2010s, as stressed assets piled up, the Reserve Bank of India experimented with new tools like Strategic Debt Restructuring (SDR) and Scheme for Sustainable Structuring of Stressed Assets (S4A). These initiatives were innovative, encouraging lenders to convert debt to equity or bifurcate into sustainable versus unsustainable debt.

In theory, SDR allowed banks to take control of companies and bring in new promoters. In practice, banks lacked the appetite, capability, and bandwidth to run businesses or find serious buyers. Similarly, S4A, while clever in financial engineering, rarely addressed core operational problems.

The recurring theme remained the same: financial restructuring without operational turnaround is incomplete. You can push liabilities out, reprice debt, or even swap equity, but unless the business model itself is fixed, the company will limp back into distress. That is what happened to many companies whose debt was restructured and defaulted again over the years until the government decided to promulgate IBC to provide a clean slate.

2016: IBC, a clean slate for a fresh start

The passage of the Insolvency and Bankruptcy Code in 2016 marked a turning point in India's credit culture. For the first time, there was a credible, time-bound process with teeth. Promoters who were earlier shielded from consequences now faced the possibility of losing control if they defaulted. Lenders, once fragmented and hesitant, found a legal framework to act decisively.

The IBC has been far from perfect, with delays in tribunals, litigation tactics, and uneven recoveries posing challenges. But its impact on borrower behaviour has been transformative. The very threat of losing the company has pushed many promoters to avoid default at all costs. Credit discipline has improved, and a new ecosystem of resolution professionals, distressed investors, and turnaround advisors has emerged.

For lenders, IBC has shifted the mindset from "evergreening" to resolution. For promoters, it has reinforced the message that equity comes with accountability. And for India's financial system, it has created transparency in the recovery process.

The Rise of Private Credit

Alongside regulatory reforms, the last decade has seen the rise of private credit funds, which I have had the privilege to build and lead. These funds have brought a new dimension to India's financing landscape with patient, bespoke capital that can step in where traditional banks hesitate.

Private credit has played a dual role:

1. Rescue Capital – stepping in with comprehensive funding solutions to help viable companies restructure, refinance, and survive.
2. Growth Capital – providing flexible structures that support acquisitions, expansions, and promoter buybacks even in stressed contexts.

The success of Kotak Special Situations Fund and peers demonstrates that India has an appetite for this asset class. It also highlights how alternative capital can partner with lenders and promoters to unlock value in complex situations.

Lost Opportunities: Why We Need Turnaround Experts

Looking back, one of the greatest missed opportunities has been the underutilization of turnaround professionals and CROs (Chief Restructuring Officers). Globally, CROs have been central to revivals; i.e., they bring operational rigor, independence, and the credibility to engage with multiple stakeholders.

In India, however, both promoters and lenders have been reluctant. Promoters often fear loss of control, while lenders worry about liability or optics. As a result, many companies that could have been saved slipped into insolvency.

The lesson has been clear: financial engineering alone cannot rescue a sinking ship. It takes operational expertise, tough decisions, and day-to-day execution. CROs, with their hands-on approach, can anchor this process by bridging the gap between boardrooms and shop floors, between strategy and action.

The Road Ahead: Optimism with Caution

I remain optimistic about the future of corporate turnarounds in India. Several forces are converging in a positive way:

- Strengthened legal frameworks with IBC and RBI oversight.
- Maturing credit markets with banks, ARCs, and private credit funds co-existing.
- Promoter awareness that governance and timely action are no longer optional.
- Emerging talent pool of turnaround advisors, interim managers, and CROs.

What India needs now is a cultural shift to embrace turnaround as a value-creation opportunity rather than a stigma. Promoters must shed their reluctance to bring in external experts. Lenders must go beyond balance sheet repairs and insist on operational fixes. And regulators must continue to refine frameworks that encourage early detection of stress.

If we can collectively act with urgency, transparency, and professionalism, I believe the next decade will see more businesses revived than liquidated, more jobs saved than lost, and more value created than destroyed.

Closing Thoughts

As someone who has walked this journey i.e., from a banker to an ARC head to a private credit investor, I can say with conviction: India now has the ingredients to make corporate turnaround a sustainable profession and practice. What is needed is courage from promoters, discipline from lenders, and the steady hand of turnaround experts to guide the process.

This book is a timely contribution to that dialogue. It not only documents the past but also provides a framework for the future. My hope is that it inspires all stakeholders like entrepreneurs, bankers, investors, and policymakers, to approach distress not as the end of the road, but as an opportunity for rebirth.

The Indian growth story is still being written. As our economy aspires to touch new heights, the ability to rescue and revive businesses will be central to preserving capital, fostering entrepreneurship, and creating long-term value. In that effort, turnaround experts and CROs must no longer be seen as outsiders, but as partners in renewal.

Bharat is a living example of someone, whose life was changed by a book. In October 2006, while pursuing an MBA from prestigious London Business School, he stumbled upon a book on Corporate Turnarounds. That set him off on almost a 20-year journey, pursuing the most challenging and difficult corporate situations in India and the Middle East.

To find himself a suitable turnaround and restructuring opportunity, Bharat co-founded and became the first President of the Turnaround Management Club at London Business School. The club was so successful, it became one of the fastest growing clubs at LBS with a significant positive cash balance within first year of launch. Post his MBA in 2008, Bharat has spent last 17+ years honing his craft in UK, Middle East and India, most recently as a Partner with EY LLP, where he led their Operations Restructuring practice for several years.

Overall, Bharat brings close to 30 years of diverse work experience in India, Southern Africa, UK and Middle East. During this period, he has worked for A. F. Ferguson & Co., SABMiller India & Southern Africa, worlds top turnaround & restructuring firms Alvarez & Marsal, AlixPartners and EY.

By education, Bharat is a Chartered Accountant and MBA (London Business School). He has also completed several AI & Digital Transformation courses.

Outside of work, Bharat enjoys running (several half marathons in India and UAE), mountain climbing (several high passes and peaks of over 5000 mtrs in India, Nepal, Tibet, France & Tanzania), reading (non-fiction) and listening to lounge-music. Bharat is also building India's largest repository of quotes by Indian leaders, visionaries and spiritual gurus, which you can find at *www.Indian-Wisdom.com*

You can learn more about Bharat at:
https://www.linkedin.com/in/guptabharat/ and
https://au-rrangeventures.com/

9 789360 701307

Printed at Repro India Ltd.